PARENT POWER

To my parents

ABOUT THE AUTHOR

Ray Massey has been Education Correspondent of the *Daily Mail* since 1990. He previously held the same post with the Press Association, the UK's national news agency, where he also covered politics and general news. He entered the education field just as the 1988 Education Reform Act became law. Born in Newcastle upon Tyne in 1960, he was educated exclusively in the state sector. After passing the eleven-plus, he moved to Walbottle Grammar, sited on Hadrian's Wall in Northumberland. He left to join the north east's biggest growth industry – the drift south. He studied English and German literature at the University of Warwick, during which time he spent a year teaching at a German grammar school in the Black Forest. His journalistic career began on the *Coventry Evening Telegraph* and his work has taken him to schools at home and abroad, including Siberia, Germany, China and Japan. He is a Fellow of the Royal Society of Arts and lives in Kingston upon Thames, Surrey.

PARENT POWER

Securing the best schooling for your child

Ray Massey

Education Correspondent of the *Daily Mail*

Harmsworth
PUBLICATIONS

ISBN 1 85324 773 1

Harmsworth Publishing Ltd, Bateman
Street, Cambridge CB2 1LZ

Printed and bound in Great Britain by Clays
Ltd, St Ives plc, Bungay, Suffolk.

A CIP catalogue record for this book is
available from the British Library.

Ref L133/zz10qq/J/JC

Cover illustration by Tony Husband

CONTENTS

Preface

The idea for this book took root because of constant pestering from friends and colleagues who had suddenly become parents. 'What should I do about my child's schooling?' was their frantic refrain. I am indeed indebted to them.

I should particularly like to thank the *Daily Mail* for allowing me to draw on some of my work as its education correspondent and to use illustrations by its cartoonists Mac and Ken Mahood, as well as its photographers.

My heartfelt thanks also go out to Elizabeth Clinton for her proofreading skills and moral support throughout the endeavour. Professor Alan Smithers, Dr Pamela Robinson and Joanna Bragg of Manchester University's School of Education gave me much expert help and encouragement in carrying out the survey of parental attitudes. The survey could not have taken place without the co-operation of Donald Naismith, Edward Lister and the schools and parents of the London Borough of Wandsworth.

On the computer front, I am grateful for the technical expertise of Ms Dominie Steed of Just Macs and to my *Daily Mail* colleague Chris Cherry, both of whom got me out of the clag when, at critical moments, my Apple Mac became temperamental. And to Bridget Perez whose valued efforts at organising my filing – no mean task – made the eventual writing so much easier.

Thanks also to Madalane Moore of the School Examinations and Assessment Council, Paul McGill of the National Curriculum Council, and all those at the Department for Education and OFSTED press offices who patiently answered my queries.

As this book was written against a background of rapid change and intense controversy in education, I must acknowledge the efforts of my commissioning editor. I would also like to thank the book's editor who, despite my own personal hobby-horses, stressed the need for the book to be fair and balanced. There should now be something in *Parent Power* to irritate everyone!

Finally, may I thank all those heads, teachers, parents, pupils, academics, Ministers of the Crown, politicians, officials, celebrities and others mentioned within the covers – as well as those who are not – for sharing with me their thoughts, enthusiasms, ideas, prejudices and favourite dodges.

Ray Massey

September 1993

WHAT DO PARENTS REALLY WANT FOR THEIR CHILDREN?

In writing a book like *Parent Power*, it would have been churlish not to have asked the people for whom it is intended – parents – what they think. This I have done, to a modest degree. In the spring of 1993, with the valued help of Professor Alan Smithers and Dr Pamela Robinson of Manchester University's School of Education, I conducted a survey of the views of nearly 300 parents who had children at 32 primary schools. All the pupils were about to move up to secondary schools in the state or private sector, so their parents had just been through the process of making critical decisions. What they told me casts a fascinating light on the realities of parental choice.

PARENTS TAKING PART

Of the 297 respondents, 124 (48%) were parents of boys and 173 (58%) of girls. Nearly 8 out of 10 (78.5%) intended sending their children to state schools, 1 in 8 (12.8%) specified the independent sector, 7.1% were unsure and 1.7% did not specify anything.

GETTING A SCHOOL PLACE

The children of three-quarters of parents (75.8%) were accepted by their first choice school, but 1 in 6 (16.5%) were not. At the time, some 7.7% said they did not yet know the outcome of their applications. Of the 49 parents who were NOT accepted by their first-choice school, some 18 (37%) said they would appeal against the decision, while 32 (65%) said they would settle for the school allocated to them. The rest did not answer.

Looking at the figures overall, with roughly three-quarters of all parents getting their first-choice school, and 10.8% of the total saying they would settle for the school allocated to them, some 86.6% of parents were generally satisfied. These findings are broadly in line with government estimates that 9 out of 10 parents settle for the school to which their child is allocated.

D IS FOR DISCIPLINE — THE FACTORS THAT INFLUENCE CHOICE OF SCHOOL

Good discipline appears to be the main factor that parents take into account when choosing a school for their child (see Table 1). It was certainly one of the most common factors cited by parents who chose to remove their children from the state system and send them to fee-paying independent schools. The important point to note is that it is the parents' perception that matters, whether or not their criticisms are justified. For it is the parents' perception that will influence choice.

One parent said 'The school I have chosen has less children in each class and there's a lot more discipline than in state schools.' Another commented 'The local state school is too rough, and not good enough academically.' 'Social control' was offered by another parent as a reason for sending a son to a particular school. 'Sounds awful, but he needs it. Our two older children went to a state school and it was rough.' The comments of these parents who

opted out of the state education system are particularly important. For these are exactly the sort of people state schools must attract back from the fee-paying sector if confidence is to rise.

Apart from good discipline, a number of other key factors were cited by parents as being 'important' in influencing their choice of school. Among these were the following: a personal impression gained by visiting the school; the sense that there was more to education than simply passing exams; a feeling that the school would best suit the aptitudes of their particular child, and the fact that the children themselves wanted to go there. Only then came concerns that the school had good exam results and that the pupils were properly stretched.

TABLE 1: FACTORS PARENTS CONSIDER IMPORTANT WHEN CHOOSING A SECONDARY SCHOOL FOR THEIR CHILD

Parents were asked to grade each factor from 'important' to 'played no part'. Here are the factors they considered most important when choosing a secondary school.

1	Good discipline	89.6%
2	Personal impression of the school	82.2%
3	Recognition that there is more to education than just good exam results	81.5%

4 It best suits the aptitudes
   of my child   80.7%
5 My child wants to go there 79.3%
6 Good exam results   78.1%
7 Pupils are stretched   77.6%
8 Warm and caring
   atmosphere   77.6%
9 Emphasis on high
   academic achievement   74.8%
10 School's reputation   61.7%
11 The head-teacher   59.5%
12 Stress on moral, religious
   teaching   51.2%
13 School uniform   50.2%
14 Performance in 'league tables'
   of exam and test results   46.1%
15 Close to home   45.2%
16 Church links   38.1%
17 Brother or sister already
   at the school   27.7%
18 Media reports   24.6%

'LEAGUE TABLES'

Despite the outrage generated by teachers and educationalists about the use of 'league tables' of exam and test results, parents in the survey showed they were far less hot under the collar about their use. Indeed, 6 out of 10 thought them 'a good thing', while 2 out of 10 were neutral on the issue (see Table 2).

Teachers have argued that parents are not sufficiently expert to use 'league tables'. Almost 6 out of 10

parents in the survey (59.8%) disagreed with this. Only 1 in 10 accepted the assertion. The rest were neutral. More than 9 out of 10 respondents (92.1%) agreed that parents should not rely solely on exam league tables, but should take other factors into account. Nevertheless, almost 7 out of 10 (68.9%) believed that tables provide useful information that helped them make an informed choice, although some have reservations about the way 'league-table' information is used and presented. Most parents wanted the tables to give more information (73.3%).

Parents appear to be divided on many aspects of this issue. Some 40% agreed with the statement that the tables don't tell them anything they don't already know, yet an almost identical number (39.3%) disagree, and say they do offer new information. A similar split occurred when parents were asked whether tables are 'unfair'. Some 35.5% agreed, compared with 33.6% who disagreed. However, the idea of banning the tables seems to carry little support among parents. Only about 1 in 8 parents (13.2%) agreed with the statement that exam league tables should be banned. By contrast, more than 6 out of 10 (65.4%) disagreed.

TABLE 2: PARENTAL ATTITUDES TO 'LEAGUE TABLES'

Parents were asked to state whether they agreed, disagreed or remained neutral on a range of questions connected with the controversial issue of 'league tables'.

	% Agree	% Neutral	% Disagree
Exam 'league tables' do not tell parents anything they don't already know about a school	40	20	39.3
Exam 'league tables' are unfair	35.5	28	36.6
'League tables' give additional information that helps parents make informed decisions	68.9	15.3	15.7
Exam 'league tables' should give more information	73.3	19.4	7.4
Exam 'league tables' should be banned	13.2	19.4	65.4
I welcome exam 'league tables'	59.4	24	16.6
Parents should not rely solely on 'league tables' but should also take other factors into account	92.1	4.7	3.3
Parents are sensible enough to use exam 'league tables' wisely	59.8	29.5	10.7
Parents are not sufficiently expert to use exam 'league tables' wisely	29.5	30.2	40.3
Overall, exam 'league tables' are a good thing	61.4	27.1	11.6
Overall, exam 'league tables' are a bad thing	15.7	25.6	58.7

DEALING WITH GOBBLEDEGOOK

Jargon and gobbledegook are the curse of the British education system. Despite the work of the Plain English Campaign there is still too much jargon about. Mrs Chrissy Maher, the campaign's director and a mother of four said: 'This educational gobbledegook isolated me as a parent when I went to see teachers about my own children. You become totally confused, but you don't want to seem like a dingbat.' Some people have suggested that the use of jargon may be a conspiracy by the professionals against parents. Most likely it is just a combination of convenience and self-importance.

WHAT TO DO IF FACED BY GOBBLEDEGOOK

- If in doubt, ask.

- Don't be frightened of appearing stupid. Much of the jargon is a handy form of shorthand for people in the know, and you couldn't be expected to be familiar with it.

- If the words or phrases used by teachers or officials don't make sense, tell them. Explain politely that you are not fully versed in all the educational jargon, and could they please go over it again.

- Remember that jargon is often a result of lazy thinking. A gentle reminder that not everyone speaks it could help eliminate the problem.

- If you encounter jargon or gobbledegook in official documents, ring up the office concerned and ask them to explain it to you. If they decline, ask firmly but politely to speak to the boss.

The Plain English Campaign awards Crystal Marks for clarity and Golden Bull prizes to the worst printed examples of jargon and gobbledegook. The prizes receive national coverage in the media and have done wonders by embarrassing organisations into using clear English.

Send examples of educational gobbledegook to:

The Plain English Campaign
Outram House, Canal Street
Whaley Bridge
Stockport SK12 7LS

1 SCHOOLS TODAY

INTRODUCTION

THE POWER TO SURVIVE

This book is a survival guide. Massive changes to the way our school system is run mean that parents need, now more than ever, a reliable map through the maze. They need to be armed with the facts, figures and a certain amount of streetwise 'nous' which will help them secure the best possible education for their children, whether in the state or private sector. The aim of this book is to give parents a clear overview of the school system as it stands, in its state of flux, so that they can draw their own conclusions and make informed decisions.

It is the inevitable lot of parents that the bygone school days they remember, for better or worse, probably bear little relation to the schooling their own children will experience. Parents educated in the rather traditional 1940s and 1950s, with eleven-plus selection and grammar schools, are unlikely to have predicted the progressive methods that their children would encounter in the more relaxed 1960s and 1970s as the comprehensive experiment became the norm.

> ❝The whole theory of modern education is radically unsound. Fortunately in England, at any rate, education produces no effect whatsoever. If it did, it would prove a serious danger to the upper classes, and probably lead to acts of violence in Grosvenor Square. ❞

Lady Bracknell in Oscar Wilde's
The Importance of Being Earnest

Similarly, as the 21st century dawns, those post-war 'baby-boomers' and 'thirtysomethings' now raising their own families are confronted by a scene very different to the one in which they themselves were taught.

INTO THE 21ST CENTURY

Among the changes with which you as a parent must now get to grips are state schools 'opting out' of town hall control to run themselves, published 'league tables' of exam results, a national curriculum setting down what every child must learn and be tested on, and the creation of special 'hit squads' to take over the running of failing schools.

Most schools do constantly adapt themselves to keep up with the ever-changing nature of education, but the revolution that has overtaken them in recent years has completely rewritten the rules.

The revolution began in earnest with the introduction of the Education Reform Act in 1988, which set out the broad principles. It continues with the 1993 Education Act, which puts the funding and inspection of schools on a new footing. Although many of the details of the changes are being fought tooth and nail, the National Curriculum and testing look here to stay.

Change, however, is slow and the whole reform process will still be 'bedding-in' well into the 21st century.

KNOW YOUR PLACE

Critics of the system before 1988 said too many parents were expected to put up with what they were given, instead of being allowed any real choice. In short, they were expected to know their place and accept unquestioningly whatever was on offer from the state schools in their area. While the selective eleven-plus system had been criticised and almost dismantled in the 1960s and 1970s for creating grammar school 'winners' and

secondary modern 'losers', it was now the turn of the comprehensive system to come under fire.

Critics attacked the 'drab uniformity' of schools which taught pupils in mixed-ability classes and which failed to stretch the brightest or cater for the needs of the slowest learners. Underachievement was often linked to low expectations on the part of teachers. And parents had to like it or lump it. Unless, of course, they had money, and could help their children escape into private schools. But as adults and children grew accustomed to ever-increasing consumer choice, this 'take it or leave it' attitude was becoming outdated and unacceptable.

The result was the reform programme that Conservative leaders insist, amid howls of protest from opponents, will bring a greater choice and diversity of schools for parents and their children.

> ❝Parents know best the needs of their children, certainly better than educational theorists or administrators, better even than our mostly excellent teachers. ❞
>
> *Education Secretary John Patten in the 1992 White Paper 'Choice and Diversity'*

THE CUSTOMER AS KING

Parents are now seen as 'consumers' or 'customers' whose wishes must be taken more fully into account by the 'producers' – those teachers, governors and education chiefs who run our schools. Indeed, the state system is now being geared in such a way that those schools which fail to pay sufficient attention to their customers will lose out financially.

TEACHER KNOWS BEST?

It is against this background that the phrase 'parent power' has become a slogan. Politicians seized on it to describe the philosophical thrust behind the government's reform of the nation's schools. It embraces everything from what is taught and how it is taught, to devolving more cash and the responsibility for spending it down from town halls to the schools themselves. Behind this idea was the urge to give parents a much bigger say in the school system. Ministers argued that if parents are to entrust their offspring to a school to be educated, they should be allowed to influence the outcome.

The government provoked particular outrage among many teachers and educationalists when it said that parents, and not the professionals, know what is best for their children.

'Teacher knows best' was the reply of some of the professionals. 'Partnership is crucial,' said the majority.

THE POWER GAME

There should indeed be a partnership between parents and the educational professionals, a balance of power. In the best schools, that is already the case. But sometimes these 'partnerships' can be a little one-sided, with the professionals holding all the key cards – often a little too closely to their chests.

Countless official and independent reports testify that some schools are simply not up to scratch, and the result is that thousands of parents – as many as one in three – are seeing their children getting a raw deal. This book will hopefully help redress the imbalances of power and enable parents to have a greater say in their children's education.

HEART VERSUS HEAD

Nothing is so precious as a good education, but where is a good education to be found? Many parents support, in principle, the state system, but when it comes to their own children their hearts rule their heads. If the local state school does not seem to offer what they want they are prepared to go elsewhere. Often this means choosing another state school, but it can mean looking outside the state system at private schools. Other parents support the private system as a matter of principle, yet are now finding the pressure of fees propelling them toward state schools. Choosing the best school can only be done with firm information. Education officials have long used their knowledge to ensure that their own children get into the best schools. Where do teachers at your child's school send their children? Have you ever dared ask them why? And you might be surprised at how many state school teachers, local authority officials and Education Department bureaucrats send their children to independent schools.

INSIDER DEALING

The truth is that those working inside the system have always been privy to more information of better quality than those left outside it. And whatever their political or ideological views, most caring parents will let their hearts overrule their heads when it comes to their own child's future, however uncomfortable the subsequent wrestling with conscience may prove.

It would be wonderful if all schools were equally good. Sadly they are not. Some are so bad that a cycling proficiency certificate is considered a worthy substitute for academic

triumph and so rough that teachers fear for their lives. The problems may well be sociological, but, at the end of the day, would you want your child to go to such a school?

EVERYONE AN EXPERT

It is important to remember that when it comes to education all those who have been to school consider themselves 'experts'. What the experts tell you will depend on where they stand as much as on the 'facts'. As a parent you will be told that standards are spiralling up, and that they are plummeting. You will hear vigorous arguments for one educational policy, only to hear it demolished by opponents. What is crucial is that you have enough knowledge to be able to sift through the points of view you hear and are able to choose for your children the sort of education you think best.

> ❝If politicians stray from the acceptable and necessary ground of policy into laying down details of what should be taught and how it should be tested, dangers lie ahead.❞
>
> *Elizabeth Diggory, Head of St Albans' High School, addressing the 1992 annual conference of the Girls' School Association*

Former head-teacher Peter Dawson, who went on to lead the Professional Association of Teachers for many years, always had a wry sense of what parents wanted. He often told with glee the tale of one mum at Eltham Green Comprehensive, in a robust area of South London, who deposited her youngest son, the latest in a line of scallywags, into his charge. But the mum knew what he wanted. And that was to give her children the chance of a better life than she'd had.

'Mr Dawson,' she said, 'I want 'im to read proper, write proper, add up sums and behave 'is bleedin' self.'

❝There are no easy correlations these days between income, occupations and class. Parents' aspirations for their children can be high in any income group or occupation. I remember a recent conversation with a British Rail ticket collector. He had got a copy of the Parents' Charter from the library, compared the local primaries, been quite unable (despite writing to his MP) to get his daughter into the school locally accounted the best, and had tackled the head of the school she did go to, to ask why it wasn't better.❞

Averil Burgess, Headmistress, South Hampstead High School

A Short History Lesson

SCHOOLS THROUGH THE CENTURIES

To help understand where schools are going today, it is worth spending time on a short history lesson to see where they have already been.

Education for all has only existed in England since the latter part of the last century. And secondary education, as we know it today, has only been a right since the Second World War.

Formal schooling began with the Church in the early Middle Ages to prepare young boys from poor backgrounds for the priesthood.

By the middle of the 19th century there were many so called 'ragged schools', charitable institutions that provided a basic schooling, industrial training and religious education for destitute children. But with the nation at the height of the Industrial Revolution, the need for a better-educated workforce was obvious to everyone from politicians and capitalists to social campaigners.

The change came with William Forster's 1870 Education Act, which allowed authorities to introduce compulsory schooling for pupils up to the age of 11, with some exceptions. Some London boards took the step of making it compulsory to age 13.

Local school boards, elected by ratepayers, were set up to manage schools in areas where the Church had not established its own. The boards were given the power to make local authorities raise a rate to pay for the schools, and could also ensure that pupils attended.

By 1902 local councils had taken over the responsibility for all elementary, secondary and technical schools in their areas, replacing thousands of school boards. Thus public money was used to educate all children, although Church schools still retained some autonomy.

Even so, the majority of pupils attended only elementary schools from the ages of 5 to 14. Only a minority – in 1938 fewer than half a million pupils – stayed on for a genuine secondary education at a grammar or technical school. Of those, the majority had to pay full or partial fees, so millions of pupils missed out because their families could not afford the money.

MODERN TIMES: 1944 – 88

The truly universal school system, which has shaped the education of most of today's younger adults, had to wait until 1944. Tory Education Secretary Rab Butler's landmark Education Act was passed by the wartime coalition government with all-party support. It set up a tripartite system of grammar schools, secondary moderns and technical schools. The schools were run by the local education authorities (LEAs) in what experts described as 'a national education system, locally administered'.

Pupils sat an exam at the age of 11: the 'eleven-plus'. Those who passed gained a place at the local grammar school for a very academic and usually academically traditional education. Everyone who had 'failed', was destined for the far less academically challenging secondary moderns and vocational technical schools.

The system gave a great boost to post-war social mobility by providing thousands of bright boys and girls from less privileged backgrounds with the sort of schooling that had previously been the preserve only of the wealthier, fee-paying middle and upper classes.

But just as the 'grammar school boy made good' was making a mark on society, along with his female counterpart, the writing was already on the wall for their schools. Critics complained that while the 20% who passed the eleven-plus exam and went to grammar school would do well as 'winners', the remaining 80% who went off to secondary moderns were considered 'losers'. The solution, even if it meant compromising the academic high-flyers, was a school that would cater for pupils of all abilities. Matters really moved up a gear in the 1960s as Labour politicians and educationists, favouring what they termed a more 'progressive' system, oversaw the creation and massive expansion of the comprehensive school. A Labour government sounded the grammar school's death-knell in 1965 when Education Secretary Anthony Crosland's controversial 'Circular 10/65' told education authorities to push ahead with the comprehensive programme. In April 1974 another Labour government circular told education authorities to start planning the removal of selection procedures for entry into secondary schools.

This was compounded in November 1976, when Labour Education Secretary Shirley Williams presided over a new Act which legally required authorities to admit pupils 'without reference to ability or aptitude'.

This outlawing of grammar schools was to have been the final nail in the selection coffin, but the Act was revoked when the Tories came to power in 1979. Today only about 150 grammar schools survive, many of them having played for time by fighting legal actions against the Labour government's policy in a desperate bid to avoid closure. Ironically, Tory governments have probably presided over the closure of more grammar schools than Labour, as LEAs pressed ahead with their comprehensive programmes.

The arrival of the comprehensive school in the 1960s and 1970s coincided with a general mood in some sectors of society against anything that smacked of competition, success or what some termed 'élitism'.

School sport was one of the most visible manifestations of this phenomenon. Some teachers began rejecting 'competitive' sports like football, rugby and cricket, which produced clear winners and losers, in favour of less confrontational activities. The result of this policy became all too clear in later years as national sports squads bemoaned the lack of sporting talent coming up from state schools – just look at Welsh rugby and English cricket.

Traditionalist critics were furious at what they branded a perverse form of social engineering, which appeared to owe more to waging class warfare than teaching children anything useful.

Over time some truly outstanding comprehensives have developed, whilst others appear to have lost their way. Many unfortunate parents have seen their children suffer terribly in schools that have failed to stretch bright children to the full, or have let slower children wallow helplessly out of their depth. There was one escape route if your local state secondary school was abysmal: private education. But only if you could afford it.

Nor was the situation in some primary schools much healthier as, in the wake of the 1967 report by Lady Plowden, some primary schools went overboard in their enthusiasm for progressive methods. They turned their backs on the traditional 'chalk and talk' lessons, in which pupils sat in rows facing a blackboard, in favour of a more 'child-centred' approach. This was characterised by pupils sitting together in groups around tables working, for a large part, on all-embracing topics rather than specific subject-based lessons.

KEY DATES

1870

William Forster's Education Act introduces schooling for all children. Local school boards, elected by ratepayers, are set up to manage schools in areas where the Church has not established its own. The boards have power to make local authorities raise a rate to pay for the schools, and ensure that pupils attend.

1902

Local councils take over responsibility for all elementary, secondary and technical schools in their areas, replacing thousands of school boards. Public money used to educate all children, although Church schools will retain some autonomy.

1944

Rab Butler's 1944 Education Act.

It introduces the tripartite system of grammar schools, secondary moderns and technical schools. The latter subsequently fail to take off.

School-leaving age raised from 14 to 15.

1948

In September Britain witnesses the birth of a new kind of school, the 'comprehensive'. Middlesex County Council opens the first three.

1965

Labour Education Secretary Anthony Crosland sends out his department's 'Circular 10/65' to push the development of compre-hensive schools, then educating only about 1 in 10 pupils.

1967

Plowden Report leads to fashion for 'child-centred' and 'progressive' methods in primary schools.

1970

New Tory Education Secretary Margaret Thatcher revokes Labour's comprehensive 'Circular 10/65'.

1971

Tory Education Secretary Margaret Thatcher announces plans to end free school milk in schools and is dubbed 'Thatcher the Milk Snatcher'.

1973

School-leaving age raised to 16.

1974

In April Labour government sends out 'Circular 10/74' requiring education authorities to submit plans for ending selection to secondary schools.

1975

Labour legislates to phase out Direct Grant schools.

1976

In October Labour Prime Minister James Callaghan opens his 'Great Debate' on education at Ruskin College, Oxford, following deep concern about falling standards.

1976

In November Labour Education Secretary Shirley Williams presides over new Act, which outlaws grammar schools by requiring authorities to admit pupils 'without reference to ability or aptitude', to be revoked by the Tories after their 1979 victory.

1988

Tory Education Secretary Kenneth Baker introduces the landmark Education Reform Act, the biggest shake-up of the school system since Butler's 1944 Act.

It introduces for the first time a national curriculum, regular testing at ages 7, 11, 14 and 16, and allows state schools to break free of town hall control to run themselves as self-governing, grant-maintained schools with direct funding from Whitehall.

1993

John Patten's 1993 Education Act sets out the structural framework for schools into the 21st century and introduces 'hit squads' to take over or close failing schools.

Children of mixed ability began to be taught in groups in what has been dubbed a 'thematic' approach, with some doing maths in one corner, while others did reading, writing or painting in another.

Though progressive theories had much to offer, teachers were often unfamiliar with the new planning and organisation required, and in practice many children floundered under this experimental system. However, most schools adopted a mixture of styles and avoided the worst errors of some of their colleagues. Labour leader Jim Callaghan saw the problem only too clearly in 1976 when, against a backdrop of concern about falling standards, he opened his 'Great Debate' on education during a speech at Ruskin College, Oxford:

'There is no virtue in producing socially well-adjusted members of society who are unemployed because they have no skills.'

'I am concerned to find complaints from industry that new recruits from the schools sometimes do not have the basic tools to do the job that is required.'

Mr Callaghan believed these tools were 'to be basically literate, to be basically numerate, to understand how to live and work together, and to have respect for others and respect for the individual'.

Conservative politicians, too, were alarmed. They, however, blamed the 'dull uniformity' of the comprehensive system and pledged to reform it once they got into power. They did achieve power, in 1979, but it still took them another nine years to tackle schools with the 1988 Education Reform Act: the biggest classroom shake-up since the war.

A NEW ERA – THE REFORM YEARS 1988 – 93

Driving the government's school reforms was the political will to end what ministers perceived to be the monopoly on state education held by the local education authorities. Policy-makers felt this was crucial to pushing up standards and giving parents more choice.

When the landmark Education Reform Act became law in 1988 the government seized on its initial letters to spell out the new political agenda. This was to be a new era.

In fact this was only the beginning, and the past few years have seen even more changes which, as Britain enters the 21st century, will shape the educational landscape quite profoundly.

THE KEY CHANGES IN THE 1988 EDUCATION REFORM ACT INTRODUCED BY EDUCATION SECRETARY KENNETH BAKER WERE:

- the introduction of a national curriculum, setting down for the first time what every pupil must learn and be tested on from the ages of 5 to 16.

- regular testing of pupils at ages 7, 11, 14 and 16, with publication of results.

- the right for schools to 'opt out' of local education authority control to become grant-maintained with direct funding from Whitehall.

- delegating cash down from town halls to the schools themselves, allowing heads and governors to decide how 85% of the money should be spent and managed.

- scrapping artificial pupil limits which councils had set on popular schools.

- the creation of City Technology Colleges in inner-city areas as a result of a partnership between industry and government.

INTO THE FUTURE

The 1993 Education Act serves to tie up the loose ends left by previous reforms. For example, it creates a new funding framework to cater for what ministers predict will be a much enlarged sector of grant-maintained schools. As these state schools are now self-governing and receive their funding from Whitehall, this could spell the disappearance of local education authorities in some areas.

Earlier, the 1992 Education (Schools) Act brought in a new system of regular school inspections that began in September 1993. Private teams of inspectors now monitor standards in all schools and identify those which are at risk of failing. Under the 1993 Act, schools that significantly fail these standards will be taken over by 'hit squads' of experts who will try to rescue the school or, if that proves impossible, close it down.

The two words at the heart of the government White Paper announcing these proposals were 'choice' and 'diversity'. Ministers want to expand the different types of school available to parents by encouraging pupils to specialise in different areas. This follows the idea behind the 'magnet' schools in America. These attract pupils by specialising in the arts, science, technology and modern foreign languages.

THE 1992 EDUCATION (SCHOOLS) ACT SAW:

- the creation of a new watchdog, the Office of Standards in Education (OFSTED), to oversee a system of regular inspections in schools from 1993.

- plans for every school to be inspected every four years by properly validated private inspection teams, with reports published and sent directly to parents.

Many of the ideas behind the reforms were floated by the Tory London borough of Wandsworth.

Ministers also claim to have started an 'information revolution' by giving parents the right to hard facts on which to base their choice of school. The information comes in a variety of forms, including 'league tables' of school exam performance and truancy rates, inspection reports, and annual reports on their own individual child's performance. It means parents will not only know how their own child or school is doing, they will be able to compare that performance against national bench-marks.

More generally, primary schools are now being advised to teach pupils in 'sets', which means dividing pupils up into groups according to their ability in each subject. In addition, there may be more 'whole-class' teaching instead of smaller group work, more individual subject teaching and less topic work. This is because schools are being asked to consider whether they are using an appropriate balance of these teaching styles.

Teacher training, which has in the past been concentrated in colleges, will progressively shift into the schools themselves. Schools will in future receive cash to run as 'teaching schools', in the same way that we have teaching hospitals. The idea is to give trainee teachers more practical experience and less theory.

Ministers privately wish they had tackled this area much earlier, as Tory education experts believe the training colleges have been the breeding ground for many of the more 'progressive' ideas that have been passed down through generations of new teachers and taken root in schools.

❝If you have a school at risk, a St Trinian's in your patch, then parents should be made aware.❞

Professor Stewart Sutherland, Her Majesty's Chief Inspector of Schools at the launch of his new Office for Standards in Education

---

THE 1993 EDUCATION ACT MEANS:

- greater flexibility for schools to specialise in particular areas, such as science, technology and modern foreign languages.

- special 'hit squads' of experts and retired head-teachers will be sent in to salvage or shut down failing schools. Their official title is Education Associations.

- a better deal for children with special educational needs.

- a new framework for funding schools in areas where grant-maintained schools become a real force.

- the creation of funding councils to channel funds to grant-maintained schools and take a strategic planning role alongside or in place of the local education authority.

- measures to make it easier for schools to opt out and to reduce the risk of schools deterring parents who want their schools to go grant-maintained.

NATIONAL CURRICULUM

WHAT IS THE NATIONAL CURRICULUM?

The National Curriculum sets down what all pupils in state schools throughout England and Wales should learn between the ages of 5 and 16. It details the subjects that must be covered and the targets that should be achieved.

Linked to this is a programme of regular testing at ages 7, 11, 14 and 16. Results are published so that parents can compare the performance of their own child, and his or her school, against local and national bench-marks. Progress in each subject will usually be assessed by a combination of these national tests and teachers' assessments of work.

Results from tests at 7, 11 and 14 will help identify each pupil's strengths and weaknesses, and pinpoint areas that need more attention. This leads up to GCSE exams at age 16, which give pupils formal qualifications in National Curriculum and other subjects.

The results of all tests, examinations and teacher assessments in National

Curriculum and other subjects will be sent to you in the annual report on your child's progress, which all schools must now produce. In some cases you will not only receive your child's overall mark or 'level', but also details of how your child fared in the areas that make up that subject.

Until the 1988 Education Reform Act created the National Curriculum, schools in England and Wales were free to decide for themselves what should be taught. The law had little to say except that religious education was compulsory. This is in stark contrast to many of our European neighbours, who introduced either national or regional curriculums years ago and are now moving toward less rigid systems.

The 1988 Education Reform Act was introduced to raise standards in state schools, and in 1993 inspectors from the Office for Standards in Education reported that it was successfully doing that in maths, English and science. But its introduction also heralded years of controversy as rival camps argued over what, and how much, should be in it. The result is that from now on the National Curriculum should concentrate on the basic building blocks of each subject, be less detailed and prescriptive, and give teachers more flexibility about what they teach. The National Curriculum is no longer set in stone and can be adapted as required.

The 1988 Education Reform Act says the curriculum should:

- be balanced and broadly based.

- promote the spiritual, moral, cultural, mental and physical development of pupils at the school and of society.

- prepare pupils for the opportunities, responsibilities and experiences of adult life.

As a parent, the best way to keep up with the changes as they happen is to read newspapers, which report them in detail, and to keep in contact with your child's school.

WHAT IS IN THE NATIONAL CURRICULUM?

The National Curriculum was designed to stress 'positive achievement' rather than failure. It consists of three core subjects – English, maths and science, plus seven foundation subjects:

technology, history, geography, a modern foreign language, art, music and physical education. The modern foreign language is compulsory only from the age of eleven.

The National Curriculum and its associated tests are being slimmed down substantially as a result of the review in August 1993 by Sir Ron Dearing, Chairman of the School Curriculum and Assessment Authority. The main thrust of the reform was to ensure that the essentials of each subject are taught in all schools, while giving teachers more flexibility to teach what they think best. For younger pupils the emphasis is firmly on the three Rs.

Some questions remain to be settled, but the main changes made by the government are that:

- Pupils up to the age of seven are to concentrate on the basics of reading, writing, spelling, handwriting and arithmetic.

- Pupils aged 8 to 11 continue to study nine compulsory National Curriculum subjects: English, maths, science, technology, geography, history, art, music and PE, but lesson content is being slimmed down. (Religious education and now sex education are also compulsory, though parents have a right to withdraw their children).

NATIONAL
CURRICULUM

SEE ALSO:
The Big Debates
Sex Education
RE and
Collective
Worship

- A modern foreign language continues as part of the curriculum for 11 to 14 year-olds.

- The existing curriculum remains in force until the school year 1994 – 95. The first slimmed down subjects are brought in for the school year 1995 – 96.

- The government says it will produce optional banks of tests that teachers may use to support their own assessment, as already happens in Scotland.

The National Curriculum plus religious education is known as the 'basic curriculum'.

In Wales, schools in Welsh-speaking areas study their native language as a core subject. Schools in areas where English is the main language treat Welsh as a foundation subject.

The National Curriculum will not be fully in place until 1996, and that deadline may slip. The first 'graduates' to have studied the National Curriculum in full from 5 until 16 will not emerge from a British school until the year 2003.

CROSS-CURRICULAR THEMES AND SKILLS

The government's curriculum advisers have also identified five cross-curricular 'themes', which all pupils should study in order to make their study 'broad and balanced' as the law requires.

These are:

- economic and industrial understanding

PROGRESS THROUGH THE YEARS

AGE	YEAR	KEY STAGE	AGE	YEAR	KEY STAGE
5	Reception		12	Year 7	
6	Year 1	1	13	Year 8	3
7	Year 2		14	Year 9	
8	Year 3		15	Year 10	4
9	Year 4	2	16	Year 11	
10	Year 5				
11	Year 6				

- health education
- careers education and guidance
- environmental education
- citizenship.

KEY STAGES

There are four 'Key Stages' – 1, 2, 3 and 4 – covering the 11 years of compulsory education. A Key Stage is simply a block of years.

THE TEN-LEVEL NATIONAL CURRICULUM SCALE

Most National Curriculum subjects are assessed against a ten-level scale except music, art and physical education.

- An average 7 year-old should achieve level 2.

- An average 11 year-old should achieve level 4.

- An average 14 year-old should achieve level 5 or 6.

- An average 16 year-old should achieve level 6 or 7.

An average seven year-old should reach level 2, while a bright child could achieve level 3 or even 4. Only the very brightest 16 year-old pupils will reach level 10. However, the scale has drawn a lot of flak from

❝ When, in 1976, the then Prime Minister, James Callaghan, in his speech at Ruskin College, set out the notion of a national curriculum and national standards, he provoked some hostility among teachers and local education authorities. But there was undeniably a feeling among politicians, parents and the press that something was wrong in our schools and that something needed to be done. ❞

John Rowland, President of the National Association of Schoolmasters/Union of Women Teachers, 1993 – 4

some education experts who say that you simply can't measure pupil performance in all subjects this way. So the future of the ten-level scale is in doubt for some, if not all, subjects.

WHY HAVE A NATIONAL CURRICULUM?

The argument for a national curriculum in England and Wales really took hold following a landmark speech by Labour Prime Minister James Callaghan at Ruskin College, Oxford, in 1976. His call for 'the so-called core curriculum of basic knowledge' came in response to rising concerns about low standards in schools. But Mr Callaghan's 'Great Debate', which raised the notion of a national curriculum, was opposed by many teachers and local education authorities. When the Tories took power in 1979 they developed the idea of a national curriculum, and it became a reality in 1988 with the Education Reform Act.

The government wanted to ensure that all children are taught what they really need to know and that their progress is checked regularly. The continuous monitoring of performance should help teachers set a pace suitable for each child, while building on strengths and tackling weaknesses. Of course, good teachers should already make their own informal assessment of students' progress in order to pitch their teaching correctly.

It is hoped that by publicly specifying what students should achieve, the problem of teachers' low expectations of what their pupils can achieve – highlighted by a host of inspectors' reports – and of wide differences in standards in similar schools across the country will be eliminated.

Britain needs brain-power, not muscle-power. But the nation has won for itself a reputation as the 'thick man of Europe' with one of its worst-educated workforces –

particularly in areas of science, technology, basic mathematics and language skills. The high drop-out rate has been one significant worry. Many pupils were specialising too early and missing out on a broad and balanced curriculum. Some 75% left school without attempting an exam in a balanced science course, two-thirds of 16 year-olds failed to attempt exams in history and almost as many did not do modern foreign languages or geography. Few girls took technological subjects and few boys studied modern foreign languages.

Fee-paying independent schools do not have to follow the National Curriculum. Ministers originally advanced the view that the failure of independent schools to follow the National Curriculum would alert them to the fact that there was something wrong with it.

> ❛ The strait-jacket of the National Curriculum, with its concomitant time-consuming tests, may be necessary to improve state school standards, but no independent school worth its salt should have to use it. ❜
>
> *Sir Robert Balchin, Chairman of the Grant Maintained Schools' Foundation*

SO WHY THE CONTROVERSY?

Arguments about the National Curriculum and its associated testing have persisted for years. But, curiously, the reasons given by those who oppose them have shifted subtly over the years.

At first the argument was whether we needed a national curriculum at all. In 1987 the National Union of Teachers voted not to co-operate with the government in setting one up. This echoed the stance they had taken more than a decade earlier when Labour Prime Minister James Callaghan urged its introduction.

But Britain's poor showing against its international competitors and the great disparity in standards between similar schools mean that the argument for a national curriculum has now been won. Few teachers or educationalists, despite their initial reluctance, now argue that it should be scrapped. The battleground has shifted instead to what should be in it.

Now, here's the rub. The original idea floated by many Conservative supporters had been for a 'no-frills' national curriculum that set down the minimum basic that children should know. This would be checked by simple 'pencil and paper' tests to ensure that pupils at least knew the three Rs, the rudiments of science

and a smattering of a foreign language by the time they left school.

But many teachers and educationalists objected to this approach, believing it too 'simplistic'. The educationalists wanted more emphasis to be put on the pupils' acquisition of 'skills'. They wanted to ensure that pupils not only absorbed information, but knew how to apply it. In short, they believed it was as important to see what a child could do as to discover what he or she knew. They objected to what they saw as a return to crude rote-learning and 'teaching to the test'.

This view was not universally held. Others, with a more traditional view thought this approach was too 'woolly' and failed to give sufficient weight to the teaching of knowledge or facts. Nevertheless, this 'skills' philosophy was the one which initially drove the early content of the embryonic national curriculum.

A 'YES MINISTER' NATIONAL CURRICULUM?

Instead of the 'no-frills' national curriculum first envisaged, Education Secretary Kenneth Baker decided in 1988 that his version should lay down in detail what children should know in ten key subjects. Some observers suggest he was overly influenced – or 'got at' – by his

Whitehall advisers. A host of Conservative education secretaries going back to Margaret Thatcher have viewed with grave suspicion and mistrust their own top civil servants, fearing their sympathies lie more with the educational theories and practices of the 1960s and 1970s than with the radical changes the government was trying to implement in the 1980s and 1990s.

These same civil servants, nevertheless, helped to hand-pick the members of working groups to decide what should be studied for each subject. A third of those chosen were university professors or lecturers.

"APPEARS THAT THE INITIAL WORKING PARTY WAS INCORRECTLY FORMULATED".

There were, however, few working teachers to say what would work in the classroom, and only a handful of industrialists. Most were members of what ministers and others have referred to subsequently as the 'Education Establishment'. Teachers often complain, with hindsight, that they were not given a chance to help draw up the National Curriculum and argue that if their advice had been heeded, many of the later problems would have been avoided.

This is a fair comment as far as it goes. But it also ignores the fact that the teachers' trade union leaders and representatives were at best lukewarm about, and in some cases virulently opposed to, the reforms. Ministers

THEY OBVIOUSLY COULDN'T GET THEIR ACT TOGETHER!

20

> 6 Nobody is challenging the principle of the National Curriculum. It is an accepted development and there is recognition that it is beginning to raise standards. 9

Sir Ron Dearing, Chairman of the School Curriculum and Assessment Authority, beginning his National Curriculum Review in May 1993

therefore viewed such offers of 'help' with suspicion. As it was, a few early members of the subject working party groups resigned from their posts in disgust, complaining that m any of their co-members were actually philosophically opposed to the government's reforms and were out to sabotage them from within. Civil servants within the Education Department were also accused of hampering the spirit of the reforms, in the manner immortalised by television's 'Yes Minister', by subtly doing the opposite of what ministers intended.

GROWING LIKE TOPSY

The subject groups of experts set up to advise on what should be taught got down to their tasks with gusto. But as each and every educational lobby group – including teachers – threw in their five-pennyworth about what MUST be included, an ever more complex web emerged. Individual subjects became over-loaded. The result was that the National Curriculum grew like Topsy as more and more detail was added. The extent of the problem remained hidden for a while. But as more subjects came on stream, the cumulative effect of the overload became critical.

Critics also complained about the 'woolly' and jargon-ridden nature of the lesson blueprints. For instance, a huge row erupted over the early history blueprint in which pupils were expected to 'empathise' with historical characters. This meant that instead of remembering that the Battle of Hastings took place in 1066, a pupil would be left with the impression of how he or she would have 'felt' as one of King Harold's or William the Conqueror's fighters.

14 year-olds, describing them as 'elaborate nonsense'.

But drawing up simpler, objective written papers didn't help ministers win over the disgruntled teachers either. They had opposed the first task-based tests because they found them too bureaucratic and time-consuming. They then opposed the slimmed down, more traditional style tests because they believed them too 'simplistic' or 'mechanistic'.

By now, ministers were beginning to suspect that teachers would seek any excuse to oppose tests. This belief played a part in shaping their future behaviour towards the teachers as attitudes hardened on both sides. The teachers, by contrast, insisted they had always tested pupils as and when they needed to. What they

NEVER MIND THE QUALITY, FEEL THE WIDTH

By April 1990 even the then Prime Minister Margaret Thatcher was complaining that this complex creation was not what she had in mind. The first of a series of 'slimming-down' exercises got under way. Kenneth Clarke, as Education Secretary, subsequently scrapped some of the early task-based tests drawn up for

6 It is one thing to support the National Curriculum and its general aims, quite another to support in any way the greedy monster represented by the ten National Curriculum subjects with their ten levels each and their unnumbered and innumerable attainment targets. 9

Harry Isaac, President of the Association of Teachers and Lecturers, 1993 – 94

21

objected to were nationally imposed tests which, they argued, taught them nothing they didn't already know. Tests should be used as 'diagnostic tools' to support their own teaching, not as the basis for creating 'league tables' of schools.

Ministers insisted national tests were essential if parents were to be able to judge their child's and the school's performance against nationally laid down bench-marks. They suggested that some teachers were simply afraid of having their performance monitored in a way that might highlight deficiencies which the reforms were designed to eradicate. Education Secretary John Patten said 'This small band of educational Luddites has opposed every single step that has been taken to raise education out of the abyss into which it had fallen in the Sixties'.

NATIONAL CURRICULUM AT KEY STAGE 4	
AGE 14 – 16 subject to review	
CORE SUBJECTS★	
Maths	Full course
Science	Single, double or three separate sciences
English	Full course
FOUNDATION SUBJECTS★	
Technology	Full course
A modern foreign language	Full or short course
History **Geography**	Full course in ONE or short combined courses in BOTH
Physical education	Compulsory
Art	Optional
Music	Optional

★WALES
In schools where Welsh is a CORE subject, it remains compulsory.
In schools where Welsh is a FOUNDATION subject, pupils may take either a full or a short course.
Religious education continues to be compulsory up to the age of 16.

STOPPING THE JUGGERNAUT

By March 1993, however, the government was also under attack from right-wing critics who said it had allowed the Education Establishment to undermine its original vision and create 'a juggernaut' that was out of control. At a heated meeting of the right-wing Centre for Policy Studies think-tank in March 1993, Mr Patten was told to his face that he had let too many 'half-baked' ideas take root. Donald Naismith, Director of Education for the Conservative flagship borough of Wandsworth, who briefed Mrs Thatcher on the original idea for a simple, straightforward national curriculum and testing programme, said 'What we have now is not what was intended. Chickens are coming home to roost. The government will have to rethink it along original lines.'

Critics said the fundamental problem was the ten-level scale against which all pupils were to be measured, in every subject, throughout their school life. The idea was flawed, they said. Now it is under review.

By 1993 ministers were paying dearly for past errors and compromises. Teacher boycotts against the tests were solid. Despite the confrontation, the overload in the curriculum was at least one point on which ministers, teachers and educationists were agreed. The real row was about how best to put things right.

WHAT OF THE FUTURE?

The National Curriculum is still being phased in, and will not be properly bedded in until the beginning of the next century – which is not too far away. The massive review ordered by ministers in 1993 set about slimming down the National Curriculum even further to create more flexibility in the system. This means giving both teachers and pupils more time and responsibility to choose what they think best suits them. Some observers say the National Curriculum should take up no more than 70% of teaching time, leaving space to teach other subjects like economics, Latin and Greek. The topic is nevertheless likely to remain one of controversy for some time to come.

THE APPLICATION OF SCIENCE

There are now three options for older secondary school pupils studying science towards GCSE.

- Single science, which takes up about 12.5% of the timetable and is worth a single GCSE.

SEE ALSO:
GCSEs and
A-Levels

- Double or 'balanced' science, which takes up about 20% of the timetable and is worth two GCSEs.

- Three separate sciences, which take up about 30% of the timetable.

The majority of state school 14 to 16 year-olds are expected to take double or 'balanced' science, which, say its supporters, contains all the essential knowledge and concepts of the separate sciences.

Pupils unable to manage double science, or who want to concentrate on another subject, may take single science, which still embraces all three disciplines.

Ministers retained the option of the traditional three separate sciences – physics, biology and chemistry – following pressure from public school heads.

BENEFITS OF THE NATIONAL CURRICULUM

Apart from raising standards, the government says the combination of clear targets and national tests will ensure that:

- Parents can see the progress and standards being achieved by their children, and hold their schools to account.

- Pupils can move more easily from one school to another without disrupting their education.

- Teachers have the highest expectations of their pupils.

- Schools raise their standards across the country.

OPPOSING VIEWS

The Times said:

'Inspectors report that children are faring better in three out of four subjects since the advent of the national curriculum.'

15/3/93

While The *Guardian* reported:

'The Education Inspectorate yesterday undermined government claims that the national curriculum has raised performance in schools by reporting that it did not significantly improve educational standards in its first two years of operation.'

30/12/92

A GUIDE THROUGH THE JARGON

KEY STAGE

Pupils following the National Curriculum progress from age 5 to 16 through four 'Key Stages' numbered 1, 2, 3 and 4. The law says they must be assessed at the end of each Key Stage at ages 7, 11, 14 and 16.

STANDARD ASSESSMENT TASKS (SATs)

Another name for National Curriculum tests taken at ages 7, 11 and 14. The GCSE exam is the test for 16 year-olds.

ATTAINMENT TARGETS (ATs)

National Curriculum subjects are broken down into smaller sections called Attainment Targets. These set out the knowledge, skills and understanding pupils of different abilities and motivations are expected to have at the end of each Key Stage. In mathematics the Attainment Targets are: using and applying mathematics, number, algebra, shape and space, handling data. Confusingly, these are not precise targets, but areas that should be studied.

PROGRAMMES OF STUDY

What your child must cover in lessons. Programmes of study set out the 'matters, skills and processes that must be taught to pupils'. Curriculum advisers describe them as the teacher's 'planning tools'.

YEAR GROUPS

Remember when secondary school teachers and pupils referred to the 'fourth form'? That's all changed. Many now call it Year 10. The new scale begins at age 5 with the 'Reception' class, followed by Year 1, Year 2 and so on up to the 16 year-olds in Year 11. Don't worry. Many teachers have to think twice, too.

LEVELS

All pupils have their progress in National Curriculum subjects measured against a ten-level scale which covers the whole of the 5 to 16 age group. An average seven year-old should achieve level 2. He or she would be expected to progress about one level every two years. Only the very brightest 16 year-olds would progress to level 10. However, the controversial ten-level scale is under review because critics say it is not possible to measure achievements in all subjects on one uniform scale.

STATEMENT OF ATTAINMENT

A precise statement of what pupils should be able to do.

AIMING FOR THE TARGETS

The National Curriculum sets clear targets for children to achieve in each subject at different ages. Here are some of the targets for pupils at key ages, plus the levels that children of average ability would be expected to reach.

AGE 7

Target score for pupil of average ability : level 2

ENGLISH

- read a range of material with some independence, fluency, accuracy and understanding

- produce, independently, pieces of legible writing using complete sentences

- spell simple words such as 'and', 'take', 'them'

MATHS

- read, write and count numbers in order to at least 100

- work out change

- know the common units of measurement

- understand the meaning of 'a half' and 'a quarter'

- solve simple additions and subtractions such as 3 + 6 = 9, or 8 - 3 = 5

SCIENCE

- know that plants and animals need certain conditions to live

- know the relationship of the Earth to the Sun and Moon

- know the effects of pushes and pulls

- know that magnets attract some materials but not others, and that they can repel each other

AGE 11

Target score for pupil of average ability : level 4

ENGLISH

- read aloud expressively, fluently and with increased confidence from a range of familiar literature

- write stories that have an opening, a setting, characters or series of events and an ending

- spell words that display the main rules of English spelling

- match style of writing to different audiences

MATHS

- recognise and understand simple fractions and percentages

- know multiplication or times-tables up to 10 × 10 and use them

in multiplication and division problems

- know basic algebra

- work out areas, perimeters and volumes

- work out calculations mentally or on paper

- make 3-D objects

SCIENCE

- draw conclusions from the results of experiments

- construct simple electric circuits

- know about the formation of soil

AGE 14

Target score for pupil of average ability : level 6

ENGLISH

- read a range of fiction and poetry, explaining preferences and showing critical and analytical skills

- produce, independently, pieces of writing in which the subject matter is organised and set out clearly and appropriately

- check final drafts of writing for misspelling and other errors in presentation

MATHS

- calculate with fractions, decimals and percentages

- use formulae to find the circumference and area of a circle

- design and use a questionnaire for an opinion survey and analyse the results

SCIENCE

- know how organisms are adapted to survive in their natural environment

- understand the difference between solids, liquids and gases

AGE 16

Target score for pupil of average ability : level 7

ENGLISH

- talk and write about literature and other texts giving evidence of a personal response to the work

- show an awareness, in discussion and writing, of what is appropriate and inappropriate language use in written English

- argue a point of view using evidence from texts

- spell, and understand the meaning of, common word 'roots' that have been borrowed from other languages

NATIONAL CURRICULUM

SEE ALSO:
The Information
Revolution
Pupil Reports
GCSEs and
A-Levels

MATHS

- solve different types of equations

- use Pythagoras's Theorem to work out the unknown lengths of triangles

SCIENCE

- understand how the volume, pressure and temperature of a gas are related

- know how gravity works and determines the movements of planets

- understand the molecular basis of inheritance

- understand the movements of the Earth's crust

- use symbolic equations to describe chemical reactions

CHILDREN WHO HAVE SPECIAL EDUCATIONAL NEEDS

Children with special educational needs will usually follow the National Curriculum and take the tests at 7, 11 and 14 and exams at 16. These will be specially adapted, where necessary, for individual pupils.

School Curriculum and Assessment Authority (SCAA)
Newcombe House
45 Notting Hill Gate
London W11 3JB

Tel: 071-229 1234
Fax: 071-243 0542

Save the trees

Teacher Sue Rogers startled a conference when she wheeled in on a trolley the five-foot high pile of National Curriculum documents and advisory papers that every schoolteacher must study. Trainee teachers at Warwick University similarly saw their shelves groan under the weight of official bumph they have to wade through.

Though it has already been slimmed and simplified, the National Curriculum still has a long way to go to match the slim foreign rivals. Critics refer to the workload it imposes as 'death by ring-binder', after the folders in which the papers are stored. It was a relief to teachers when the National Curriculum review of 1993 set out plans to slim it down considerably. So Britain should be a little more in line with other countries that have opted for much less detailed lesson plans.

NATIONAL CURRICULUM

GERMANY

In the southern German state of Bavaria, teacher Angelika Schmid can hold aloft all her curriculum documents in one hand. There are just five volumes: one for primary schools, one for special needs, and three for secondary education. The Bavarian 'Lehrplan' – literally 'teaching plan' – was recently revamped to make it more parent-friendly. Frau Schmid, who teaches English and German at the Oskar-von-Miller Grammar School in Munich, said 'You read it once through and you know it.'

FRANCE

Marguerite Gentzbittel, Head of the Lycée Fenelon in the Paris Latin Quarter, has her copy of the French national curriculum in paperback form on her shelf. Contrary to popular myth, the French minister of education cannot look at his watch and know exactly what every child is studying in every classroom. But it's not far wrong. Madam Gentzbittel, whose own pupils have included the children of movie star Catherine Deneuve, film director Louis Malle, and the grandson of former French President Georges Pompidou, said 'I don't know how you survived without a national curriculum. But yours is a bit complicated.'

TESTING

TESTING TIMES

Controversy has dogged the progress of the new National Curriculum tests since they were introduced by the 1988 Education Reform Act. Arguments raged first about whether they should be introduced at all, and then about what should be in them. Matters came to a head in the spring and summer of 1993 when the three main classroom teachers' unions voted to boycott the planned tests for 1.2 million 7 and 14 year-olds. Motives for the action varied. The main reason stated by the teachers' leaders was 'excessive workload'. The tests were simply too complicated, too bureaucratic, too time-consuming and technically 'flawed'. Even some right-wing education experts who helped draw up the tests spoke of 'a monster of byzantine complexity'. This argument drew much public sympathy and support, even from traditionally Conservative-supporting newspapers. The consensus of opinion – backed by opinion polls of parents – was that the vast majority of people supported the principle of tests, but had severe reservations about the way the 1993 crop had been introduced. The government responded by agreeing to slim down the tests from 1994 to concentrate on 'the basics' of English, maths for seven year-olds plus science for older pupils.

However, some teachers made clear publicly and privately that they were philosophically opposed to the whole idea of national tests, and wanted the system scrapped altogether. They argued that teachers had always organised their own tests in the classroom to help monitor pupils' progress, and that this should be enough. The National Union of

❛ It is a misguided notion on the part of some educational theorists that if work is graded some children and their parents will think of themselves as failures. Pupils need to be told when they are doing badly just as much as they need to be when they are doing well. Praise or encouragement loses value if it is lavished on every piece of work.❜

Education Secretary John Patten in his 1992 White Paper 'Choice and Diversity'

TEST QUESTIONS – extract from *The Sunday Times*

MATHS TESTS
Age 7:
Mental arithmetic sums may include adding up scores in a tiddlywinks match or working out the price of food on a snack-stall. Algebra questions include: 4+2=?, 5-?=4 and ?+7=8.
Pupils would be expected to fill in the missing number from a sequence running: 2, 4, ?, 8, 10.
They may be shown a picture of a tennis ball, priced 25p and asked 'How many balls can you buy for £1.25', or 'Cakes are 7p each. How much will five cakes cost?'
Bright children may answer questions on long division, multiplication, percentages and fractions.

Age 11:
'Calculate how many worms there are in a field measuring 225 square metres, given that each square metre contains 75 worms.'

Age 14:
Pupils may be asked to work out how much carpet is needed to fit a floor of given size, or how many rolls of wallpaper are needed to redecorate a room. They may have to use Pythagoras's Theorem to work out the lengths of a side of a flag.

Teachers said the government should simply produce 'banks' of tests which teachers could, if they wished, draw on to support their own assessments of each pupil's progress, as happens in Scotland.

This clash of philosophies has led to much of the trouble over testing. Some parents also expressed reservations about testing pupils at age seven, fearing that they may be overcome by stress. Ministers pointed out that the tests for seven year-olds were the ones running most smoothly, having had time to 'bed-in'. They also highlighted research which showed that most children actually enjoy taking the tests, and that the results showed that many teachers were underestimating what their pupils could achieve.

BACK TO BASICS?

The government's original idea had been for traditional and straightforward 'pencil and paper' tests that could be sat by whole classes at the same time and administered easily by teachers. This would ensure all pupils left school with at least a firm grasp of the three Rs, and, it was hoped, enough flexibility to do their own thing.

'Pencil and paper' tests are probably what most parents will think of when the word 'test' is mentioned. Many independent schools set them as a matter of course at the end of each term. Most state schools insist they too set regular internal tests to help inform teachers about pupil progress.

Teachers' leaders and many educationalists were, however, horror-struck by the idea of such tests being introduced nationwide to judge not only the performance of pupils, but also of schools. Such tests were too simplistic, they complained. They would not help teachers diagnose faults or weaknesses. They would lead to teachers 'teaching to the test' by cramming pupils with information that would get them a high mark, instead of helping them to understand fully the principles behind what they were doing.

The government took many of these concerns on board. The result was that the first tests, for seven year-olds, were not the simple 'pencil and paper' tests first envisaged, but much more complex task-based exercises that teachers had to administer to pupils one at a time or in groups. They were given a special jargon name Standard Assessment Tasks, or SATs, to emphasise the importance of the 'task' element.

Committees of expert academics and educationalists drew up the tests according to the brief set by the government. Some of the earliest examples, however, were ludicrous. Journalists giggled when they were shown them. Teachers, who had to administer them to classes of 30

6 The original intention of testing in schools - that information should be available for all pupils and schools for core subjects at ages 7, 11, and 14 using short paper and pencil group tests which are simple to administer and easily under-stood has been substantially undermined.
'The testing system which has been developed since the Act was passed is so complex and so full of anomalies that is virtually incapable of being explained simply to the public.9

Dr John Marks, Standards in Schools, *Social Market Foundation, 1991*

children found less to smile about, even though their own leaders had been among the loudest voices against the 'pencil and paper' tests. The teachers' main grumble was that no one had consulted them – the people who had to administer the tests – about making them manageable. Other critics complained that the tests had been 'hijacked' by the 'Education Establishment'.

Lord Skidelsky, who later became a key government adviser on testing before resigning dramatically in a blaze of publicity, said of the National Curriculum system of testing that emerged: 'The source of its byzantine complexity comes from two sources – teachers and government. Between them they have created a monster.'

The government's advisory body on testing from 1988 was the School Examinations and Assessment Council (SEAC), set up to construct, administer and monitor testing procedures. In September 1993 it merged with the National Curriculum Council (NCC) to form the new School Curriculum and Assessment Authority (SCAA), which now advises ministers on both testing and curriculum matters.

WHY TEST CHILDREN?

Whenever I talk to parents about the school system and education in general, they are almost certain eventually, and in exasperation, to raise one key point: 'Why is there all this fuss about testing? We were always tested at school.'

The government's aim is absolutely clear. Ministers believe that regular national tests, in key subjects, taken by every pupil at the age of 7, 11, 14 and 16, are the best way of monitoring progress and raising standards for individual pupils, individual schools and the nation's children as a whole.

Publishing the school-by-school and area-by-area test results gives parents an idea of how their own children – and their current or prospective schools – are performing against local and national averages, argue ministers.

The government also argues that the tests will:

- give pupils a chance to show what they know and can do.

- give parents and teachers important information about each pupil's strengths and weaknesses.

- help teachers and parents plan together the next stage of each child's schooling.

Until recently, the only public test a child might sit before taking GCSEs (or previously O-levels) at age 16 was the controversial eleven-plus exam for entry into grammar school or secondary modern. This now exists in only a few parts of the country.

By contrast, the National Curriculum sets targets for pupils of all ages and abilities to achieve between the ages of 5 and 16 in the ten curriculum subjects. These consistent standards are often referred to as national bench-marks. Some will be assessed by the teachers on the basis of each pupil's performance in class. Others will be assessed by formal tests.

TESTS AT 7, 11, 14 AND 16

Each pupil will be formally assessed four times throughout the compulsory years of his or her school life – at ages 7, 11, 14 and 16. The assessment will take two forms:

- tests
- teacher assessment.

The balance between tests, set externally, and the teacher's own assessment will alter depending on the individual subjects. At age 16, the main test will be the GCSE exam in each subject. The GCSE exam is compulsory for almost all students in the three core subjects of English, maths and science. It had been intended that technology would join this list of compulsory exams at the end of the two-year GCSE courses beginning in September 1993, with other subjects coming on stream in subsequent years.

Classroom disruption looms as teachers vote to boycott testing

The government announced a range of fundamental changes to testing in the wake of the review by Sir Ron Dearing, Chairman of the School Curriculum and Assessment Authority, in August 1993. Not all the issues were settled and the future of the ten-level National Curriculum scale to measure pupil performance remained in doubt. Here are how the changes affect your child.

AT AGE 7

- Pupils sit a reduced number of tests concentrating on reading, writing, spelling, handwriting and arithmetic.

- Science tests scrapped and replaced by teacher assessment.

- No 'league tables' of school-by-school performance are to be published.

- Instead, parents are to be told how their child and school has fared. The Education Department is to publish annually a national aggregate bench-mark against which parents can check performance.

- Teacher assessments of pupils' schoolwork in English, maths and science are to have equal status with the test results, and will be reported alongside them.

AT AGE 11

- Pupils sit tests in maths, English and science.

- Voluntary pilot tests take place in May 1994.

- The first compulsory tests take place in 1995.

- Parents receive the results achieved by their children and the overall results of the school.

- 'League tables' of school-by-school results will be published by the government only 'once the tests are established'.

- Tests in maths and science will each take 75 minutes of classroom time.

- Pupils will take two tests in English: one in reading and one in writing.

- Teachers themselves will assess lower ability pupils, while extension papers will be available for the brightest.

- Teachers will not be required by law to assess pupils in technology, geography, history, art, music and physical education.

- Teacher assessment and test results will have the same status and must both be reported to parents.

AT AGE 14

- Pupils take tests in English, maths and science. There will also be teacher assessment of schoolwork.

- Further tests may be added, but not until 1996. This depends on the success of slimming down the rest of the curriculum. In the meantime there are to be optional tests in technology.

- Testing time is almost halved from a total of $12\frac{1}{2}$ hours in 1993 to $6\frac{3}{4}$ hours in 1994.

- ENGLISH – A test of an hour and a quarter assessing pupils' understanding of a set Shakespeare text and a comprehension test lasting one and a half hours.

- MATHEMATICS – Tests reduced from three to two hours contain 'more broadly based questions'.

- SCIENCE – Tests reduced from three to two hours.

- There is to be no compulsory testing or teacher assessment in history, geography or technology.

- Parents are to be told about their own child's performance in the three core subjects in annual reports.

- No 'league tables' of school-by-school results will be published.

AT AGE 16

- GCSE continues to be the main means of assessing 16 year-olds.

- The A★ to G scale will continue until at least 1995.

- Results are published by the government in school-by-school 'league tables'.

- The number of compulsory subjects pupils must take is still subject to review.

HOW ARE THE TESTS GRADED?

The tests at 7, 11 and 14 are graded according to the ten-level National Curriculum scale, which measures pupils' performance throughout their schooling.

- An average 7 year-old should achieve level 2.

- An average 11 year-old should achieve level 4.

- An average 14 year-old should achieve level 5 or 6.

- An average 16 year-old should achieve level 6 or 7.

The ten-level scale was to have been extended to the GCSE exam at age 16, where the top level would have

been 10, and the bottom level 4. But in spring 1993 the government decided to postpone this move indefinitely. The GCSE grades now run A★, A, B, C, D, E, F, G. The A★ is higher than the former GCSE A-grade and is achieved only by the very brightest pupils.

School Curriculum and Assessment Authority (SCAA)
Newcombe House
45 Notting Hill Gate
London W11 3JB

Tel: 071-229 1234
Fax: 071-243 0542

❝ There is a philosophical quarrel. Government and probably most parents see testing in a traditional way: short 'paper and pencil' tests modelled on the spelling and arithmetic we had to undergo as children, which showed what we could or could not do at a point in time. Teachers now see testing as developmental and designed to help learning. So we have two quite different approaches to testing.❞

Lord Skidelsky, in the Evening Standard, *after resigning as a member of the now defunct School Examinations and Assessment Council*

A SHORT HISTORY OF THE TESTS

MARCH 1985

Education Secretary Sir Keith Joseph publishes White Paper 'Better Schools' setting out broad guidance for a curriculum, but leaving details to schools.

DECEMBER 1986

Education Secretary Kenneth Baker announces that a national curriculum is to be legally imposed on schools.

DECEMBER 1987

Government-appointed team of experts draws up ten-level scale against which progress of all pupils can be checked from age 5 to age 16. It is called the 'TGAT model' from the initials of the team, the Task Group on Assessment and Testing.

JULY 1988

Education Reform Act sets up National Curriculum under which pupils will be tested at age 7, 11, 14 and 16.

FEBRUARY 1990

Education Secretary John MacGregor announces that pupils aged 7 and 11 will sit compulsory tests only in English, maths and science, and not all ten subjects.

APRIL 1990

Prime Minister Margaret Thatcher raises doubts about the detail and complexity in the National Curriculum and tests.

SUMMER 1990

Tests for seven year-olds are piloted in schools amid much controversy and claims by some head-teachers that they 'make pupils cry'. One test requires every pupil in a class to perform 251 tasks. Government promises simpler tests.

SPRING 1991

All seven year-olds tested on the 'basics' – reading, writing and arithmetic.

SEPTEMBER 1991

Ministers promise that future national tests for seven year-olds will be made shorter and easier to administer following evidence that some took up to four weeks to conduct.

SPRING 1992

Education Secretary Kenneth Clarke postpones compulsory tests for 14 year-olds after criticising pilot papers as 'elaborate nonsense'.

JUNE 1992

Trial tests for 14 year-olds in maths and science carried out in 72% of secondary schools. Trial English tests for 14 year-olds at 100 schools.

JULY 1992

Education Secretary John Patten announces that 14 year-olds will sit compulsory questions on Shakespeare's plays, poems and extracts from the classics.

SPRING 1993

Three main classroom teachers' unions vote to boycott National Curriculum tests. Government insists 1993 tests will go ahead as planned, but announces radical review of testing for 1994.

AUTUMN 1993

The government's chief test and curriculum adviser, Sir Ron Dearing, unveils his plans to slim down the content of the National Curriculum and make the mini exams more manageable.

TYPES OF SCHOOL

Just as there is no such thing as a free lunch, there is no such thing as a free school. All schools have to be paid for somehow, and there are about 35,000 of them in the United Kingdom teaching about nine million pupils.

The vast majority are state schools paid for by tax-payers and free to the pupils who use them. Of those state schools, more than 26,000 are primaries catering for pupils up to the age of 11, and about 5,000 are secondaries teaching pupils from 11 to 16, or 18 if they have a sixth form. There are also about 2,500 independent or private schools, for which parents pay a fee which can be as high as £12,000 a year.

The division between the state and the private sector has, however, been blurred in recent years with the advent of the grant-maintained school, which was born as part of the 1988 Education Reform Act. Although parents vote for these schools to 'opt out' of council control, they remain state schools funded by the tax-payer, but have a degree of independence more akin to their fee-paying rivals. Many independent heads admit privately

that the self-governing grant-maintained state schools pose a serious threat, especially as many parents feel the financial pinch and begin to question the affordability of a private education.

Not everyone who pays taxes has children, and not everyone who sends their children to school pays taxes. But anyone who does have children must by law ensure that they are properly educated between the ages of 5 and 16. This is usually in a school, although a small minority of parents do have their children taught at home which, subject to a few rules, they are entitled to do.

CHOICE AND DIVERSITY

The key words behind the 1993 Education Act were 'choice' and 'diversity'. These are reflected both in the new types of school that have already been created and those which may yet emerge.

Following the slow strangulation of grammar and secondary modern schools, the comprehensive has established itself as the dominant model for state secondary schooling. But the government, while insisting it has no plans to return to old-style eleven-plus selection, does want to see new and different types of school develop.

THE 'S-WORD'

Another pointer towards such change is what has been dubbed the 'S-word'. It stands not for 'selection' but for 'specialisation'. The government is keen for schools, particularly comprehensives, to specialise in particular fields. Indeed, there are cash incentives for them to do so. In December 1992 the government announced that 118 state schools had bid successfully for a share of £23 million to develop themselves into Technology schools. Each received sums ranging from £85,000 to £300,000 from the government's Technology Schools Initiative, which aims 'to develop technology teaching with a strong vocational emphasis'. The announcement took the total of such schools to well over 200, with more likely in future.

TECHNOLOGY SCHOOLS

The original City Technology College programme, which aimed to set up a network of 20 'beacons of excellence' offering a hi-tech vocational education to pupils in the

nation's inner cities, appears now to have run its course with 15 such institutions set up. But the philosophy behind the scheme will continue, though in a modified form. As well as giving cash incentives to encourage existing state schools to specialise in technology, ministers have also shifted the emphasis away from big business and towards the creation of local education authority, grant-maintained and even Church-aided City Technology Colleges.

Given the enormous amount of money ploughed into the CTCs for a relatively low number of pupils, critics have dubbed the CTCs 'white elephants' and a 'waste of money'.

But even critics have been forced to concede that some of the approaches to teaching they have generated for pupils in inner-city areas are truly pioneering.

SELECTION MAKES A COME-BACK

Selection in schools has begun to make a come-back. In March 1993 grant-maintained Queen Elizabeth Grammar School in Penrith, Cumbria, was given permission to select all its pupils by an entrance exam at age 11. Despite its name, the self-governing state school had until then been a comprehensive school, taking pupils of all abilities. Just weeks earlier, ministers had given girls' grant-maintained comprehensive Southlands School in Reading, Berkshire, permission to select nearly 20% of its pupils on academic ability.

In 1992, ministers announced that schools would be able to select up to 10% of their pupils in three subjects: music, art and PE. This would be according to their aptitude and motivation, but not according to their academic ability. Later they signalled that such selection would also apply to technology. Critics said this was part of a 'secret agenda' to bring back grammar-school style selection. The charge was vigorously denied by ministers, who insisted there would be no wholesale return to the eleven-plus. But obviously, each case will be judged on its merits.

SEE ALSO:
*Primary Schools
Secondary
Schools*

WHAT MAKES A GOOD SCHOOL?

There is no magic formula for creating successful schools. But experts are pretty clear about the key elements that are present in any well-run school. Probably the most important factor is leadership. The head-teacher, by setting the educational, managerial and moral tone, lays down the foundations for success on which all else can be built.

The White Paper '*Choice and Diversity*' lists four other key elements:

- clear and widely understood objectives

- consistently high expectations of pupils

- thorough monitoring and review of performance

- a high level of parental and community support.

Many of the pointers to help parents identify good schools will be explored later.

❝Parent power can be one of the most positive and worthwhile influences in improving the performance of individual children. It is a collaborative force, with parents using their special knowledge and relationship to compliment the work of schools.❞

Pat Partington, Head of Bramcote Hills Primary School, Nottingham, and President of the National Association of Head Teachers (NAHT), 1993 – 4.

INDEPENDENT OR 'FEE-PAYING' SCHOOLS

PRE-PREPARATORY SCHOOLS

Pre-prep schools are normally attached to prep schools. They take pupils from four to seven and provide primary education for children going on to prep schools.

PREPARATORY OR PREP SCHOOLS

Teaching pupils aged 7 to 13, these schools literally 'prepare' pupils for the Common Entrance exam, which is the passport – apart from the fees – into public schools. It could cost you up to £5,000 in tuition fees to put your child through prep school; boarding fees would be an additional expense. Prep schools do not have to teach the National Curriculum.

PUBLIC SCHOOLS

To many lay observers, the term 'public school' simply means a fee-paying school for older pupils. By the late 19th century the phrase applied to just seven independent schools: Eton, Harrow, Winchester, Rugby, Westminster, Marlborough and Charterhouse. Then it broadened to include any school which was a member of the Headmasters' Conference (HMC), the association for leading senior independent school heads. But now, at a time when many of them are taking in girls and going co-educational, the definition has widened even further in many quarters to encompass members of the Girls' School Association.

Results prove going private may not pay

TYPES OF STATE SCHOOL

Many of these schools will be familiar to you, but some may be less so.

STATE SCHOOLS

What most parents refer to as 'state schools' give pupils a free education, paid for by locally and nationally raised taxes. They are often, confusingly, referred to as 'maintained' schools. This is because they are maintained financially by such taxation. More than 90% of children attend state schools, of which there is now a growing variety of types.

PRIMARY SCHOOLS

Primary schools cater for pupils from the age of 5 to age 11, when they transfer to secondary school. Many pupils start a little younger than five, in the term at which they reach their fifth birthday. There are two types of primary school:

- Infant schools, for children aged five to seven, although some have nursery schools for younger children.

- Junior schools, for children aged 7 to 11.

MIDDLE SCHOOLS

Some education authorities are organised so that pupils attend a primary or 'first' school at age 5 and then transfer to a middle school at age 9 and stay until 12 or 13. Their secondary education then begins. Opinions vary as to whether the organisation of this works effectively.

SECONDARY SCHOOLS

Secondary schools teach pupils from the age of 11 to 16, or 18 if there is a sixth form. Different types of secondary schools now exist, not all of which may be available in your area.

COMPREHENSIVE SCHOOLS

Comprehensive schools accept pupils of all abilities, but can differ markedly in their style and organisation of teaching. Some have embraced many of the progressive ideas expounded about mixed-ability teaching, others have retained a more traditional ethos, and do break classes down according to pupils' ability. Most probably lie somewhere in the middle.

GRAMMAR SCHOOLS

Grammar schools educate pupils of above-average academic ability, usually the top 15 to 25%, in areas which still operate a selective system. Selection is usually by an eleven-plus exam involving verbal reasoning tests. Only about 150 grammar schools remain spread across a small number of LEAs.

SECONDARY MODERNS

Secondary modern schools admit pupils of average and below-average ability who fail to get into grammar school, usually about 75% of pupils in areas where all schools are selective.

SIXTH-FORM COLLEGES

Sixth-form colleges, as the name suggests, teach students from 16 to 18. Pupils usually study A-levels, but may also take some additional GCSEs and all vocational qualifications. These colleges offer teenagers the chance to study in an atmosphere away from that normally associated with school.

SPECIAL SCHOOLS

Special schools cater for children with what educators have termed 'special needs'. In real terms, this translates into severe learning difficulties, physical or emotional disabilities, or problems with their sight or hearing.

LOCAL AUTHORITY OR 'COUNTY' SCHOOLS

Local councils have been responsible for running the majority of state primary, middle and secondary schools in England and Wales. They are often called 'county schools' because in more rural areas it is the county council which has responsibility for overall planning, although the schools themselves are increasingly responsible for their own day-to-day running. In many large urban areas the metropolitan borough council takes planning responsibility.

The powers of councils have been severely reduced by central government giving schools under local authority control responsibility for 85% of their budgets. Education authorities have been able to retain a maximum of 15% for central administration, but this will drop to just 10%. Local government reorganisation will see power shift even more.

VOLUNTARY OR CHURCH SCHOOLS

About 1 in 3 children attend what are called voluntary or Church schools. Their running costs are paid by LEAs, but they have a

continued

distinctive character, usually because they were founded by a religious or voluntary body such as the Church of England or the Roman Catholic Church. In many cases it is the governors who employ the staff and decide which pupils to admit. They may have an agreement with the council to limit the number of pupils who are not of a particular faith.

These schools fall into three categories: voluntary aided, voluntary controlled and special agreement schools.

GRANT MAINTAINED OR 'OPT-OUT' SCHOOLS

This is new category of school was created by the 1988 Education Reform Act. Parents at these schools have voted to 'opt out' of LEA control. This may be to escape the clutches of a council that is slashing budgets, or simply to increase the sense of independence. They remain state schools, but are completely self-governing under the control of their governors and receive direct funding from Whitehall. Their arrival has been surrounded by controversy and can arouse intense passions both for and against them. Many parents have complained of being victims of 'dirty tricks' campaigns during ballots. The majority of grant-maintained schools are secondary, but more primary schools, which may opt out in small 'cluster' groups, have started to go it alone.

CITY TECHNOLOGY COLLEGES (CTCS)

- This new type of secondary school was created by a partnership between the government and business sponsors.

- These colleges, which place special emphasis on science and technology teaching, are extremely hi-tech, with pupils often using computers in place of conventional pen and paper. Their school day may be longer.

- They are state schools, free to pupils, but completely independent of the local education authority.

- Pupils can be selected according to aptitude and motivation, rather than ability, and the college usually interviews the parents, too, to ensure commitment to the type of schooling on offer.

- Originally, there were to be 20 CTC 'beacons of excellence' paid for with sponsorship from business and industry. But the programme has stuck at 15.

TECHNOLOGY SCHOOLS

Certain secondary schools have bid for and won extra government cash with the aim of giving greater emphasis to work-related technology teaching. They have pledged to become 'centres of excellence' in technology teaching, while still following the requirements of the National Curriculum.

TECHNOLOGY COLLEGES

Similar to CTCs, these colleges are not confined to urban areas. Any state school will be able to apply to become a grant-maintained Technology College. Business sponsors will be strongly represented on the governing body. Existing or newly created Church schools will also be able to set up as Technology Colleges.

State School Success
Headmaster John McIntosh and some of the 180 boys from the London Oratory School, Earls Court, London, who sat the first National Curriculum tests for 14 year-olds in maths, science, English and technology. 'I think 75% of us thought it was a breeze,' said Sean Rowe (back row, left).
Picture by Steve Poole, courtesy Daily Mail

★ GOLD STAR CELEBRITIES ★

★ LORD ARCHER ★

OCCÚPATION
Author

SCHOOL
Wellington School, Somerset

SCHOOL REPORT
'Archer must stop telling everyone Keats couldn't spell. Keats isn't taking his A-levels.'

TEACHER WHO MADE A BIG IMPRESSION
My English master Alan Quiltel, who went on to be headmaster of Wells Cathedral School, for his love of Shakespeare and his ability to make it come alive.

MOST IMPORTANT LESSON LEARNED AT SCHOOL
It is the quality of the teacher that determines whether you enjoy a subject.

SOMETHING I WISH I'D DONE DIFFERENTLY AT SCHOOL
Worked harder

BEST MOMENT AT SCHOOL
Winning the reading prize

WORST MOMENT AT SCHOOL
Caught following a girl, Wendy, across the playing fields. Reward: six of the best.

SWOT POINTS
Captain of athletics

EMBARRASSING MOMENT
Caught wearing a double-breasted blazer. Fined.

QUALIFICATIONS AT SCHOOL
Not enough

QUALIFICATIONS AFTER SCHOOL
Not much better (Dip Ed, Oxford). Educated by my wife Mary since leaving school.

CHILDREN
William aged 20, James aged 18, both educated at independent schools. 'Their choice.'

POINTS TO CONSIDER WHEN CHOOSING A SCHOOL
Whether it will lead to a place at university • Good for arts • Good for sport • No drugs, drink or reputation for bullying • Bad food

MY VIEW OF TODAY'S EDUCATION SYSTEM
It has produced a generation better educated, more mature and more caring than my own.

Picture by
Bill Cross,
courtesy Daily Mail

★ NIGEL DEMPSTER ★

OCCUPATION
Daily Mail diarist and author

SCHOOLS
St Peter's, Lympstone, Devon, and Sherborne, Dorset

SCHOOL REPORT
'Nigel has a character which will need curbing.' St Peter's report, 1949.

TEACHER WHO MADE A BIG IMPRESSION
Michael Gardner, the English master at St Peter's, who taught the subject with passion and encouraged boys to expand their word power and become writers.

MOST IMPORTANT LESSON LEARNED AT SCHOOL
How to avoid being punished. This was especially useful as both schools used the cane for any number of offences. Prefects, masters, housemasters and the headmaster at Sherborne were all allowed to administer corporal punishment.

SOMETHING I WISH I'D DONE DIFFERENTLY AT SCHOOL
Left school earlier and of my own volition

BEST MOMENT AT SCHOOL
Being selected for the Colts Rugby XV and participating in a two season unbeaten run

WORST MOMENT AT SCHOOL
Being asked to leave

SWOT POINTS
Athletics, tennis and rugby teams.
No academic achievements.

EMBARRASSING MOMENT
Being found to have a bar account at the Plume and Feathers pub.

QUALIFICATIONS
3 O-levels. None after school.

CHILDREN
Independent school for Louisa aged 14

POINTS TO CONSIDER WHEN CHOOSING A SCHOOL
Small classes, a variety of extras like music, a convenient location and a good ethnic mix of pupils

MY VIEW OF TODAY'S EDUCATION SYSTEM
Pretty abysmal. Independent schools aside, the great mass leaving state schools seems unable to read or write a simple sentence – obviously a necessity when applying for jobs – and have little knowledge of syntax or grammar.

Picture by Neville Marriner, courtesy Daily Mail

2 POWER TO THE PEOPLE

WHO RUNS STATE SCHOOLS?

END OF EMPIRE

A lot has changed since Councillor Buggins and his town hall cronies were the king-pins of the education scene. Local education authorities, which once ruled the roost, as well as the schools, are now fighting for their very survival. Having once been responsible for running vast educational empires, many are now seeking a new role as commercial agencies providing services for schools that have been given responsibility for running their own budgets, each of which can run from hundreds of thousands of pounds to £3 million or more.

Some local education authorities, like Hillingdon in west London, have all but disappeared as the majority of their schools voted to go grant-maintained. Hillingdon made headlines by announcing plans to merge its education committee with social services. The 1993 Education Act removed the legal obligation for councils to have an education committee at all.

Power is shifting. There is no doubt that ministers – in particular the Education Secretary – have armed themselves with many more powers. The National Curriculum, testing, and the funding for opted-out schools are all controlled centrally. Schools complain that they have been put into a strait-jacket.

Yet despite the concentration of power centrally, it is also being devolved down to the individual schools. The schools – not the local councillors or bureaucrats – decide how cash will be spent. The losers are the local education authorities and those who work for them. Ministers have used the image of a wheel to describe this shift in power, which they see as moving from the hub to the rim.

School revolution ousts bureaucrats

HE WHO PAYS THE PIPER CALLS THE TUNE

The vast majority of people with school-age children are products of a school system run, in practice, by the local council. It was described as a national system, locally administered. The government set the overall policy, but the councils ran the schools. In some areas, where there was a proper partnership between town hall and schools, it worked well. In fact, as far back as the sixties some schools did enjoy some financial responsibility devolved from the town hall. In other areas relations were more strained.

For a start, the amount of cash a school received was down to the local education authority. There was no real logic as to why one school got more money than another, and there was wide scope for favouritism to creep in. Politicians being politicians, there was also a great temptation to switch cash to schools in marginal council wards with a view to winning over the voters.

Schools were in a difficult bargaining position, even if they were extremely popular with parents. Since councils could set artificial limits on pupil numbers, often far below a school's physical capacity, schools could be prevented from increasing their per capita funding. This use of artificial limits was used by some councils to spread pupils around evenly, in the name of 'fairness'. But it also worked to deny parents the school of their choice.

Heads and teachers have described how their budgets could be affected after visits by the local authority's inspectors. Sometimes the inspectors would want a school to go along with a new educational fad of which the head might be extremely sceptical. The head then faced a dilemma. Should he or she voice objections and risk seeing the school's budget adversely affected? Or would it be better to pay a certain amount of lip-service to the idea, go along with it officially, but quietly let it drop in practice?

The schools which survived best were those whose heads could think and act like politicians. The system was ripe for reform.

HOW IT WORKS TODAY

The idea of giving schools the cash to run themselves was pioneered in Cambridgeshire in the early 1980s. The leader of the council was Baroness Blatch, who went on to become an Education Minister in the early 1990s. She said she formed the idea while carrying out a job interview for a prospective head. She asked the candidate what she thought the school's annual costs were, and was shocked when the reply bore no relation to reality. The broad principle then became government policy from 1988.

FOLLOW THE MONEY – LOCAL MANAGEMENT OF SCHOOLS

Broadly speaking, a school now receives the bulk of its cash according to how many pupils it can attract. The exact sum per pupil can differ according to the age of pupils and the area. The average cost of educating a primary school pupil in England and Wales is £1,430; a secondary education costs on average £2,200 per pupil.

So the more pupils a school can attract, the more cash it will receive. The technical jargon term you will hear to explain this is LMS. It stands for 'Local Management of Schools'. Ministers phased it in over a number of years, making it compulsory in all council-run state schools from April 1994. LEAs were originally able to retain 15% of a school's income for central administration, but ministers later announced that this was being reduced to 10%.

Most state schools prefer their freedom to take key spending

decisions for themselves. Many schools are now pondering whether to take that extra step and sever links completely with their local council, and go grant-maintained, with 100% direct funding from Whitehall. The opportunity to manage their entire budget is the carrot for taking that extra step to complete independence within the state sector. Head-teachers of schools which opt out to become self-governing tell me that once they have got to grips with LMS, the switch to becoming grant-maintained is easy.

CHARGING FOR SCHOOL ACTIVITIES

Schools may charge for activities that are provided wholly or mainly outside school hours, as long as these are optional extras. Schools are not allowed to charge for books, equipment or trips and outings during normal school hours and which form an essential part of the school curriculum. Schools must make their charging policies available to parents and set out a summary in their prospectuses.

WHO'S WHO?

SECRETARY OF STATE FOR EDUCATION

Based at the Department for Education in London, the Education Secretary sets the overall national policy for schools in England and has powers to intervene in some circumstances. The Welsh Secretary has the same role in Wales.

LOCAL EDUCATION AUTHORITY (LEA)

Local education authorities now have a much reduced role. Where only a small number of schools vote to opt out, the local education authority retains a strategic responsibility for planning school places in the area. The authority also acts as a postman by channelling cash budgets down to schools that have not opted out. It has to provide an education welfare service, issue statements setting out how pupils with special needs should be educated, and organise home – school transport. Schools that opt out of local education authority control must balance the financial gains with the loss of LEA support services such as a library service, child psychologists, school meals and cleaning.

FUNDING AGENCY FOR SCHOOLS (FAS)

The Funding Agency is a new national body, a quango, set up to channel cash budgets to the growing number of state schools which have opted out of town hall control to become grant-maintained.

SEE ALSO:
Becoming a
Governor or
Lay Inspector

Where 75% of the pupils in an area attend grant-maintained schools, the Funding Agency will automatically take over the local education authority's responsibility for ensuring enough places exist for pupils. When 10% of pupils in an area attend opted-out schools, the responsibility will be shared between the LEA and the Funding Agency.

SCHOOL CURRICULUM AND ASSESSMENT AUTHORITY (SCAA)

Advises the Secretary of State on tests, exams and the National Curriculum.

OFFICE FOR STANDARDS IN EDUCATION (OFSTED)

Watchdog which monitors standards, organises school inspections and advises the Secretary of State. Headed by HM Chief Inspector of Schools.

SCHOOL GOVERNORS

The governing body is like a company's board of directors. It comprises elected parents, governors nominated by the local council, teacher governors, a representative from industry or commerce and a number of 'co-opted' members. Now there is a new category of 'sponsor governor' for representatives from firms which want to forge closer links with schools. The governors should set the overall policy for the school, but leave the day-to-day running of the school to the head-teacher. In some celebrated cases they have failed to do this. They have new powers to hire and fire staff. The head-teacher may choose whether or not to be a governor.

HEAD-TEACHER

The head-teacher is probably the most important person in the success or failure of a school. He or she, through leadership and force of personality, sets the tone that others follow. If governors are the equivalent of a board of directors, the head is like the managing director. The loss of a good head can be disastrous, and the appointment of a good head can see a school's fortunes transformed.

THE DEPUTY HEAD

Though their efforts are often over-looked by parents, it is increasingly the deputy head-teachers who are the real movers and shakers in today's schools. For while the head may take the overview, it is usually the deputies – the school's middle management or maids-of-all-work – who have to go out and put theory into practice. Increasingly deputy heads are specialising to take over specific duties such as finance.

A witty but useful manual produced for deputy heads by their association picked this up in its title *If it Moves....* The point was that deputy heads can be expected to do almost anything.

TEACHERS

Teachers do not just teach. They plan lessons, mark homework, supervise extra-curricular activities and carry out important administrative tasks, such as keeping records of pupils' work and test results. For some time they have complained of being bogged down with paperwork and of not having enough time to teach. Teacher's pay will increasingly be determined by their performance in the classroom and by the extra duties and responsibilities they take on. This can include being part of a 'management team' to plan lessons, cash spending, and exam and test timetables.

PARENTS

Last but by no means least, parents play an important part in a number of ways. They can join a parent/teacher association, making their views known at the annual meeting. They can stand for election as governors, offer their help as volunteers with primary classes, and take part in ballots to determine whether their child's school should sever links with the local education authority by opting out to become grant-maintained and self-governing. Any of these roles would be in addition to their fundamental role of supporting their own child's learning.

HOW ARE SCHOOLS RUN?

Schools are now big businesses. That is not to diminish their role as educators of children. It simply acknowledges the fact that they, and not the local council, are now responsible for how huge sums of money should be spent to the best advantage of the children. A small village primary school might have a budget of about £500,000, while a large comprehensive might receive £2 – 3 million each year.

The biggest expense is teachers' salaries and other staff wages, but repairs, books and equipment all have to be taken care of too. And that means schools have to make often difficult decisions about spending priorities whilst ensuring that the books balance and the school receives value for money. Will it be a new lick of paint for the building or a new set of textbooks? An additional teacher or investment in a language laboratory? Hard choices. But now the schools themselves, and not the town hall bureaucrats, have to make them.

HEADS AND THEIR MANAGEMENT TEAMS

The complexities of running a modern school mean that today's head-teachers increasingly see themselves as leaders of a management team. Responsibilities for particular areas of school life are delegated to key senior staff. The head decides the school's priorities and directions, while the management team of deputies and senior teachers deals with the detail.

Special courses on financial and management skills are now common-place. Some state schools follow the example of their independent rivals and use their new-found financial flexibility to appoint a bursar to oversee budgetary matters. Most have appointed a staff member to deal with publicity, public relations and press enquiries. The fact that school budgets are now tied to pupil numbers means schools must market themselves to parents. Courses teaching these skills to teachers are extremely popular.

Some heads have taken to their new role like ducks to water. Others are uncomfortable with it and long for a return to the simple life.

MANAGEMENT STYLES

You should not run away with the idea that, just because schools are employing the techniques of the business world, Bash Street Comprehensive has suddenly turned into Bash Street PLC.

Good head-teachers and their staff know their priorities: the pupils come first. Management techniques are being employed to make schools more efficient and to help raise standards. They are used to spot wasted cash and missed opportunities, and ensure they are put to better use in future. They are not being used to turn children into units of production. Independent schools, with centuries of running their own budgets, have certainly not let that happen. So there is absolutely no reason to suppose that individual state schools would lose their unique identities, ethos, character or customs.

THE SCHOOL DAY

There was a time when the bell rang at 9 am and pupils worked through until home-time at 3.30 pm or 4 pm, with lunch and breaks in between. But changes have been afoot for some time. Some schools have introduced a continental day which begins at 8 am and finishes just after lunch-time. Some education authorities, like Hammersmith and Fulham, want to see this in all the schools under their control.

City Technology Colleges often open their doors as early as 7.30 am for breakfast and run a longer day. This means that pupils in the CTCs receive, on average, some 31 hours of timetabled lessons a week, compared to 24 hours in mainstream state schools. Most CTCs start teaching at 8.30 am and continue through to 4.30 pm. A report for the City Technology Colleges Trust noted: 'The early start is advantageous for parents who can drop off their children for breakfast before going to work'.

HOW TEACHERS SPEND THEIR TIME

It is not just teaching which takes up a teacher's time. In fact a study by Warwick University Professor Jim Campbell showed that less than a third of a secondary teacher's working week is spent in front of a class. Teachers have increasingly complained about this in the wake of the National Curriculum and testing.

The survey, carried out for the Association of Teachers and Lecturers, said teachers worked on average 54 hours a week – double the 1,265 hours per year for which they are contracted. Yet only 17 hours (or 31% of the total) is actually spent instructing children, compared to more than 18 hours on administration and low-level managerial duties.

Nevertheless, Professor Campbell noted that if teacher-time could be used more effectively, there could be raised standards in the classroom.

Many conscientious teachers do work incredibly hard and they are probably the majority. But those who work in the profession admit it has its fair share of shirkers, too. They say that, until recently, it was possible to work flat out while another colleague might be coasting. There was little incentive to break into a sweat, other than the sense of professionalism and vocation that drives the best teachers on. Duff teachers survived in the past because there was no way of getting rid of them other than to promote them. Head-teachers have confessed to writing glowing references for totally useless teachers, just to get them out of their school and into even more senior positions in someone else's. But now governing bodies have powers to hire and fire. And pay is increasingly being determined according to each

> ❝ Teaching is really too important to depend on the lack of job opportunities elsewhere. Every effort must be made to make it a first choice profession.❞

Professor Alan Smithers, Manchester University School of Education

individual teacher's performance. The days of the flat-rate pay award, for strivers and slackers alike, are over.

The Labour Party, too, has conceded that there is no place for bad teachers in our schools. Those with problems should be given help to improve. But if that fails, they should be asked to leave.

A legitimate grievance

Jonty Driver, headmaster of Wellington College in Berkshire, took great delight in telling of an experience at a previous school when he disciplined two boys. Soon afterwards he happened upon them in the lunch queue where, unaware of his presence, they were discussing their punishment.

'He's a bastard,' said the first reprobate. 'Yeah, he's a bastard,' said the other, before pausing for a few moments and then reflecting, 'but I suppose he was fair'. 'Yeah, I suppose he was, really,' said the first boy.

Having heard enough, the imposing Mr Driver slipped away, quietly satisfied that there can be few greater honours bestowed upon a headmaster than to be thought of by his pupils as a 'fair bastard'.

THE SECONDARY SCHOOL DAY

Activity	Min		
Teaching	203	Lesson preparation	53
Departmental/school admin	49	Marking, recording pupils' achievements	61
Examination admin	14	Organising	11
Pastoral/discipline	13	**Extra curricular**	
Parental consultation	10		
Working on wall displays	2	Weekend preparation, marking, etc	106
Supervision	7	Other (including sport, orchestra, clubs)	35
Liaison	6	**Training**	
Assembly	5	Courses/conferences	10
Breaks (free of work)	21	Travel	6
Breaks (not free of work)	20	Baker Days (staff planning days)	2
Non-contact time (free of work)	3	Meetings	22
Registration, dinner money, transition between classes	10	Reading	8
		Total	677

A TYPICAL TEACHER'S ROUTINE

Ann O'Brien, 28. Bonner Primary, Bethnal Green, East London
7.30 am: Arrive, prepare lessons
8.50 am: Staff meeting
9 – noon: Teaching and 15 mins playground duty
Noon – 1.30 pm: Rush lunch to attend meetings and finish paperwork
1.30 – 3.30 pm: Teaching
4 – 6 pm: Staff meetings twice a week,
8 – 10 pm: Preparation for next day
Sunday: Three hours' preparation/ paperwork/administration
Voluntary work: One hour a week aerobics class for pupils' mums.
Average: 55 to 60 hours a week.
Ann recently left her school to teach in Russia.

Illustration by
Tony Husband

SIX OF THE BEST?

The head-teacher is the single biggest influence on a school. Heads come in all shapes, sizes and styles. But some do conform to certain basic stereotypes.

Here are a few tongue-in-cheek fictitious versions of the types you may encounter. Any similarity to real head-teachers living, dead or retired is purely coincidental.

MR PROFFITT

Appearance: Smart suit marred by a Rotary Club badge

Behaviour: Hi-tech and marketing junkie, who thrives on industry links. A wheeler-dealer who talks mission statements, sponsorship deals and bottom lines. Wants to put an 'Inc' after the name of his school. Likes 'power breakfasts'.

Favoured habitat: Technology schools, City Technology Colleges

Educated: Grammar school, London School of Economics, now studying for MBA part-time

Favourite TV programmes: 'The Money Programme', 'Blockbusters'

Daily newspaper: *The Financial Times*

Magazines: *Investor's Chronicle, The Economist*

Musical tastes: Abba

Holidays: Cottage in Normandy

Hobbies: Playing the markets

Favourite tipple: Bucks Fizz

Car: BMW

Role models: Richard Branson, Robert Maxwell

Favourite sayings: 'Let's do lunch', 'It's got 40 Megabyte RAM.'

How to deal with him: Give him your business card and suggest your secretaries fix up an appointment to talk strategies.

MS TAKEN

Appearance: Baggy ethnic-print dresses with big pockets. Short hair, dangly earrings, little or no make-up.

Behaviour: Objects to the word blackboard because it is racist, manhole because it is sexist and thinks Enid Blyton should have been drowned at birth.

Favoured habitat: Inner-city schools, particularly in London

Educated: Ropey state comprehensive or top notch girls' public school

Favourite TV programmes: Anything on Channel 4 after the 9.30 pm 'watershed' or with subtitles

Daily newspaper: Doesn't trust any of the media

Magazine: *Spare Rib*

Musical tastes: New Age

Holidays: Lesbos, Greenham Common

Hobbies: Greenpeace, anti-vivisection, Terence Higgins Trust

Favourite tipple: Herbal tea

Car: Citroen 2CV

Role models: Germaine Greer, French and Saunders, Janet Street-Porter

Favourite saying: 'That is not a word we use here.'

How to deal with her: Make sure it is mum, not dad, who does all the talking.

2 b

MISS POWERS

Appearance: Shoulder pads and power-dressing, a cross between Miss Jean Brodie, Margaret Thatcher and Alexis Carrington in 'Dynasty'

Behaviour: Pure Dallas meets Debenhams. The business-like clack of stiletto heels on corridor tile has the male masters quaking in their Hush Puppies.

Favoured habitat: Formidable in girls' schools, particularly independents; deadly in co-eds

Educated: Grammar school and red-brick university

Favourite TV programme: 'Newsnight' (but only with Jeremy Paxman)

Daily newspaper: The *Independent*

Magazines: *Marie Claire, Cosmopolitan*

Musical tastes: Opera

Holidays: Florida, African safaris

Hobbies: Golf, rally-driving, a Chippendales show

Favourite tipple: Gin and tonic

Car: Peugeot 205 GTI, VW Golf GTI

Role models: Anita Roddick, Esther Rantzen, Lady Denton

Favourite sayings: 'Girls, Girls' and 'Don't run....walk.'

How to deal with her: Politely

MR 'THRASHER' CAINE

Appearance: Tall and imposing in his black academic gown

Behaviour: Sweeps through the corridors like a ship of state. High Church. Sings baritone in choir. Stentorian voice booms across the quad. Distinctly old-fashioned. A Latin lover of the Ancients variety who mourns the passing of corporal punishment and fagging. Keen on sport and cold showers.

Favoured habitat: Grammar schools or comprehensives with pretensions, grant-maintained and independent schools

Educated: Oxford, Cambridge or Hatfield Polytechnic

Favourite TV programme: Never watches it. Much prefers the wireless.

Daily newspaper: *Daily Telegraph* or *The Times*

Magazines: *Spectator*

Musical tastes: Wagner

Holidays: Florence, bird-watching

Hobbies: Watching rugger and cricket, fly-fishing

Favourite tipple: Good claret or vintage port

Car: An old Bentley, family inheritance

Role models: 'Whacko' Jimmy Edwards, Sir Rhodes Boyson

Favourite sayings: 'Spare the rod, spoil the child', 'Give me a child at seven, and I will show you the man.'

How to deal with him: Robustly

Mr 'Call me Ken' Trend

Appearance: Red spectacles, mid-40s, loud shirt

Behaviour: 'Right-on', Politically Correct, appears totally reasonable and sincere, but his smilingly smug know-it-all approach can verge on the condescending. Despite his comfortable white middle-class upbringing, he considers himself an expert on working-class and ethnic culture.

Favoured habitat: Suburbia

Educated: Minor public school

Favourite TV programmes: 'The Late Show', 'Thunderbirds'

Daily newspaper: The *Guardian*

Magazines: *New Statesman, Viz*

Musical tastes: Genesis, Rolling Stones, Credence Clearwater Revival

Holidays: Mikonos

Hobbies: Dinner parties

Favourite tipple: Perrier water, real ale, Frascati

Car: Volvo Estate

Role models: Ken Livingstone, Ben Elton, Che Guevara

Favourite saying: 'This is an ongoing learning experience.'

How to deal with him: Ask when the children last had a spelling test.

Miss Bramble

Appearance: Middle-aged, middle class, middle income and hard core Middle England. Probably head of a village school and a pillar of the community. Her first name is as dark a secret as Inspector Morse's, and as mysterious as the number of John Major's O-levels.

Behaviour: Outgoing, a bit eccentric, but dearly loved. Cycles to school on an old black Raleigh with a basket on the front.

Favoured habitat: Rural schools, particularly those with a Church connection

Educated: Probably the same school she teaches in

Favourite TV programmes: 'Poirot', 'Inspector Morse'

Daily newspaper: *Daily Mail*

Magazine: *Good Housekeeping*

Musical tastes: Manuel and the Music of the Mountains, James Last

Holidays: Norfolk Broads, Cornwall, Wales

Hobbies: Rambling, local history

Favourite tipple: Elderberry wine

Car: No. Prefers a bicycle or a moped.

Role models: Agatha Christie's Miss Marple, Mrs Major

Favourite saying: 'It would be so nice if you could help with the tombola.'

How to deal with her: Offer to run the tombola.

61

Flying kites for quality

Kates Hill primary is the first state school in the UK to fly the British Standards kite-mark for quality assurance. It is a measure of how far the management techniques of business and industry are now permeating the world of education. The award aimed to improve management quality in industry, but has since been extended into the service sector, and now into schools. The inner-city, multiracial school in Dudley, West Midlands, applied for and won the British Standards Institute's BS 5750 Quality Assurance Certificate. Head-teacher Pearl White said 'By following procedures which the standard dictates we have more time to plan and teach, and there is less chaos, less stress and less confusion. So much of what we do has in the past been carried around in our heads. Now everyone knows what is happening.'

Troubleshooter in the classroom

Garibaldi School has pulled itself back from the brink, raised standards and made £100,000 'profit' after taking a leaf from TV troubleshooter Sir John Harvey-Jones. In 1990 head-teacher Bob Salisbury arrived at the comprehensive at the heart of a recession-hit mining community in Mansfield, Nottinghamshire, to find a school in crisis. 'The school suffered from a poor image, high levels of vandalism, poor morale and poor examination results. Truancy was rife, and there were problems with pupil behaviour,' he said. Troubled parents in feeder primary schools were sending their children elsewhere. The school was losing about 50 of its predicted annual intake.

As the head sweated over an action plan to save his school, he began reading the book *Making It Happen* by former ICI chairman, management guru and television pundit Sir John Harvey-Jones. 'The lessons learned transformed the school's fortunes. There has been a 300% increase in the number of A to C passes at GCSE; the cost of vandalism has fallen from £40,000 a year to just £250; attendance does not dip below 90%, and less than 1% of absences are unauthorised. Pupils have started coming back in droves. The sixth form alone has risen from just 8 to 112.'

PARTNERSHIP?

HOWDY PARTNER!

The balance of power between schools and parents has shifted significantly since the Education Reform Act of 1988. Before then, many schools did talk of forging 'a partnership with parents'. Many were no doubt motivated by a genuine desire to power-share. But there was also a lot of lip-service paid by the professionals to the demands and wishes of parents. They tended to get what they were given, rather than what they necessarily wanted.

A NEW DEAL

Now schools depend for their cash on attracting as many pupils as possible. So, even on a purely mercenary level, schools, like it or not, now have to treat pupils and parents as their 'customers'. And if they get a reputation for treating their customers badly, they risk losing business.

This change also means that the 'partnership' between home and school is a little more equal than it was before the reforms. But it has led to some friction as different camps have debated just who does know what's best for children: their teachers or their parents?

SIGN ON THE DOTTED LINE

Good schools have been swift to adapt to the new climate. Some have pioneered 'home – school contracts' in which staff and pupils literally sign a deal. In return for being taught something useful and being treated with respect, pupils pledge to turn up on time for class, behave reasonably and do their homework. Parents, too, have signed up, pledging to ensure that their children get enough sleep, don't watch too much television and arrive at school properly dressed having had a decent breakfast on which to start the day.

Ministers have been so impressed with such schemes that they have looked

❛ It is a mistake to under-estimate the willingness and capacity of many parents to work with the school, and an even bigger mistake to cling to old ways which although cosy and comfortable do not meet present and future needs. ❜

Policy discussion paper by Bob Fisk, Head of Coquet High School and Pat Partington, Head of Bramcote Hills Primary School

63

into expanding them nationwide as part of the Parents' Charter.

THE DYNAMIC DUO

Bob Fisk, Head of Coquet High School in Northumberland, and Pat Partington, Head of Bramcote Hills Primary School in Nottinghamshire, have been at the forefront of moves to make parents more equal partners.

In a discussion document, these two leading lights of the National Association of Head Teachers conceded that the prospect of parents helping shape school policy still sits uncomfortably in many staffrooms. 'This is still an idea capable of making heads and teachers go pale and raising the hackles of professionalism. Yet why is it that so many of those who work in schools feel threatened by the thought that parents of the children whom they teach should have some say in the way schools function?', they asked. 'Parents do not want to 'take over' schools,' they said, 'but are entitled to a legitimate say when school policy is being drawn up'.

These head-teachers believe that if schools are to serve their 'customers' well, they must embrace the sort of 'quality management' principles that have grown up in the commercial world. Central to this is good communication.

❝ The question of parental influence on school policies and practices raises all kinds of issues, prejudices and anxieties. The role of the professional may be threatened and the aspirations of certain parents frustrated. ❞

Policy discussion paper by Bob Fisk, Head of Coquet High School and Pat Partington, Head of Bramcote Hills Primary School

Three simple indicators can be used to check how well schools are communicating with parents and, perhaps more importantly, getting feedback, say the heads. As a parent, you might want to use it to see how your own school's efforts measure up.

1 How many 'meaningful' parent contacts does each class or department make each term?

2 What proportion of parents have taken advantage of opportunities to attend school-based meetings?

3 How much of the written communications that has been sent to parents has:
a) arrived?
b) been read and responded to?
c) been written in a style and language appropriate to a parent audience? This might best be judged by a group of parents.

COQUET HIGH SCHOOL, AMBLE

CONTRACT

NAME OF PUPIL...

CONTRACT TERMS

(To be read aloud to pupil and parent/guardian before the pupil is asked to sign the agreement.)

I agree:

1. to attend lessons as set out on my timetable, arriving punctually, and on no occasion deliberately missing a lesson.

2. to behave during lessons, lunch-time and breaks in a civilised and controlled way that will not cause undesirable disturbances or interfere with the way in which any other pupils may wish to spend their time.

3. to control my temper and the way in which I speak to other pupils and adults so that there can be no misunderstanding over my intentions, ie not to adopt a threatening, impertinent, overbearing or resentful manner.

4. to use common sense in deciding what is acceptable and what is not, and to report to my head of year at least once per week to explain how this contract is working.

Signed ....

Date ....

Witnessed for the school...

Witnessed for the parents...

HOME – SCHOOL CONTRACTS

Pat Partington stressed that there is no benefit in simply asking parents and pupils to sign a home–school contract and then expecting miracles. Nor must the contract be one-sided in favour of the school.

'The hard work is done long before the pen ever touches the paper. In one sense the contract itself is irrelevant. The signing is symbolic of the work that has already been done and really sets the seal on the agreement.'

The NAHT discussion document published in 1988 notes: 'Home–school partnerships can exist without any kind of contractual agreement. Nor will a contract on its own create a partnership which must essentially be founded on goodwill and shared commitment.' But it adds, 'A contract can enhance a partnership by giving it a clarity of meaning and framework of reference'.

Children's contract

FOUR-YEAR-OLDS SIGN PLEDGE TO PUT HOMEWORK BEFORE TV

AN INSPECTOR CALLS

INSPECTING OUR SCHOOLS

Schools must now by law be inspected once every four years by approved teams of independent inspectors. This is part of a new system of inspecting schools that was introduced in a bid to identify more of those which are failing, and either save them or shut them down. When ministers first announced the changes, they admitted they already had a short list of between 100 and 200 of the worst schools which government inspectors had identified as needing serious attention. The main aims of inspections are to monitor standards, report to parents and raise standards generally. The regular inspections should also enable the elimination of the 1.5 million surplus places, that is empty desks, in schools.

THE OLD SYSTEM

In the past, schools were subject to two kinds of inspection. First, there were visits by the local education authorities' own inspectors. But ministers felt that these were insufficient, and maybe even contributed to the problems, rather than providing the solution. Nor did they think education authorities could be wholly impartial in judging the performance of their own schools.

The real guardian of the nation's standards up to now has been the 150 year-old Her Majesty's Inspectorate, known as HMI. These watch-dog inspectors regularly visited schools, producing reports on general subjects as well as individual schools. Their individual school reports were first made public in 1983.

OFFICE FOR STANDARDS
IN EDUCATION

2. MAIN FINDINGS

Standards, Quality, Efficiency and Ethos

4.　　　This is a very good school. Standards of achievement are good and at times outstanding. Examination results at GCSE and A-level are well above national averages. Written and oral expression are good. Pupils are confident and competent in the use of mathematical skills.

Ilkley Grammar School, Ilkley, Bradford Education Authority, 15–19 March 1993, OFSTED report.

Her Majesty's Senior Chief Inspector of Schools advised the Education Secretary directly, and published an annual 'state of the nation' report, which often made uncomfortable reading for ministers.

THE PROBLEM

With only 400 inspectors and 24,000 schools, it would have taken decades to visit every one systematically. It was estimated that each secondary school could, on average, expect a full inspection every 60 years. As it was, some schools were visited regularly, some hardly at all. Ministers wanted schools to be inspected once every four years, meaning 6,000 inspections each year. The solution, set out in the Education (Schools) Act 1992, has proved to be radical and controversial.

THE NEW SYSTEM

The new system relies on private enterprise and the free market to work.

Properly registered independent inspection teams throughout the country now compete for the business of vetting 6,000 schools a year in a market worth about £100 million.

At the head of the new system is Her Majesty's Chief Inspector of Schools. He presides over a new body called OFSTED, the Office for Standards in Education. This has a full-time central staff of about 200 inspectors, slimmed down from the 400-strong Her Majesty's Inspectorate, who will preside over the running of the market-led system as a sort of imperial guard.

NOW FOR THE CONTROVERSIAL PART

The school inspections will be carried out by specially licensed private or 'freelance' inspection teams, which must tender for the contract to inspect each individual school.

2. MAIN FINDINGS

Standards, Quality, Efficiency and Ethos

5.   This school is a cause of concern. Standards of achievement, both in lessons and in public examinations, are too low and the quality of learning is often unsatisfactory. Pupils are poorly supported by the school's procedures for assessment, which lack rigour. The school has no policy for special educational needs and therefore fails to support adequately the less able. Attendance is poor.

6.   Management is generally ineffective. No procedures exist for documenting good practice and senior management has allowed itself to become preoccupied with administration to the point where it is failing to provide leadership.

Dyke House School, Hartlepool, Cleveland Local Education Authority, 25–29 January 1993, OFSTED report.

WHO ARE THE INSPECTORS?

REGISTERED INSPECTORS

Each team must be led by a 'registered inspector'. This may be a former local authority or government inspector, an education or management consultant or a university academic with a strong educational background. He or she must be judged a 'fit and proper person'. They must actually conduct each inspection and cannot just organise it for others.

TEAM MEMBERS

These are people who want to be professional inspectors. They will have expertise in a particular field of education and have satisfactorily completed a five-day training course. Many will also have been local authority or government inspectors.

'LAY' INSPECTORS

These are inspectors who have no experience of working in school or education, other than as governors or voluntary helpers. They are in the team in order to give a commonsense perspective. They can come from all walks of life: industry, commerce, trade unions, etc. These government inspectors are vetted and trained, and can be 'struck off' if they are found to be unsuitable, incapable or guilty of corruption.

The new system works broadly on the same principle as the annual MOT test. Just as a motorist must, by law, put his or her car through a regular mechanical check, so head-teachers and governors must, by law, put their schools through a regular inspection. And just as any number of properly registered, privately owned garages can carry out the MOT test, so properly registered, privately owned teams of inspectors can compete for the contract to inspect a school.

Originally schools were to be allowed to choose which inspection company would vet them. But because the House of Lords felt this would be open to abuse, it is now Her Majesty's Chief Inspector of Schools who decides which company's tender wins, on the basis of efficiency and value for money.

69

THE INSPECTION

Before the inspection parents may be sent a questionnaire about the school. There must be a meeting between the registered inspector and parents, so that their views can be aired. The inspector cannot respond directly to any complaints, but will take them into account as evidence when visiting the school. Published reports must state whether the inspection findings support the parents' worries. The OFSTED *Handbook for the Inspection of Schools* says: 'Where the team's findings differ markedly from that of parents, this should be carefully justified in the report by reference to the evidence.'

Registered inspectors will report on:

- the quality of education provided.

- the educational standards achieved.

- how efficiently each school manages its cash.

- the spiritual, moral, social and cultural development of pupils.

The inspectors' reports will be published, and a summary of their findings sent direct to parents at their homes, so they can see for themselves how their own schools are performing.

These reports, available for inspection at the school and local libraries, will be particularly useful to parents who

6Parents with children at these ailing schools often feel powerless and frustrated. Children only have one chance of a school career; they should not be allowed to suffer from the long drawn out demise of a failing school.9

The government's 1992 White Paper 'Choice and Diversity'

have not yet settled on a choice of school for their children. Parents can ask for their own copy from the school, the LEA or OFSTED. A charge may be made for photocopying.

Once a school receives its report, the governing body will be required to draw up and publish an action plan setting out how it proposes to deal with any criticisms or weaknesses uncovered by the inspectors. This action plan must also be made available to parents and others who want to read it.

SCHOOLS THAT ARE NOT UP TO SCRATCH

Schools that are failing to deliver a reasonable standard of education to their pupils will be deemed to be failing, or at risk of failing, and given the choice of putting themselves in order or risking closure.

Any number of problems may be responsible for the school's failure:

- sloppy teaching

- low expectations of what pupils should be achieving

- failure to teach the curriculum

- bad organisation

- poor financial management

or even, as has happened:

- revolution in the staffroom, with the head, teachers and governors all at loggerheads with one another.

Often a combination of such problems appears in schools where standards are deteriorating.

If a county or voluntary controlled school is deemed to be 'at risk', the school governors and the local education authority will be expected to take 'urgent remedial action'.

2. MAIN FINDINGS

2.1 Standards, Quality, Efficiency and Ethos

2.1.1   Standards achieved are poor. Results in public examinations are very poor. There is too little oversight of what takes place in the school and within lessons. Classroom management is often weak and there is need for relevant professional development. Pupils' motivation and attitude to work in Year 7 are good. This must be cultivated and maintained. Teacher expectation is low and pupils lack an expanded vision of what they can accomplish. Attendance is poor, particularly in Year 11.

2.2 KEY ISSUES FOR ACTION

2.2.1   The school's governing body and senior management team (SMT) should give urgent attention to the following serious issues:

* Pupils under-perform in class. Teachers should understand better the academic standards of which pupils are capable and how to help pupils achieve them.
* There is too little emphasis on developing an ethic of hard work leading to personal satisfaction and self–esteem. Pupil achievement needs to be recognised and rewarded: a whole school policy to guide practice in NC assessment is needed.
* Levels of literacy are low. Many pupils require a planned programme for improvement with targets set and individual progress monitored.
* Lessons are insufficiently lively and challenging. Activities need to have intrinsic interest and match pupils' abilities more closely in order to engage their full attention.
* Pupils need opportunities to show initiative and exercise responsibility and develop self–esteem.
* The school gives insufficient emphasis to equality of opportunity as a principle for raising achievement. The needs of girls, low attainers and those with learning difficulties should be addressed.

St Chad's School, Tilbury, Essex Local Education Authority, 9–12 November 1992, OFSTED report.

Where the governing body is reluctant to comply, the local authority will be allowed to appoint its own additional governors. It also has powers to withdraw the delegation of cash from the town hall to the school. By taking over the budget the council has greater influence over the running of the school.

The government's Chief Inspector of Schools will tell the Education Secretary in Whitehall of all schools that are deemed 'at risk'. Within eight weeks of the inspectors' report being delivered, the local education authority is required to supply the Education Secretary with:

- a copy of the governors' action plan

- the education authority's views on the plan, along with any additional steps the council proposes taking.

If the Education Secretary is satisfied that the governors and the education authority have come up with an effective course of action, he can allow them up to a full academic year to improve the school's performance.

If, after that one year's grace, it is obvious that the rescue plan is not working he can send in what have been dubbed 'the hit squads' to take over the running of the school in a bid to save it.

Alternatively, he can send them in immediately if he feels that neither the local education authority nor the governing body will be able to improve the school sufficiently.

ENTER THE 'HIT SQUADS'

The proper name for a 'hit squad' is an Education Association. Ministers describe it as 'a small and cohesive body' usually comprising a chairperson and five part-time members, appointed in any geographical area that needs one, by the Education Secretary in Whitehall.

Many of the members will be former or retired head-teachers with experience of running schools, prompting some to call them a committee of 'Mr Chipses'. But some of the members will also have experience of management, possibly in the commercial sector.

The Education Association will be set up in each local area whenever the first 'at risk' school appears as a candidate for its services. It will be able to take over the running of as many schools in an area, or neighbouring area, as are found to be failing.

HOW THE 'HIT SQUADS' WORK

The Education Association works in a similar way to a firm of receivers sent in to rescue or shut down a company that goes into liquidation or suffers bankruptcy.

THE NEW INSPECTION SYSTEM IN BRIEF

HER MAJESTY'S CHIEF INSPECTOR OF SCHOOLS:

- heads the system

- runs OFSTED

- keeps a list of registered private inspectors

- can 'strike off' inspectors who are not up to scratch

- advises the Education Secretary.

OFSTED, THE OFFICE FOR STANDARDS IN EDUCATION

- OFSTED has a full-time staff of about 200 Her Majesty's Inspectors and is a separate government department with its own budget.

- It oversees and regulates the inspection system and licenses private inspection companies.

PRIVATE INSPECTION COMPANIES

- Each must be headed by a 'registered' inspector.

- Team members must be experts in the school system or the curriculum.

- Team members must pass a five-day training course.

- One inspector must be a layperson who is not an education professional, to give a commonsense view.

- They will inspect 6,000 schools a year.

EDUCATION ASSOCIATIONS OR 'HIT SQUADS'

- Comprising former head-teachers, education or management experts, these normally six-strong teams will take over the running of any school that neither the governors nor the local education authority can save.

- If successful, the school will become grant-maintained. If not, it will be shut down.

It receives a grant direct from the Education Secretary, and has powers broadly similar to those of a board of governors at a grant-maintained school. It will, in particular, have powers to hire and fire staff, including the existing head-teacher, and to change the character of the school, if this is deemed to be necessary. This could mean making the school

73

specialise in a particular subject area such as technology or introducing some form of selection. The Education Association will be given a defined period, which can be extended, in which to improve the school.

Some observers close to ministers have noted that local authorities could theoretically lose control of all their schools if the 'hit squads' strike, since, most controversially, schools that are rescued in this way will normally be expected to become grant-maintained. Those which cannot be rescued will be shut down. The final decision will rest with the Education Secretary.

The government's White Paper 'Choice and Diversity' setting out the new framework says: 'Education Associations will be expected to provide the essential leadership and management that has previously been lacking at the school. That may require staffing changes at the senior management level and within its teaching force.'

> **❛It's like sending in Dad's Army to tackle Saddam Hussein. ❜**
>
> *Nigel de Gruchy, General Secretary of the National Association of Schoolmasters/Union of Women Teachers, on hearing of the 'hit squads'*

HOW THE SYSTEM WORKS IN TEN STEPS

1 Private inspection teams bid to inspect each school.

2 Office for Standards in Education (OFSTED) awards a contract to the inspection team offering the best value for money.

3 Registered inspector meets the parents so their views can be taken into account.

4 Inspection takes place.

5 Inspectors' reports published and summaries sent direct to parents.

6 School publishes an 'action plan' setting out how it will deal with inspectors' criticisms.

7 This action plan must be made available to parents.

8 Governors and the local education authority can be given a year's grace to rescue any school the inspectors deem to be 'failing or at risk of failing'.

9 If this doesn't work, the Education Secretary can send in Education Associations or 'hit squads' of experts to take over the running of the school.

10 If school is saved it becomes grant-maintained. If not, it is shut down.

JUDGING A SCHOOL TO BE 'AT RISK OF FAILING'

Evidence of several of the following factors would lead inspectors to judge a school to be 'at risk of failing'.

ACHIEVEMENT OF PUPILS

- Low standards among the majority of pupils.

- Low standards consistently among particular groups.

- Poor exam results compared to similar schools.

BEHAVIOUR

- Regular disruptive behaviour.

- Serious truancy.

- Pupils at physical risk from other pupils or adults at the school.

- Pupils at emotional risk from other pupils or adults at the school.

- Racial harassment; high levels of racial tension.

STAFF AND TEACHING

- Demoralised or disenchanted staff.

- High level of unsatisfactory teaching.

- Low expectations.

- High levels of staff turnover.

- Abrasive and confrontational relationships with pupils.

MANAGEMENT

- Head and senior management display ineffectiveness and insensitivity.

- Staff, parents or governors lose confidence in the head.

- Extensive friction between staff and senior management.

- Schooling is being seriously affected by poor level of, or management of, cash and other resources.

- Inspectors look out for signs that these factors are causing widespread underachievement, a risk to pupils, or the likelihood of breakdown of control.

OFSTED
The Office for Standards in Education
Elizabeth House
York Road
London SE1 7PH

Tel: 071-925 6800

How to Complain

It is unlikely that your child will go through school without you, at some point, having to wrestle with a tricky issue, whether it is worries about your son's or daughter's work, bullying, exams, poor teaching, what is being taught, or worse.

The exclusion of your child from school, worries over special educational needs provision, dissatisfaction over the content of morning assemblies, religious or sex education and racial or sexual discrimination can all spark a dispute between parent and school.

IGNORANCE IS NOT BLISS

A survey by watchdogs at the National Consumer Council in November 1992 revealed widespread ignorance and confusion about schools' complaints procedures. By law, schools must have these to deal with parents' worries about the curriculum or religious worship, and they must be set out in the school prospectus. You also have very specific rights of appeal in the case of complaints about special needs, expulsion, poorer than expected GCSE marks or A-level grades.

SECTION THREE
SCHOOL ORGANISATION & ADMINISTRATION

Complaints procedure

We hope that parents will feel able to approach the school about any concerns they have over their children. However, if a complaint concerning the curriculum, collective worship, charging, or the provision of information cannot be dealt with satisfactorily through discussion with the Headteacher, there is a formal procedure by which parents can pursue the matter. Information concerning this is available from the Headteacher. Most difficulties can be resolved without discord providing they are identified early, kept in proportion and approached in such a way as to achieve a solution which is in the best interests of all concerned. In many cases anxieties are based on misunderstandings which be prevented if parents make contact with the school.

Coquet High School Prospectus, 1993, School Organisation & Administration

The NCC survey by senior law lecturer Dr Neville Harris of Liverpool University said the Act was being interpreted differently in different parts of the country.

'Parents' ignorance of the procedures and the inadequate publicity that schools and local education authorities are giving to them may be partly responsible for the very small number of formal complaints so far recorded,' said his report.

He noted that in 1989 – 90 there were 63 complaints to governing bodies, of which just six were upheld. In 1990 – 91 there were 71 appeals, of which 19 were upheld. In 1989 – 90 local education authorities received 25 complaints, of which two were upheld. The following year complaints dropped to 14, of which again two were upheld.

Dr Harris said that while more than 9 out of 10 parents were willing to complain, nearly 6 out of 10 had no idea that special procedures now exist for dealing with complaints about the curriculum or religious worship.

FORMAL OR INFORMAL COMPLAINTS?

The government's wish is for all complaints to be dealt with at as local a level as possible. But to be effective you first need to know HOW to complain, which is largely common sense, and then WHERE to direct your complaint.

CLASSROOM TEACHER

Many misunderstandings between parents and school can swiftly develop into rows if they are not quickly sorted out. So where problems do arise, it is best to tackle them as soon as possible by talking first to the classroom teacher. Often problems can be dealt with to your satisfaction at this level, whether they relate to reading methods, pupil progress, or your child having problems settling in at school. It is courteous to ring up first to make an appointment or to drop the teacher a letter. Schools do differ in their levels of formality. But it is helpful for the teacher to establish in advance what the subject for discussion will be.

> ❝ Parents will not necessarily be fobbed off with form masters, tutors or housemasters; the nice ones occasionally, and the awkward ones always, insist on going to the top. ❞
>
> *Eton Headmaster Dr Eric Anderson in* Head to Head, *John Catt Educational Ltd*

Bramcote Hills Primary School Prospectus 1993 – 94

HEAD-TEACHER

If you are still not satisfied, or if your complaint relates to wider issues than your child's rate of progress, you can talk to the teacher's head of department or direct to the head-teacher. Sometimes head-teachers will delegate such duties to a deputy, who will hear your complaint. But if you feel strongly enough about matters, you are quite within your rights to insist upon seeing the head.

GOVERNING BODY

Beyond this point, the school's board of governors can be asked to investigate. The school will supply you with a list of governors, and the name and address of the chairperson and the clerk to the governors. You may want to have an informal chat with a parent governor, perhaps even at the school gates, to test the water before making a formal approach.

You can ask for an item to be raised by the governors at their regular meetings, but you cannot demand it; that needs the support of three governors. If a group of parents feel sufficiently strongly about a matter, they can have it raised as a resolution and voted on at the school's annual meeting, provided 20% of parents are attending. At this stage matters are becoming much more formal and can take a number of turns.

DIRECTOR OF EDUCATION

For general complaints against local authority schools, your next stop is the director of education. You can get his or her name and address from the town hall or county hall.

THE OMBUDSMAN

If you think your local education authority has failed to follow proper procedures you should seek out the local government ombudsman. His office investigates cases of 'maladministration' in which local councils act unfairly against the public. He does not investigate every complaint. Complaint forms are available from Citizens Advice Bureaux.

New tribunals hearing appeal cases on special educational needs will, from 1994, include an independent member to help ensure that parents receive a fair hearing.

SECRETARY OF STATE

The final arbiter, before you seek justice in the courts, is the Secretary of State for Education. But the minister will only consider cases that have been through the proper complaints procedures.

Parents who believe that their school or local education authority has acted 'unreasonably' and failed in its legal duties can make a formal

---

Secretary of State for Education
Department for Education (DFE)
Sanctuary Buildings
Great Smith Street
London SWIP 3BT

(Your name and address)

(Date)

Dear Secretary of State,

I wish to make a formal complaint and would like you to use your powers under section 68 and/or 99 of the 1944 Education Act to investigate and remedy the matter.
I believe (name of local education authority or school) has acted unreasonably/illegally by (state complaint).

Yours faithfully,

A model letter

complaint under sections 68 and/or 99 of the 1944 Education Act. If the minister agrees you have a case, he has powers to direct the local education authority or the school's governing body.

You are also entitled to complain to the Secretary of State (see previous page) if the school or local authority fails to deal properly with any complaint lodged by you under the curriculum complaints procedure.

HOW TO COMPLAIN

Complaining effectively can be an art form. Here is a seven-point plan:

1 CALM DOWN

No matter how furious you might feel about a particular issue or incident, try to calm down and distance yourself mentally and emotionally from the issue in dispute. Cool, rational thought will help you win your argument more effectively than a hot temper.

2 MARSHAL YOUR THOUGHTS

Go over in your mind and then draft your arguments in writing, separating out your complaint into individual points. Play devil's advocate with yourself and ask how you would respond to your complaint if someone else made

it against you. Defensively? Anticipate the answers you might receive so you are ready to follow through with other questions.

3 COLLECT YOUR EVIDENCE

Collect together as many pieces of evidence that might support your case. If your concern is bullying, do you have witnesses? Keep a diary, noting meetings, what was discussed and decided. If you have phone conversations, note the dates and times, and keep notes of who said what to whom. It could prove valuable. If you think your child is achieving less at school than you think he or she is capable of, note down your reasons. You may be able to point to previous sound reports from other teachers, good performance in other subjects and so on.

4 PUT IT IN WRITING

Before storming down to the school and demanding an explanation, consider putting your concerns down in writing. By all means communicate the depth of your feeling in writing, but try not to jump to an immediate conclusion or demand a specific course of action. Use the letter as a means of setting out an agenda that you want the school to talk through with you. Try to concentrate on

COMPLAINING ABOUT THE CURRICULUM

- All local education authorities must, by law, set up complaints procedures for parents unhappy about aspects of the curriculum. These must be approved by the Education Secretary.

- The key legislation is section 23 of the 1988 Education Reform Act.

- Complaints against the governing body should first be heard by that same governing body. If still unhappy, the parent can put the complaint to the local education authority.

- Parents can use the complaints procedure where they think the local authority or the governors are failing in their duty to:

  - provide the National Curriculum in school for a child

  - follow the law, on what can and cannot be charged for in school

  - offer only approved qualifications and syllabuses

  - provide religious education and daily collective worship

  - supply information they are duty-bound to provide

  - carry out other statutory duties relating to the curriculum.

- They can also use the formal complaints procedure where the governors or local education authority are acting unreasonably in any of the above cases.

the facts, rather than speculating on why it happened. Even if you decide not to send the letter, the act of committing ideas to paper will help order your mind.

5 KEEP RECORDS

Even though it is a real chore, always try to keep copies of letters and documents in case you need

them later to support your case, should a dispute drag on. In extreme cases disputes can drag on through the school's internal hearings to appeals, the courts, the High Court and even the House of Lords.

6 TRY NOT TO BECOME OBSESSIVE

There is nothing more depressing than the sight of the obsessive

SEE ALSO:
School Appeals
Appealing against
Poor Grades
Children with
Special Needs
Exclusions
RE and Collective
Worship

parent clutching a white plastic bag full of documents charting every cough and spit of some interminable dispute. As Charles Dickens noted in *Bleak House*, lives can be destroyed in this way. Try and keep a sense of proportion. As long as you have the evidence to back you up, you need only use it in summary form. Remember, if you can't sum up your argument in a sentence, you haven't got an argument.

7 ALWAYS BE POLITE

Good manners will usually get you a lot further than a raging row. So try not to blow your top. Keeping your temper means you are keeping control.

Advisory Centre for Education (ACE)
1b Aberdeen Studios
22 Highbury Grove
London N5 2EA

(Free telephone advice line 2–5 pm each weekday on 071-354 8321)

Commission for Local Administration
(The Local Government Ombudsman) England
21 Queen Anne's Gate
London SW1H 9BN

Tel: 071-222 5622

❝ You do not have bad schools, you have bad parts of schools. If the matter concerns your child rather than a particular academic subject, see the head of year or the pastoral teacher. If your complaint is to do with the teacher, ask directly for the head. School secretaries can be very protective, so do persist. ❞

John Dunford, Headmaster, Durham Johnson Comprehensive, County Durham

Commission for Local Administration
(The Local Government Ombudsman) Wales
Derwen House
Court Road
Bridgend
Mid Glamorgan
CF31 1BN

Tel: 0656 61325

Department for Education (DFE)
Sanctuary Buildings
Great Smith Street
London SW1P 3BT

General telephone: 071-925 5000
Public enquiries: 071-925 5555
Fax: 071-925 6971

★ NICKY FOX ★

OCCUPATION
TV presenter, programmes include 'Top Gear', TV-AM weather, 'Fun in the Sun'

SCHOOLS
St Peter's C of E Primary, Poole, Dorset and Talbot Heath, Bournemouth

SCHOOL REPORT
'Nicola is unrealistic about her future plans.' Mostly I was a good girl but wanted to be more creative. I did get pulled up for daydreaming and doodling in class.

TEACHER WHO MADE A BIG IMPRESSION
For better, my primary teacher, whom I loved. For worse, or just sadder, my art teacher, who after A-levels said: 'You will come back sometime, won't you, to tell us what the outside world is like?'

MOST IMPORTANT LESSON LEARNED AT SCHOOL
Don't panic about what you are going to be at 16 or 18.

SOMETHING I WISH I'D DONE DIFFERENTLY AT SCHOOL
I wish I'd not been afraid of being good at things. I learned that very British thing of trying to underachieve so as not to be called a creep or to stand out.

BEST MOMENT AT SCHOOL
Leaving

WORST MOMENT AT SCHOOL
Being told I was not 'university material'. I was.

SWOT POINTS
Direct-grant scholarship to Talbot Heath. Crack over-arm bowler for the under-13s cricket team in the Southern Championship.

EMBARRASSING MOMENTS
Being told constantly that I was a second-class citizen because I didn't tie back my hair or do up my top button. Fortunately, I saw the ridiculous side of this.

QUALIFICATIONS
10 O-levels, 3 A-levels, BA (Hons) in Comparative American Studies from Warwick University

CHILDREN
Ideally my children will attend a good state school. We abhor the public school system.

Picture by Steve Poole, courtesy Daily Mail

3 WHICH STATE SCHOOL?

NURSERY

THE UNDER-FIVES

If you want to start well, start early. Most experts agree that the earlier a child begins to learn, the better. Of course, parents can do a lot for themselves. But sometimes, whether because of working commitments or simply a desire to see their child mix and learn with other children, a more structured approach is sought by parents.

Despite the recent recession, increasing numbers of women with children under the age of five are going back to work. The problem for many parents, however, is that state-funded nursery provision varies widely from area to area. According to a survey by the Labour Party, based on official figures, some 58% of three and four year-olds in Cleveland will get a state-funded place in nursery school. That compares with just 2% in Somerset and none in Gloucestershire.

There is no compulsion in law for national or local government to provide education for children under the age of five. Most international comparisons show that Britain is not terribly well served for state-funded nurseries. The bad news is that the situation is likely to worsen.

So where state-funded nurseries do exist, competition for places is usually intense. And where the local council does not offer many places, you will have to dig into your pocket and pay for it yourself. The quality of what is on offer, whether in the public or private sector, can vary widely. As usual, the politicians argue about this state of affairs. Former Prime Minister Margaret Thatcher did promise that there would be a nursery place for every child whose parents wanted one by the end of the 1980s. But ministers later had to concede that this was one promise that just could not be fulfilled.

Broadly speaking there are two main types of provision for children under five:

- nursery schools

- day nurseries or playgroups.

Nursery schools are usually attached to a primary school and cater more obviously for the child's education. An early start will probably be made with exploring shapes, colours, size and reading. Getting into a good primary school can be much easier if you are already sending your child to the nursery, though this is by no means automatic.

85

Day nurseries concentrate on play, but should help children gain a grasp of basic skills and concepts. They are a place where children can be left to play, mix and learn in a slightly less formal setting while, hopefully, developing socially and emotionally. A variety of activities and games usually takes place. The best groups will include a strong educational element.

Playgroups are really just another name for day nurseries. Again, the best of the bunch will ensure that part of the time is spent in some educational pursuit.

The National Campaign for Nursery Education has noted that parents are coming under increasing pressure to enrol their four year-old children into school reception classes, rather than local nurseries. It says the reasons are not always to do with the child's best interests, but are a bid to boost numbers.

EARLY LEARNING BOOSTS STANDARDS

Professor Philip Gammage, Dean of Nottingham University's Education Faculty, has no doubts about the benefits of early learning. Recently appointed to the Royal Society of Arts Early Learning Enquiry, he said

'By early learning we mean the formal and informal learning of young people up to the age of seven – language and literacy, number and shape, co-ordination and self-control, problem-solving and other aspects.' He added 'Currently about 40% of our children have some nursery education at the age of three. It is through a combination of playgroups, nursery classes, nursery schools and private schools. France has had a fully articulated system, which 98% of its children attend, since 1871. We are a long way behind.'

FACT FILE
In 1992 in England there were 3.2 million children aged under five.

41% of the three and four year-olds were attending pre-school playgroup sessions.

PRE-SCHOOL PLAYGROUPS ASSOCIATION

Founded more than 30 years ago, this registered charity is the largest single provider of care and education for under-fives in the country, running more than 20,000 groups for 750,000 children. More than 75% of playgroups belong to the association. Most are run by parent management committees, but some are privately owned and others are organised by the Church.

This umbrella organisation says that, overall, groups receive from local and national tax-payers about £8.35 million; the equivalent of £12.12 per child. But it estimates that parents contribute a staggering £100 million a year out of their own pockets. The amount parents pay per year varies according to their area, from just 23p to several hundred pounds.

Margaret Lochrie, Chief Executive of the Pre-School Playgroups Association, has said 'Families, local communities and government have depended on the existence of play-groups to provide young children with the advantage of a good educational start in life. They have provided the experience and support that have enabled parents to feel more confident about their ability as parents.'

The association organises national training for group leaders and volunteer helpers. Most playgroups use a combination of trained staff and parent helpers. As one of their reports points out, 'Children learn at an early age about co-operation and acceptance of authority and, because parents are involved, the playgroup works as an extension of the home. Parents who help in playgroup are

able to learn about their own child's development and find support from other parents.'

The association estimates that although there are already 25,000 children with special needs in playgroups, another 120,000 with special needs could benefit from attending.

Some local education authorities subsidise the fees of children whose families are unemployed or on low incomes, but this is rare. The association has started its own fund-raising to subsidise the fees of families in particular need. Many sessions are themselves already supported by grants.

DIFFERENT TYPES OF PAID–FOR PLAYGROUPS

Playgroup sessions (similar to nursery classes) meeting for less than four hours per session	11,849
Full day-care and extended hour groups (helping working parents)	1,336
Family centres	129
Parent and toddler groups	4,828
Opportunity playgroups	136
Under-five groups	958
Others (including hospital play schemes and Armed Services playgroups)	298

CRIMEWATCH IN THE CLASSROOM

Children who attend nursery school are less likely to get into trouble in later life, experts have reported. They say the experience can help reduce the number of teenage pregnancies and cut delinquency and law-breaking. These findings were highlighted at a fund-raising meeting of the Pre-School Playgroups Association launched by 'Crimewatch UK's' Sue Cook.

Research carried out in the United States by child education group High-Scope indicates that children who attend nursery are more likely to prosper as adults. The survey of

126 children from poor families in Michigan followed their progress up to the age of 19, and has continued up to age 27. Half attended nursery schools while the rest stayed at home.

The schoolwork of those who did experience a nursery education was generally better. And when they became young adults, they were more likely to have completed school and secured jobs.

Those who did not attend pre-school classes were more likely to have been in trouble with the police, required special education classes, and scored lower on basic problem-solving tests. Girls who

'This one's a bit far fetched. A kid who has to call his teacher 'Sir' nicks something, gets a thick ear from a copper and is sent home to find his employed parents are in and not at the pub...'

missed out on nursery school were more likely to become pregnant in their teens.

The researchers also noted that for every £1,000 invested in children who attended nurseries, the American tax-payer saved £4,310 on the cost of education and social problems in later life.

Pre-School Playgroups Association President Pam Thayer, a former Home Office and Health Department inspector and a key adviser to the British wing of High-Scope, said 'The American research indicates that children who attend playgroups or nurseries, with parental involvement, do benefit in later life. There were fewer unmarried mothers and fewer children in trouble. At school they tended to be the prefects, the social backbone of the school.' The Chief Executive Margaret Lochrie agreed and pointed out the importance of the involvement of parents in pre-schooling.

Head start

Theresa James, aged five, got a head start at primary school. From the age of three she attended the on-site nursery school at Cecil Road Primary School in Gravesend, Kent, until she had the confidence to join the main school. Theresa was one of 18,000 pupils participating in an £11 million-a-year project to boost early-years learning in the county.

Her mother Iris said 'It has made Theresa more confident in every way. She has done really well with her work and I am amazed at what she can do for her age.' Mrs James added 'When she first went to the nursery she was a bit timid, but she carried on, mixed, and made friends.'

Under-fives development officer Tricia Sharp said 'Attitudes and behaviour patterns established in a child's first seven years can shape its whole later life. It is important, therefore, that early-years teachers nurture a learning atmosphere of fun and mutual discovery rather than one of dull drudgery.'

Cecil Road Primary's head-teacher Andy Sparks said the transition from the nursery created a strong foundation of progression, continuity and security for the child. This was eased by having small initial classes, with one adult to just nine children. Mr Sparks concluded 'We are pleased we have no major disciplinary problems. We are already beginning to see standards are higher than in the past. This is certainly reflected in children's reading.'

MOVING UP

On the first day at primary school the only tearful faces should belong to proud mums and dads. For your child, starting school should be a thrill not a trauma, and with your help it can be. There are various ways you can prepare your son or daughter for the big day: you can invite other children round to get your child used to making new friends; you can rehearse new situations through simple role-plays, and you can boost your child's confidence by dealing with potential worries before they come up. By discussing the transition fully and openly you can make the move from nursery to primary one of the best days of your child's school life.

To find groups in your area contact:

Pre-School Playgroups Association
61–63 Kings Cross Road
London WC1X 9LL

Tel: 071-833 0991
Fax: 071-837 4942

National Campaign for Nursery Education
23 Albert Street
London NW1 7LU

Tel: 071-387 6582
Fax: 071-383 5929

> ❝ Playgroups are a crucial national resource. Children derive tremendous benefits from playgroups, both educationally and socially. You get back what you put in, or what you don't put in. We are beginning to reap the results of that. ❞

Sue Cook of 'Crimewatch UK', whose children Charlie, 10, and Megan, 5, both benefited from nursery school

PRIMARY SCHOOLS

BACK TO THE FUTURE

Primary schooling up to the age of eleven is a crucial phase in the development of any child. But many parents will be heartily sick, if not thoroughly confused, by the rows which have surrounded the subject. Arguments about what should be taught in primary schools, and how it should be taught, have raged for a quarter of a century and more, particularly since the publication in 1967 of the Plowden Report, which led to the adoption of a more child-centred approach by schools.

But the tide appears to be turning away from what some critics have dismissed as trendy or progressive ideas, towards what they believe to be a more traditional, or common-sense, approach. Recent evidence from government inspectors and advisers suggests it is not before time. So parents must be on their guard when choosing a school for their children. Many schools insist that they use a mixture of methods. That may be true, but how rich is the mix?

THE 'THREE WISE MEN'

A report in 1992 by a trio of experts dubbed the 'Three Wise Men' proved to be the catalyst for a big shake-up in the primary sector. It criticised many of the fashionable theories that had taken root in schools and teacher-training colleges since the 1960s. And it said the expectations of many teachers were simply too low, with the result that they failed to push many pupils to achieving their potential.

Curriculum Organisation and Classroom Practice in Primary Schools – a discussion document was written by primary education experts Professor Robin Alexander of Leeds University, Chief Inspector of Schools Jim Rose, and Chief Executive of the National Curriculum Council Chris Woodhead.

A back-to-basics test on the Three Rs

It said bluntly 'Over the last few decades the progress of primary pupils has been hampered by the influx of highly questionable dogmas.'

This had led to excessively complex classroom practices and to individual subjects, like English, maths and science, being devalued. In their place was an over-reliance on 'topic work', in which pupils might do an all-embracing project that involved a bit of maths here and a touch of English there, with dabs of history and geography thrown in for good measure. Perhaps even more worryingly, the 'Three Wise Men' noted 'Standards of education in primary schools will not rise until all teachers expect more of their pupils.'

This is not to say that all schools were bad. The concern was that many, probably up to a third, simply weren't good enough. The broad picture remains one of unacceptably wide differences between schools, and between classes within schools, both in the quality of teaching and in the standards that primary pupils achieve.

MORE EVIDENCE

Ministers then took further evidence from their lesson advisers at the National Curriculum Council and the newly formed school standards watchdog OFSTED. Their reports

in 1993 broadly backed the views of the 'Three Wise Men'. OFSTED inspectors who studied 400 lessons in 74 primary schools reported 'The amount of time devoted to teaching the basic skills was not always well used.' It added 'In some classes much of what was claimed to be whole class teaching amounted to little more than drawing the class together to give instructions about the conduct and organisation of the work the pupils were expected to do, either in groups or individually. The result was ineffective use of valuable teaching time.'

'The main problem with too much group or individual work was that the time a teacher spent with each child was often fleeting,' said the inspectors. Both reports did, however, note the concerns of teachers, who were worried that overload caused by the introduction

---

❛What's this? I said.
You're starting school today.
I ain't. I'm stopping 'ome.
Now, come on, Loll. You're a big boy now.
I ain't.
You are.
Boo-hoo.❜

Cider with Rosie *by Laurie Lee, published by Chatto & Windus*

of the National Curriculum was leading to superficial teaching, particularly in the basics of reading, writing and arithmetic, which were being squeezed. This has led to moves to slim down the National Curriculum to concentrate on the basics, particularly for younger primary pupils. But the reports also noted a deep reluctance by some schools to change their topic-oriented teaching methods in order to fit in with the new requirements.

TEACHING TIME

The National Curriculum Council noted wide variation in the amount of time pupils were actually taught by teachers. Many are receiving less than the recommended levels. The government advised in 1990 that pupils aged from five to seven should receive a minimum of 21 hours direct teaching a week. It was thought appropriate for those aged 7 to 11 to receive at least 23.5 hours.

Education Department evidence indicated that almost half of 7 to 11 year-olds are receiving less than the minimum teaching time.

- 28% of pupils are receiving up to an hour a week less than the recommended minimum.

- 11% of pupils are receiving between one and two hours less than the minimum.

- 6% of pupils are receiving three hours a week less than the minimum.

- 2% of pupils are receiving up to four hours less than the recommended weekly minimum of direct teaching.

The government says primary schools should:

- organise their classes according to ability, but only subject by subject. This is called setting.

- spend more time teaching whole classes together, not in groups.

- ensure they spend enough of each school day actually teaching pupils.

- spend more time teaching specific subjects such as maths, science and English.

- spend less time on topic work.

- make greater use of specialist or semi-specialist teachers.

Check whether your primary schools do these things.

French leave

Government inspectors who crossed the Channel to see how primary schools fared in France noted a more formal approach. French teachers were far more inclined than their English counterparts to teach the whole class at the same time. However, that is not to say that the teaching was dull or undemanding. They commented 'On the contrary, much of the work in French and English was thoroughly planned, effectively implemented and challenging.'

Suki Beauchamp-Stansfield and Emily Fitton have all their lessons in French at the pioneering 'Lycée' attached to Shaftesbury Park Primary School in Wandsworth, South London.

Picture by Bill Lovelace, courtesy Daily Mail

HOW TO CHOOSE A PRIMARY SCHOOL

FIRST STEPS

Choosing the right primary school for your child means first arming yourself with as much information as possible. Two good starting points are the local education authority and the reference section of a good central library. This type of library will have a copy of *The Education Authorities Directory*, which lists LEAs and all secondary and middle schools they maintain, and independent schools. The LEA will be able to supply you with a list of all schools, including the primary schools, in your area. But don't stop there. Check whether any schools have opted out, that is adopted grant-maintained status with direct funding from Whitehall. You can do this via the Grant Maintained Schools' Foundation or the lobby group Choice in Education.

This may be important if the primary is a feeder to a grant-maintained secondary school to which you may, in future, wish to send your child. Some councils are less than forth-coming about publicising the fact that they have grant-maintained primary schools in their areas. Others, by contrast, produce annual prospectuses listing schools which are council-controlled, grant-maintained and even fee-paying.

Remember not to restrict yourself only to those schools in your council area. If you live near borough boundaries, the nearest schools to your home may actually be in neighbouring education authority areas. High Court test cases have already established that councils can't discriminate against you if you apply to a nearby school that just happens to be in another education authority's patch. The key factor is how close you are to the school. This will become apparent if you apply to one that is oversubscribed.

When choosing an infant school, you should also pay a visit to the adjoining junior school to which your child will transfer. Do your homework by taking soundings from parents of children already at schools in the area. Gossip at the school gate, while helpful in building a picture, should be put into perspective.

Check also each school's overall results in National Curriculum tests at age 7 and 11, particularly those in maths, English and science. These will probably be published in your local newspaper, but are also available from the Department for Education. What you need to check is how each school performs in relation to other schools in the area, and against the national average.

Of course, no sensible parent will choose a school solely for its performance in 'league tables'. However, published results give parents some hard facts and clear bench-marks among the mass of opinions they will hear. Use 'league tables' with caution, but do use them.

MAKING THE APPROACH

Once you have done your homework, draw up a short list of two or three schools and make your approach. The head-teacher is the most important influence on a school, so make sure you spend some time with him or her. Get a feel for the school and its atmosphere. Don't be put off by an old building if it is neat, well cared for and generally clean and

SEE ALSO:
Opting Out
'League Tables'

tidy. When you ask about the aims of the school, you should be reassured by a clear ethos and sense of direction. What is the school's attitude to teaching the basics like reading? If you are told that a mixture of methods is used, ask the head to spell that out. Are you happy with the amount of time your child would be taught with others of similar ability, ie in 'sets', and in a class of pupils of mixed ability?

INSIDE THE SCHOOL

A major study of life in 50 primary schools resulted in academics drawing up a list of key factors that can influence standards in primary schools. *School Matters – the Junior Years* by Ecob, Lewis and Stoll, Open Books, traced the fortunes of 2,000 pupils over four years. The following points are taken from the study.

General

An effective primary school tends:

- to be a voluntary or Church school.

- to be a smaller junior school with 160 pupils or fewer.

- to have classes of less than 24 pupils.

- to cover the entire primary range of infants and juniors straight through from 5 to 11.

- to have a stable teaching force and a low staff turnover.

- to encourage strong parental involvement in the school, but not just through formal parent/teacher associations.

- to have good record-keeping of pupil progress and reports.

Atmosphere

An effective school will usually:

- be in good decorative and physical order, even if it is old.

- have bright and interesting corridors and classrooms with plenty of work on display.

- have a low noise level in the classroom, but not total silence.

- have a positive climate that enthuses pupils.

Leadership

An effective primary school usually:

- has a head-teacher who has been there between three and seven years.

- has a head who plans to stay.

- has a head-teacher demonstrating purposeful leadership.

- has a good deputy head to whom the head-teacher can delegate.

- allows teachers a role in school planning.

Teaching

An effective school usually:

- has intellectually challenging teaching.

- has a 'work-centred' environment with a 'business-like and purposeful air'.

- has teachers concentrating on one theme or subject at a time during lessons.

- fosters good communication between teachers and pupils, both individually and together as a class.

- insists on a well-structured school day and well-planned lessons.

- has teachers following school guidelines consistently.

Danger signs

Possible danger signs to watch out for are:

- classes of 27 pupils or more.

- dirty and untidy surroundings, regardless of the school building's age.

- dull and uninspiring classrooms.

- little or no pupil work attractively displayed.

- noisy and over-boisterous pupils in classrooms.

- lots of apparently undirected teaching in unstructured sessions.

- too many things going on at once during lessons.

Everybody needs good neighbours

Pat Partington, head of 345-pupil Bramcote Hills Primary to the west of Nottingham says 'Most parents will accept their neighbourhood infant or junior school. They don't look to make a choice. The local community school is the one they go to.' Nevertheless, Pat, a leading light in the National Association of Head Teachers, always ensures that prospective parents see enough to make up their own minds. 'We often let pupils take visiting parents around the school. Discipline and school rules top the list of questions parents ask. They are interested in the pastoral side and want reassurance about bullying. They ask about teaching methods, class sizes and how reading is taught. They also want to know the kind of books used.' Pat is convinced most parents are happy with their children's schools, despite stories about standards slipping. 'If you ask parents about their OWN school, they are happy. But when they talk about the school down the road, they say it must be awful.'

97

SECONDARY SCHOOLS

THE GOOD, THE BAD AND THE UGLY

Do not underestimate the difference the choice of state secondary school could make for your child. Schools, as studies have shown, vary enormously in the quality of education they provide, regardless of their status. Recent exam 'league tables' have also shown that some schools in leafy middle-class suburban areas are not doing as well as their social surroundings might suggest. On the other hand, some schools in tough, inner-city areas with well-documented social problems are doing better than might be expected.

The publication of government exam result 'league tables' provoked a big debate on what makes a good school. The comparative exam data, kept hidden from parents for so many years, is one important and incontrovertible indicator. But parents must also look behind the raw figures.

MORE TO SCHOOLS THAN EXAM RESULTS

If you live in an area that has retained selection, you would expect the grammar schools to do well. But are they doing as well as they ought to,

given the fact that they cream off the top 15 to 25% of pupils? If you live in an area that has only comprehensive schools, you may think one is as good as another. That is not necessarily the case. Some are excellent, some are average and some are so downright awful that even the teachers who work there will tell you so, privately, as they try desperately to get out.

VIVE LA DIFFERENCE!

Comprehensive schools vary in terms of their teaching methods, their aims, the way in which they are organised, and their strong and weak points. The need for parents to discriminate wisely between them is more pressing than ever given that new types of schools are emerging. They are being encouraged by ministers to increase parental choice by specialising in one field, whether it's arts, science or technology. If one or more of your local comprehensives have opted out to become grant-maintained with direct funding from Whitehall, they may also have applied to the Education Secretary to change their character. This could involve something as simple as adding on a sixth form. But they might also want to select a proportion of their pupils for specific subjects. There may even be a City Technology College on your doorstep. Check it out.

In any case, a grant-maintained school will have considerably more flexibility to develop its own character and ethos. Some parents even believe that sending their child to a grant-maintained school conveys a certain cachet or snob value. This really depends on the school, but some head-teachers do play on this to a shameless degree.

SELF-FULFILLING PROPHECY

One common fear is that some schools and individual teachers have unrealistically low expectations of their pupils. Once such an idea is established, it is difficult for the teacher to recognise a pupil's potential – or for the pupil to gain credit for good work. The pupils most affected by these preconceived ideas about their ability have traditionally been those in inner cities or socially disadvantaged areas, ethnic minorities and the working class.

Be wary of this as you choose a school. If large numbers of pupils aren't being entered for GCSE exams, try to determine how the staff feel about this. Are they resigned? Is this to be

expected? Or is this something that the staff are determined to change?

LIES, DAMNED LIES AND SCHOOL STATISTICS

In the course of doing your homework, you will want to cast an eye over the school's GCSE, A-level and National Curriculum test results. Truancy rates and school-leaver destinations are also important. The government has legislated that these statistics must be set down in a standardised format in the school prospectus. This is so that parents can see, at a glance, how one school compares with another. Not all schools comply, however. Head-teachers who do present the results in the required way have complained to me about the school down the road that doesn't. The inference is that the other school is giving parents an unduly rosy picture of its performance. So beware of schools that, intentionally or not, appear to be 'massaging' the figures.

The main points to watch out for follow:

- If the school boasts a high GCSE pass rate, does this mean a high A–C rate, equivalent to the old O-level pass, or a high A–G rate?

- In National Curriculum subjects, are they giving the figure for the number of pupils in the GCSE year group, as they should be, or just those entered for the exam? If they only count the pupils entered, their figures could look better than they really are. This is because the absence of the dropouts boosts the average scores.

- Check the school's overall results against the national and local bench-mark averages. Is the school doing better or worse than other schools in the area and around the country? Find out why.

- Pay particular attention to the three core National Curriculum subjects of English, maths and science.

CHOOSING A SECONDARY SCHOOL

DOING YOUR HOMEWORK

Prepare yourself well before you have to make key decisions.

- Read school prospectuses, newsletters and magazines.

- Check schools' performances in national and local 'league tables'.

- Check newspaper cuttings.

- Visit the school on open day.

- Listen to the grapevine.

- Draw up a short list of schools.

- Arrange a formal appointment to meet the head-teacher, visit one or two lessons and have a tour of the school.

Pay a couple of visits in the early morning, at lunch-time and home-time. Look around and spend a while soaking up the atmosphere. Don't arrive at the school with a checklist of points ready to tick off one by one and don't be over-critical. Simply reread the section below before you go to the school in order to jog your memory and get you thinking along the right lines. Once you get to the school, try not to be nervous. Remember, it is the school which is on trial, not you, so just go with the flow.

SCHOOL CONDITIONS

- Regardless of the building's age, is the school generally well cared for?

- Is there a lot of litter and graffiti?

- Is the library well stocked and well used?

- Are the notice-boards full of information about academic, sporting, cultural and leisure activities?

- Are there enough computers?

BEFORE YOU START, ASK YOURSELF:

- What are my child's strengths?

- Will this school develop my child's potential?

- What are my child's needs?

- Can this school meet those needs?

- What sort of atmosphere/ environment would suit my child?

  - single-sex

  - academic, sporting or creative emphasis

  - traditional, with strong discipline

  - relaxed, no uniform

- Do I want my child to sit an entrance exam?

- Do I feel comfortable when I visit the school?

- Does the school have a good reputation?

- Does it achieve good academic results?

- Are the pupils a good advertisement for the school?

- Do I know any parents who send their children there?

- Would my child have friends already at the school?

- Is the school nearby? If not, are we prepared to move house to secure a place at the school?

- If the school has a sixth form, what is it like?

- Check the toilets. Many teachers swear you can tell a great deal about a school by the state of its loos.

- Don't be so impressed by the buildings that you fail to notice the pupils.

ABOUT THE PUPILS

- Do pupils look tidy or scruffy, regardless of uniform?

- Are they well behaved, just spirited or too boisterous?

- Is there any clear evidence of fighting, bullying, rudeness or general bad behaviour?

- Do the pupils inspire confidence or fill you with horror?

- Do pupils cheerily greet you, or shrink away, as you pass?

- What do the canteen staff and local shopkeepers say?

101

Beacons of excellence

Archbishop Blanch C of E Comprehensive School, Toxteth, Liverpool

The roof has holes, the paint is peeling off the ceiling, and a few years ago it was within a petrol bomb's throw of some of the worst inner-city riots Britain has witnessed. Yet Archbishop Blanch School has been hailed by ministers as a 'beacon of excellence' showing the way forward to boosting academic standards in the nation's classrooms. In an area where some people might expect low standards, it dispels the view that socio-economic disadvantage automatically means poor performance by pupils.

With 800 girls from a wide variety of ethnic-minority families and those from poorer areas of Liverpool, the school performed remarkably well in the government's first exam 'league tables' in 1992. Out of 39 Liverpool schools listed, it finished in overall seventh place. But as three of the schools above it were fee-paying independents, Archbishop Blanch was actually the fourth best state school in the city. On average, 48% of pupils gained five or more GCSE grades A C, well ahead of the Liverpool average of just 21% and a national average of 38%. Pupils from the school regularly go on to Oxford or Cambridge universities.

The teachers, governors and pupils I met during a visit to the school with Education Secretary John Patten insisted that it was the quality of teaching, not the age and condition of the school, that really counted. They cited traditional 'commonsense' teaching methods, good discipline, a concentration on the basics, a committed and caring teaching staff and, above all, an inspirational head-teacher.

Head-teacher Mrs Kathleen Zimak, an Oxford classics graduate who joined the school six years ago, said: 'It's not resources, it's people; we combine the traditional with new innovations. We expect the best from every girl. We emphasise traditional discipline. We insist on good manners. Girls stand up when the teacher comes into the class. We also have a really hardworking, well-qualified, professional staff.'

Mrs Zimak said great emphasis was placed on the three Rs. 'The English department is fairly traditional. Their policy is to mark very strictly and carefully. They get very good exam results. More broadly,' she added, 'we try to show every girl that she has immense worth and potential.'

Girls at Archbishop Blanch School

Picture by Paul Lewis, courtesy Daily Mail

The school teaches GCSE and A-level Latin, and has a Greek club, even though squeezing the classics between the compulsory National Curriculum subjects is difficult.

In September 1993 the school moved to a modern site, but it was clear during my visit that many would miss the atmosphere of their traditional crumbling school.

···

MEETING THE HEAD

You may not get much time with the head-teacher. But he or she has the biggest influence on a school, so make every moment count. Don't try to catch the head or staff out with trick questions. You will learn a lot more by being polite, charming and genuinely interested.

- First, get a broad feeling for the person in front of you and whether what he or she is offering coincides with what you want for your child.

- What is the school ethos?

- Does the head show conviction in the aims of the school? Do you agree with the school's aims?

- What is the school's policy on homework, sex education and religious assembly?

- How does the head deal with bullying, petty theft, smoking and drugs? Beware of heads who answer this question by talking too much about the skills of their

103

staff. You want to know how the head and the staff cope with these problems together.

- How many expulsions have there been in recent years, and for what?

- How many teachers are there to every pupil? Are classes big or small?

- What sort of child would the school NOT suit?

- How long has the head been at the school, and how long does he or she intend to stay?

- What are the strengths and weaknesses of the school?

- Does the head do any teaching?

- Does the school have a development plan?

MONEY, MONEY, MONEY

All state schools now have control over most of their budgets, which can range up to £3 million. So money is an important topic. Broadly speaking, schools with more pupils get more cash. And this money has to be properly managed.

- How is the school coping with these new financial pressures?

- Are pupil numbers rising or falling?

- How fit is the school financially?

- What capital projects new buildings or laboratories) are planned?

- Is the school well stocked with books and equipment?

- Is the head complaining about a lack of resources without doing anything about it or taking action to put things right?

- Does the school do any fund-raising, seek sponsorship or cultivate links with industry?

- At independent schools check whether the school is in debt, because if it is, the debt will probably be serviced out of your fees.

VISITING A LESSON

A few minutes will normally suffice. You should be aiming to get a flavour of the school, rather than a make or break impression.

- Do the pupils look interested or bored?

- Are they working enthusiastically, messing about or unruly?

- Are the pupils intelligently spirited and questioning, or cowed?

- How is the teacher's rapport with pupils?

ASK THE PUPILS

Pupils rarely if ever lie, according to

Eight key issues that teachers and governors at Archbishop Blanch believe contribute towards a successful school:

1 an inspirational head-teacher

2 a totally committed staff

3 close parental involvement

4 good pastoral care of pupils

5 a strong emphasis on the basics and the three Rs

6 pupils taught in 'sets' according to ability in each subject

7 shared aims and objectives

8 a good moral education.

teachers. So talk to a few children of different ages and see what they think. Ask them all the things you didn't dare ask the head.

• Is it a good school? Are they happy there? Why or why not?

• What are the school's best and worst points?

• What are the head and teaching staff like?

• Ask sixth-formers whether they considered taking their A-levels or vocational qualifications somewhere else. Why or why not?

TRICKS OF THE TRADE, AN INSIDER'S EYE

As an education 'insider', Hilary Fender, Headmistress of £9,000-a-year Godolphin School in Salisbury, Wiltshire, knows a few 'tricks of the trade' in judging a school. And the lessons of her experience, unveiled in the checklists above, apply equally to state and independent schools.

Mrs Fender advises 'Don't bring your child with you unless you are fairly certain of your choice of school. He or she might like the pets' corner and the colour of the uniform. You

Hilary Fender, Godolphin School

Picture by
Darryn Lyons,
courtesy Daily Mail

105

might hate the head and the academic record. Before you know it, you have a family battle on your hands.'

A COMPREHENSIVE CHOICE

John Dunford, Headmaster of Durham Johnston Comprehensive in County Durham and a leading light in the Secondary Heads Association, says, 'There is already immense diversity among comprehensive schools. Parents know which schools concentrate more on the academic, vocational or sporting side. You only have to go into a local pub to find out.' His own school finished enviably high in the national exam 'league tables', well ahead of many fee-paying independent schools and some state grammars. Mr Dunford set out some of the positive and negative aspects of the comprehensive system.

POSITIVE ASPECTS

1 Breadth of intake

'It gives pupils a much better preparation for life after school if they have mixed with people from backgrounds different to their own. People who live cloistered life styles don't understand what makes other people tick.'

2 Tailoring

'The system fits the individual, and does not ask the individual to fit the system. A good comprehensive will have complex but clear aims to prepare youngsters for life. They are usually good on pastoral care for the individual youngster.'

3 Lack of labelling

'Pupils are less likely to be branded failures. I started my teaching in a grammar school. I was concerned for the plight of pupils at the bottom end of the ability range in an academically selective school.'

4 Size

'Being big can have its benefits. Small is not necessarily beautiful. There are large numbers of staff on which to draw, economies of scale in terms of resources and a good-sized community.'

NEGATIVE ASPECTS

1 Tendency to be misjudged

'Comprehensives are liable to be judged by the wrong criteria. If you put comprehensives and grammar schools on the same league table, you are emphasising an apparent weakness. But the comprehensives' intake is not selected at age 11.'

Talking up your school

Pupils at Durham Johnston Comprehensive have the gift of the gab. Two of them, Amanda Pritchard and Ian Macmullen, both 16, beat opposition from some of Britain's most elite public schools to clinch the National Schools Debating Competition. Headmaster John Dunford said, of their success in the competition sponsored by the Cambridge Union and *The Financial Times,* 'It is a particular pleasure to me that a comprehensive school should win a national competition against so many well-known independent schools. It reflects the high standard of education at this school.'

Picture by
Keith Taylor,
courtesy Daily Mail

The 1,350-pupil school places great emphasis on public speaking and debating with 'mass involvement' competitions for younger pupils. 'It is a skill from which they will all benefit in later life, but which is not widely practised in state schools,' said Mr Dunford.

Mr Dunford concluded 'Our ethos is to make sure that pupils know why they are here and get on with it. Whether they are D/E or A/B candidates, they are here to do their best. We impose fairly firm discipline at 11 and then try to move towards self-discipline. We have very high expectations. So do our parents.'

2 Disaffected children

'The prevalance of disaffected children who have experienced failure in their lives may be greater in a comprehensive than in a grammar.'

3 Bright children being held back

'In some areas, a school will have such a small top-end of academic children that a bright child will be in a very small minority. That might be difficult.'

STATE BOARDING SCHOOLS

State boarding schools are described as one of the country's best-kept secrets. The much overlooked band of 41 schools who have signed up with the State Boarding School Information Service, STABIS, saw their pupil numbers rise by 1.2% this year to 4,634. And part of the reason is cost. For while fees at an independent boarding school can top £13,000 a year, those at a state boarding school are unlikely to exceed £4,500 and are usually considerably less. That is because, although the cost of boarding must be covered, the cost of tuition in state schools is borne by the tax-payer. Frank Bickerstaff, secretary of STABIS, said 'Until two years ago, most parents didn't know state boarding still existed'.

He put the current success down to two factors:

- state boarding schools advertising after years of hiding their light under a bushel.

- parents hit by the recession switching from independent to state boarding schools to reduce the cost of fees.

Some 27 of the state boarding establishments are co-ed and 14 are boys only. One of the 27 takes only female boarders, but there are no strictly girls-only boarding schools, an omission that some schools might do well to rectify. Of those schools, 28 are comprehensive, 12 are selective and one is a mixed Technology school.

FACT FILE

A report by government inspectors into boarding in state schools said:

- 58% had satisfactory or better accommodation for boarders.

- 35% had less than satisfactory boarding accommodation, 'some of it very poor indeed'.

- the rest showed 'variable' standards.

Skegness Grammar School

Skegness Grammar School opted out in 1988 and then went on to open a boarding wing. Skegness's ebullient head-teacher John Webster is clear about his motives. 'We want to give more parents the opportunity of a traditional grammar school education, and to offer pupils that edge which boarding brings.'

Of the 630 pupils, 50 are boarders, and the figure should rise. 'Prep' time is from 6.45 pm to 9 pm Monday to Thursday and Saturday morning. Lights out is at 10 pm and boarders are up at 7.15 am for breakfast. Skegness can offer weekly boarding as well.

Peter Ball aged 12 said 'They set high standards and push you that bit harder.' But it's not all work. Sixth-former Julie Stewart from Caithness said 'There's a good working atmosphere. But it is also fun. There's lots to do.'

Among the elements that help create a good boarding school, the government inspectors cited:

- a reasonable standard of accommodation.

- personal and semi-private space for pupils to 'get away from it all'.

- good relationships and sensitivity to boarders' needs.

- no stereotyping on grounds of sex or race.

- a clear complaints procedure to deal with allegations against staff.

- a system of induction for new boarders.

- good standards of housekeeping.

- adequate supervisory cover.

- involvement by pupils in decisions which affect their surroundings, such as redecoration of common room or furnishing bedrooms.

- good behaviour and friendships.

- no vandalism or graffiti.

State Boarding Information Service (STABIS) or the Boarding Schools Association both on 0883 624717.

SEE ALSO:
Independent Boarding

❝ Most people don't seem to realise that boarding education is not only for those who choose the independent sector. ❞

Jennifer Bellamy, Deputy Head, Ripon Grammar School, North Yorkshire

GETTING A PLACE

Choosing the state school you want your child to attend is one thing. Securing a place there is something else. 'Parent power' may be the educational catch-phrase of the decade; parental choice may even take precedence over the Race Relations Act, as one High Court judge ruled recently. But where demand for places is particularly intense, you need to be pretty hard nosed about the whole process. You may take heart from the fact that the majority of parents, some estimates say up to 90%, are happy with the school to which they send their child.

As a parent you should be aware of three things above all:

1 the rules and the law surrounding school admissions in general.

2 the particular school's admissions criteria.

3 the tricks of the trade that can improve your chances of getting the school of your choice for your child.

You do not initially have to give a reason for your choice, even if the education authority asks you to. But if you do give reasons, make sure they tally with the priority order of factors on which the authority will

The 1980 Education Act lays down the principles for admissions. It says parents have:

• a right to express a preference for the school they want their child to attend.

• a right to information on which to base that choice.

• a right of appeal if their choice of school is not granted.

accept or reject pupils if your chosen school is oversubscribed (see opposite).

It is worth remembering that the right to express a preference does not strictly mean that you can choose your school. In most cases the preference will be met, unless the LEA or school has good reasons why it cannot comply.

It is also important to note that you can apply for a school in a neighbouring education authority area, if it is close by. Neither the council nor the school is allowed to discriminate against you. This is as a result of what has been termed the 'Greenwich Judgement' in the High Court, upheld by the House of Lords.

EXCEPTIONS THAT PROVE THE RULE

The 1980 Act says that a child must be admitted to the school for which his or her parents have expressed a preference unless:

a) the admission of the child would prejudice the provision of efficient education or the efficient use of resources.

b) the school is a Church school that has an agreement with the local education authority or, in the case of a grant-maintained school, with the Education Secretary, to preserve its religious character.

c) the school admits pupils with reference to their ability or aptitude and the admission of the pupil would not be compatible with the admission arrangements.

COMMENT

The first is the catch-all clause. Schools and local education authorities are no longer allowed to place artificial limits on the number of pupils they accept. Since the 1988 Education Reform Act they have been required to accept pupils up to their standard number of pupils (see page 122). So the above argument cannot be used if the standard number has not been reached. However, once the number of potential pupils exceeds the standard number of places, schools are more likely to select pupils.

Broadly speaking, the second exception means that if you are not of the faith, you may not be at the head of the queue. But it doesn't mean you are barred from entry. Many Church schools, particularly Church of England schools, have large numbers of Moslem pupils. This is because Moslem families, with no state-funded Moslem schools, see Christian schools, which place greater emphasis on religious teachings and morality, as the next best thing.

According to the third exception, if your child fails the eleven-plus exam he or she won't be allowed into a grammar school, even if there are places available. This factor could become increasingly important if more comprehensive schools are granted permission to become wholly or partially selective.

ADMISSIONS CRITERIA

Schools must now publish their admissions criteria in their prospectuses. They must spell out, in order, which factors take priority when the school is oversubscribed. The priorities may differ from school to school, but all parents applying to a particular school must be able to recognise the order that applies there. The criteria must also be objective. The test for this objectivity is straightforward: if two or more independent judges were to look at the pupils' applications, they should all rank them in exactly the same order.

In a number of recent circulars, ministers have beefed up the regulations to ensure that everyone knows and plays by the same clear rules. 'Parents should be able to judge their chances of gaining admission to any particular school; if necessary they should understand the reasons for their failure to gain a place, and if they wish should be able to marshal suitable arguments for appeal.'

Courtesy
Croydon Council

WHAT HAPPENS WHEN TOO MANY PEOPLE
APPLY FOR PLACES AT A
COUNTY PRIMARY SCHOOL

PRIORITIES FOR ADMISSION

These criteria apply to the allocation of primary school places to 4–5 year olds, and also to the admission of children in any age group.

1. SIBLINGS

Priority of admission will be given same household either at the school entry, or who attended the school

The Authority makes every effort to accommodate children in accordance with the parents' preference. However, if more parents want places for their children in a particular school than the number of places available the Authority will give priority in the order shown below.

PRIMARY SCHOOLS BROCHURE
1993/94

P. Bonians B.Sc. (Econ)
Director of Education
Education Department
Taberner House
Park Lane
Croydon
CR9 1TP

CROYDON   November, 1992

CHILDMINDERS

(i)   Where a single-parent
         for a childminder to tak
         child/children attend.

2. MEDICAL CASES

Priority of admission may then be medical grounds relating to the paren certain school particularly desirable. medical certificate or letter must be Education supporting the case for

OUT OF ZONE REQUESTS

The method of deciding priority geographical basis, taking into ac offered.

3. GEOGRAPHICAL
LOCATION – ZONES

If places remain once priority is area of certain roads will be dra school. Priority (after siblings living in this area.

4. FREE AREA

As well as the zone, the school

A Free Area is made up of addit admitted once or children from vacancies still exist in the age gr

GENERAL NOTE

Any 'casual' vacancies which may occur criteria used when making the initial alloc is attending a zone school, and either the

Here are some of the criteria you may encounter:

- sibling, family or staff links
- distance from the school to home
- living within the catchment area
- having a child at a feeder primary or nursery school
- selection by ability (eg in grammar schools)
- medical, social or compassionate grounds
- grounds of educational or special needs
- wish for a single-sex education
- religious affiliation.

SIBLING, FAMILY OR STAFF LINKS

Pupils with brothers or sisters already at the school may be given priority. So may pupils with past family links, or those whose parents work at the school as teachers, administrators or ancillary staff. Check the exact nature of past family links which qualify. Does it include cousins or grandparents? This should be clearly set out to avoid doubt. The Commission for Racial Equality has also commented that family links may discriminate in the short term against pupils from ethnic minorities who have no historical link to a community.

DISTANCE FROM SCHOOL

Pupils living closest to a school may be given priority. Check how the distance is measured. Is it as the crow flies or along suitable walking routes? The government favours the latter method. LEAs must offer free transport to school for pupils under the age of eight who live more than two miles away from the nearest suitable school and for those over eight who live more than three miles away. If you live closer but can show that your child's walk to school is dangerous, you should still apply for free transport.

CATCHMENT AREAS

Subject to certain key exceptions, schools may still give priority to pupils living in defined geographical areas. Owing to the legal complexities surrounding school admissions, catchment areas are on the decline. Schools simply do not want to be challenged in the courts. Catchment areas must be defined and published well before the cycle of admissions begins, so that parents have a clear idea of their chances of getting into a particular school.

There must also be a PRACTICAL or EDUCATIONAL justification for the use of catchment areas, rather than simple distance from the school. This could include physical barriers like motorways or rivers. Particular note should be taken where a catchment area boundary coincides with a local education authority boundary.

FEEDER PRIMARY OR NURSERY SCHOOLS

Children attending named primary or nursery schools may be given priority. Although such links may be justified on educational grounds, decisions about which feeder schools are given priority must be justified on OBJECTIVE grounds. These can include the percentage of pupils who have transferred in previous years. Schools which operate this policy near local education authority boundaries must ensure that the choice of feeder school can be defended against complaints from parents whose children attend other schools across the boundary.

While state nursery schools can gain priority as feeders to state primary schools, fee-paying nursery groups cannot. This is because it is illegal to request payment in connection with admission to a state school.

SELECTION BY ABILITY

Selective schools are allowed to take into account pupils' results in tests, as well as assessments of their ability based on other factors such as head-teachers' reports or performance in interviews. Parents must be clear about relative priorities if a combination of assessment techniques is used.

Some schools and education authorities may feel that objective criteria are not flexible enough. They may want to take other subjective factors into account, such as those listed below. But if they do, they must also set out clear and detailed information about how these judgements will be made.

According to the Department for Education, interviews should not be the sole measure of a child's ability because they are too subjective. If they are used, it should be in conjunction with other evidence such as test scores and primary school reports.

MEDICAL, SOCIAL OR COMPASSIONATE GROUNDS

Parents who can demonstrate that admission to a particular school is necessary for their child's medical or social well-being may find favour with some schools or LEAs. Parents must be told about any special factors that must be made known at the time they make their application. They should also be warned if supporting evidence from doctors, social workers or education welfare officers is required.

EDUCATIONAL REASONS

Priority is given by some schools to children whose parents can show specific educational reasons why that institution is suitable for them. This may take the form of particular extra-curricular activities which interest the child, such as a school orchestra. Or there may be facilities the school offers to cater for the child's special needs.

Schools can often be skating on thin ice here. They must ensure they are not operating an unlawful selective admissions policy. Such criteria are intended to deal only with exceptional cases. Schools admitting large numbers of pupils under this heading may be changing the character of the school without proper authority.

SINGLE-SEX EDUCATION

Many single-sex schools give priority to pupils whose parents wish them to have a single-sex education. If this parental preference is to be used as a factor in deciding who gets in and who doesn't, then the school or local authority must give clear details about the basis on which judgements will be made. For instance, will parents who express an EXPLICIT desire for single-sex education be better off than those who simply assume that the application to the school speaks for itself?

At a time when research shows that girls perform better in single-sex schools, it is worth considering test-cases on the provision of single-sex schooling. In one case, a girl denied a place at a single-sex school challenged the decision on the grounds that the provision of all-girl places did not meet the DEMAND for them.

RELIGIOUS AFFILIATIONS

Schools which are supported by religious foundations usually give priority to children of particular faiths or denominations. Schools and local education authorities must make clear whether an expression of religious affiliation or commitment is enough to give a pupil priority, or whether the child must demonstrate active involvement. If the latter is necessary, parents must be told the kinds of supporting evidence that will be taken into account.

TRICKS OF THE TRADE

For the tricks of the trade I have learned, I am indebted to the head-teachers who have asked, for obvious reasons, that their names be withheld.

FIRST CHOICE?

If the admissions system you are involved in aims to accommodate parents' first preferences, the implications of that first choice NOT being met must be explained. It may seem logical that the second choice will be given automatically, but you might find your second choice filled by children whose parents placed it as their first choice. You could then be shunted to the back of the queue. That is why it is so important to have a realistic view of your child's chances of getting into the school that you nominate as your first choice.

Assessing your chances is now made easier because every secondary school is obliged to publish the number of applications it receives, together with the number of places available. Local 'league tables' will no doubt rank the most popular schools by plotting the ratios of applications against places.

PLAYING THE SYSTEM – DIVIDE AND RULE

In some areas, particularly where relations between the council and opted-out schools are strained, parents are able to hold two or more offers: one from the council-run school and others from opted-out schools. They sometimes hold offers from schools run by different LEAs, without telling one about the other. This doubles or even trebles their chances of getting a school of their choice.

'ECONOMICAL WITH THE TRUTH'

This does involve an element of deceit, since parents know it is always better to write 'no' in the application section which asks them if they have applied to any other schools. I would not condone such action. But it happens. And many head-teachers are fairly philosophical about it.

Ministers have urged councils to confer and to co-operate with the grant-maintained schools in their area to ensure there is no admissions chaos. Some already have informal arrangements, whereby each party will say which parents have accepted places at their school. The council likewise tells the grant-maintained schools which parents have accepted places at their schools.

If parents are found to be playing the system and holding more than one offer, they are given a short time to decide one way or the other. In areas where councils are waging all-out war on the go-it-alone schools, such working relationships are unlikely to exist voluntarily. If this is the case in your area, the Education Secretary may intervene and impose admissions procedures to ensure co-operation. Measures have already been taken to ensure that literature about grant-maintained secondary schools is distributed through all primary schools to draw them to the attention of local parents. This is to prevent antagonistic councils 'freezing out' grant-maintained schools by failing to provide information about them.

THINK POSITIVE

If you decide to give reasons for your choice, accentuate the positive. Do not say how awful you found all the other schools in the area, nor should you say you are choosing a particular school because it is the best one in the area. Both observations may be true, but the school you want will not take them into account.

Instead, you can stack the odds in your favour by making sure your reasons match up, as far as possible, with what your chosen school or the education authority considers a high priority. You will also gain by stressing the unique way in which your child will benefit from being educated at the school you have put top of your list.

This can be crucial if you fail to get a place and then decide to appeal. For, even if the school is full, you may still be in with a chance if you can show that the educational benefits of your child going to that particular school outweigh the disruption caused by taking on one extra pupil.

MITIGATING CIRCUMSTANCES

Entry criteria for some schools list medical reasons as a high priority.

Does your child have a particular health problem that entry to a particular school could alleviate? If your child has changed primary schools frequently, you could also argue that the secondary school of your choice would offer some welcome stability. You might say that your child will become unsettled again if he or she cannot go with his or her friends from primary school. A psychologist's report given as evidence of the likely psychological trauma could support your case.

A TEST OF FAITH

If your first choice is a Church school, you may wish to explain that your family are practising Christians and you want your child brought up in an atmosphere of sound moral and religious teaching. But be warned, the depth of your faith may be tested and you may be asked for evidence to support your claims.

THE CLASSIC CASE

Only about a quarter of comprehensive schools offer Latin. But they are often the comprehensives with the best academic reputations, and frequently oversubscribed. You may therefore wish to state in your application how crucial it is that your child studies Latin, pointing out that your chosen school is the only one in the area that offers the subject.

ARTISTIC LICENCE

If the comprehensive to which you want to send your child has the only school orchestra in the area, this could be a critical factor. If it is your wish to see that your son or daughter receives specialist tuition in music and participates fully in the musical life of the school, say so. It will help if your child is already playing an instrument and can show some talent or interest. The same argument goes for schools which may specialise in art, drama or in particular sports like rugby and cricket.

DEADLINES, DEADLINES

By law parents must be told of the admissions procedures at least SIX weeks before the deadline for sending in their forms. The deadlines do vary in different areas. Ministers say they should be AFTER the government publishes its school performance 'league tables' in mid-November. The tables include school-by-school details of public exam results, National Curriculum tests, and truancy rates.

EARLY APPLICATIONS

Schools and education authorities are at liberty to collect at any time the names of pupils expressing a preference for a particular school, but they cannot give priority to these early applications. So, there should be no real advantage to putting your application in early.

LATE APPLICATIONS

These must be considered on their merits. Schools and education authorities have a duty to act fairly according to the rules. But guidelines from ministers also note, 'Exercising discretion so as to waive these general rules in individual cases is not easy, particularly in respect of schools which are heavily oversubscribed. But special cases may warrant special treatment. Officials must, however, be prepared to defend such decisions against challenges from other parents.'

'SELECTION BY MORTGAGE'

Just because some councils replaced grammar schools with comprehensives does not necessarily mean that selection has been eliminated. Instead of selection by ability, pupils are being chosen by what some have dubbed 'selection by mortgage', and the estate agents have not been slow to exploit the phenomenon. In some cases, it has been claimed, a good school nearby has put thousands on the price of a house.

Of course, it is not always possible to move house at the drop of a hat, but any parents with young children, or couples planning a family, should be aware that one of the best ways of getting into the state school of your choice is to up sticks and move close by. Whether you are a homeowner, renting privately or from the council, the same basic principles apply. So it's worth planning well ahead.

It is also worth knowing that schools and education authorities can reserve a small number of places at the start of the school year for pupils expected to move into the area. Ministers say this is sensible where new housing is nearing completion. But the admissions documents must spell out clearly how many places are being reserved, and why. Parents applying for admission to schools outside the usual admissions cycle should be treated in the same way as those who apply in the normal way.

WAITING LISTS

Waiting lists of pupils whose parents failed to get their first-choice school should be kept by all schools and local education authorities. The names should be ranked in descending order of priority. If an offer of a place is not taken up, it can go to the parents of the pupil at the top of the waiting list. Make sure you know and understand the criteria on which spare places will be given.

BEFORE YOU APPEAL

If you fail to get the place you want, you can, of course, appeal. But before the formal appeals procedure gets underway, many areas operate

an informal procedure to deal with oversubscribed schools. The education authority should clearly identify this preliminary stage to ensure that appeals do not begin until all other means of settlement have been exhausted.

GET A HEAD START

If you fail to get the place you want, go to see the head-teacher. Do not be fobbed off by the school secretary or anyone else. Always be calm, polite, but quietly insistent. In this way you might be able to secure a place without going to a formal appeal. Most parents do not know the right questions to ask when they see the head at this stage. One head-teacher told me that parents should simply begin with the opener 'What questions should I be asking you?' I followed the advice and the head-teacher gave me a list.

PLAYING THE NUMBERS GAME

Find out the whole school's physical capacity. Ask the head if it has been reached. This could be higher than its standard number, so governors have flexibility to let more pupils in. 'If there are empty desks, ask why they can't let your child fill one of them,' said the head of a frequently oversubscribed school, who has vast experience of these matters. 'Pupil numbers are rarely even across the years. There may be more pupils in

GETTING
A PLACE

SEE ALSO:
School Appeals

the older years than in the younger year groups.

You may be able to persuade a head or an appeal panel that they can take more children in year 7 because there are fewer in years 10 and 11. Ask about the maximum class size. Heads often say about 30. Then ask if there are classes greater than 30, and, if so, how many? If there are classes of more than 30, ask why they can't have one this year too, with your child in it.

MOVING TO APPEAL

If you still fail to have your child accepted, you must be given some idea of the criteria applied by governors in reaching that decision, as well as a form on which to make your appeal, and information about how to make it. You should also be told which relevant documents you need to submit with the appeal form.

You should, however, also take time to find out about the school to which your child has been allocated in place of the one you wanted. On reflection, you might find it more suitable than you first thought. Then again, you may not.

CALLING IN THE CAVALRY

There may be times when you are at your wits' end and need some practical advice and moral support. Don't be frightened to ring the Department for Education for more information. Their response will tend to be factual. Don't expect them to take up cudgels on your behalf.

As a parent, you will also find the helpline operated by the Advisory Centre for Education (ACE) to be invaluable (see address on page 123 for details). This registered charity is the only national organisation to offer free advice, information and support to parents of children in state schools. It is independent of both national and local government. Sometimes ACE's pronouncements smack of being a touch partisan, but they are on YOUR side. They also produce a very useful and extensive range of leaflets and booklets, some of which are free of charge.

SCHOOLS THAT BREAK THE RULES

All of the following are deemed to interfere with the running of an open and fair system, and would be against the law according to ministers.

> ❝What the bureaucrats in County Hall fail to understand is the anxiety and heartache that parents go through at this time.❞
>
> *Head-teacher of a large comprehensive*

There are certain things schools may NOT do when deciding which pupils to admit.

They must not

- draw lots

- allow governors a reserved right to choose

- exclude potentially disruptive children

- exclude children with special needs

- charge fees or seek 'voluntary contributions' to school funds.

DRAWING LOTS

Putting names into a hat and pulling out the winners is just not on. As the 1992 draft circular on admissions makes clear, 'Decisions made by lot cannot be tested, and leave no basis for appeal. If there are a number of pupils who have an equal claim to a place on other grounds, distance from home to school is a simple tie-breaker.'

GOVERNORS' 'RESERVED LIST'

Neither school governors nor the local LEA can reserve the right to make the final decision on admissions. They must be bound by their admissions criteria. Otherwise parents would have no idea about the chances of their child being admitted or the reasons for refusal.

EXCLUDING POTENTIALLY DISRUPTIVE CHILDREN

This is another no-no. The government says it is not acceptable for schools to refuse pupils, or relegate them to places lower down the queue, on the basis that they MIGHT disrupt lessons. In short, they cannot act as judge and jury on the basis of second-hand evidence from other schools. However, if the child is admitted and then does actually become disruptive, the pupil can be disciplined, up to and including 'exclusion', as 'expulsion' is now termed.

PUPILS WITH SPECIAL NEEDS

Governors cannot refuse to admit a child simply because they do not believe the school can cater for his or her special educational needs. For pupils with a statement of special educational needs, the local education authority has a responsibility to ensure that those needs are met and the 1993 Education Act gives parents the right to state a preference for a school. Nevertheless, events have shown that many schools can be adept at getting around the legislation.

FEES OR VOLUNTARY CONTRIBUTIONS

No matter how it is couched, state schools are forbidden to charge fees.

Suggestions that a voluntary contribution to school funds might ease your child's application through the machinery are unlawful. Likewise, deposits to cover the administrative costs of selection arrangements are not allowed. So don't pay them, report them.

RELEVANT CHANGES SINCE 1993

- The Education Secretary will use new reserve powers to impose common admissions procedures and to arrange publication of joint admissions information where the two sides can't agree.

- The government will ensure that literature about grant-maintained secondary schools is distributed (on the same basis as that of local authority-run secondary schools) through all primary schools.

- Local education authorities will have a reserve power to direct any state school, including those which are grant-maintained, to take a pupil who has not been found a place.

- This power will pass to the new Funding Agency for Schools once 75% of pupils in an area attend grant-maintained schools.

- Grant-maintained schools will have a right of appeal.

- Local education authorities are under a new duty to provide education other than at school, such as with home tutors.

KEY DEFINITIONS

Open enrolment

Since the 1988 Education Act, education authorities can no longer set artificial ceilings on the number of pupils a school may take. Parents who choose a school for their child must have their wish met, providing there is room.

Standard number

The technical definition of the standard number is the number of pupils on the school's roll in 1979, or the number of pupils on the roll in September 1988, whichever is higher. This is effectively the maximum number of pupils a school can accommodate, and should broadly reflect the school's physical capacity. The school or local education authority must tell you what that standard number is. If the standard number has not been reached and your child meets other entry requirements, the school must accept him or her.

A school set up after 1979 will have as its standard number the number of its first full intake. Governors can set a higher standard number at their discretion, and can apply to have the figure reduced where the capacity of the school has been reduced.

APPROVED ADMISSIONS NUMBER

This is the equivalent of the standard number, but for grant-maintained schools. It is fixed when the school's application for self-governing status is approved.

Advisory Centre for Education (ACE)
1b Aberdeen Studios
22 Highbury Grove
London N5 2EA

(Free telephone advice line 2–5 pm each weekday 071-354 8321)

Department for Education (DFE)
Sanctuary Buildings
Great Smith Street
London SW1P 3BT

General enquiries: 071-925 5000

SCHOOL APPEALS

IF AT FIRST YOU DON'T SUCCEED, APPEAL

If you are one of the growing number of parents whose children fail to gain a place at the school of their choice, you will no doubt feel frustrated beyond belief. But you are certainly not alone: some education authorities process well over 1,000 appeals each year. In a rather perverse way, the number of complaints has grown in the wake of the Parents' Charter, because it made families more aware of their rights.

The bad news is that fewer than 1 in 3 appeals is successful. Education Department figures for 1990–91 show that 26,700 appeals were lodged by parents, of which some 18,700 were heard. Of this number only 7,800 parents were successful.

RUSSIAN ROULETTE

Margaret Tulloch of the Advisory Centre for Education (ACE) says going through the admissions procedures can be like playing Russian roulette. 'Those who know how to play the system manage best.' ACE, which gives free advice on schools to parents, says the number of enquiries it received on admissions procedures doubled from 1990 to 1992.

If you fail to get your child into the school of your choice, you MUST be told of your right to appeal by either the school or the LEA. If the school is run by the LEA, you should appeal to the authority. Those who fail to get into a grant-maintained school should appeal to the school directly.

ADVANCE NOTICE

You should be given at least 14 days' advance notice of the hearing and its location which, according to guidelines, should be held at premises reasonably accessible to parents but NOT at the education authority offices. At least seven days before the hearing you should receive by first-class post:

a) a written statement summarising how the school's admissions policy has been applied in your child's case.

b) a summary of the reasons for the decision.

c) copies of any documents to be put before the committee at the hearing.

Documents are supposed to be clear and easy to read. But this is not always the case.

Relax, go to it

Guidelines drawn up by local councils agree with ministerial wishes that procedures should be as relaxed and informal as possible. This is not a re-run of 'Rumpole of the Bailey'. Nevertheless, if you are not used to being in the spotlight, you may feel a little nervous about things. Try to stay calm. This is, after all, your right.

Be prepared

You will feel much more confident if you have rehearsed your case beforehand. Make sure you understand fully the basis on which the school has accepted other pupils but rejected your child. What is the order of priority for the factors that will gain a child a place? You should have already studied these factors when you applied to your first-choice school, but if you are unclear about any of the admissions criteria, ASK. It is worth reviewing them when preparing your case.

Accentuate the positive

Follow the advice of the old song and concentrate your case on the POSITIVE reasons why your first-choice school is the one that will be best for your child. Keep these arguments as much as possible in line with the order of the school's admissions criteria. With schools increasingly specialising in areas such as technology, music, PE and art, you may want to highlight at an early stage your child's particular APTITUDE, MOTIVATION, TALENT and INTEREST in whichever field is relevant. Resist the temptation to criticise the other schools. It may be justified, but appeals panels generally don't want to hear it and cannot, technically, use it as grounds for allowing an appeal.

The committee

In local education authority-run schools, it is the authority itself that sets up an independent appeals committee.

In Church schools, the governors draw up the committee, but must include a member nominated by the local education authority. This is because it is the governors, usually Church of England or Roman Catholic, who employ the staff and run the school.

Appeals in grant-maintained schools are heard by an independent committee set up by the school's own governors.

In county or LEA schools an appeals committee must consist of three, five or seven members. They will comprise councillors on the education authority and also other individuals who have experience of education. The latter must be familiar with

SEE ALSO:
Getting a Place

educational conditions in the area, or have children registered at a local school. To ensure fair play, however, there must be no conflicts of interest. So a teacher cannot sit in judgement on a pupil leaving or seeking admission to his or her own school, for example.

BRING A FRIEND OR WITNESS

If the idea of facing an Appeals Committee on your own is daunting, don't worry. You are allowed to bring a friend to support you at the appeal hearing. You may even choose to be represented; technically, there is nothing to stop you even taking a solicitor. This may, however, come across to the panel as being a little heavy-handed. The Association of County Councils says in its guidance, 'Bearing in mind the importance of maintaining an informal atmosphere, in many appeals legal representation will be unnecessary and may even be counter-productive.' But the Association concedes 'It will seldom be appropriate to deny the parent the opportunity to be represented, whether by a lawyer or by a friend, if that is what he chooses.' Parents must, however, give advance warning to the appeals committee's clerk. The same applies if the parent intends to bring a witness, although it is rare for witnesses to be called in admissions appeals.

WHAT HAPPENS INSIDE THE APPEAL HEARING?

Try not to feel intimidated. The appeal will be heard in private, and it should be fair and informal. Guidelines state 'Informality is unlikely to be assisted by the tape-recording of the proceedings, a practice which should be avoided.' Generally, the chairperson of the panel or the clerk will welcome and introduce the parties and explain the procedure. Parents must be told that the committee is independent of the LEA or governors and that its findings are binding on them.

The order of the hearing is as follows:

- an official puts the case for the school or education authority

- parents have a chance to ask questions

- the parents or their representative put their case

- the education authority officials or governors question the parents

- the education authority or governors reply and sum up their case

- the parents sum up their case.

Appeals committee members may ask questions at any time if they need particular points to be clarified.

THE VERDICT: THE 'TWO-STAGE PROCESS'

There are two stages in the verdict reached by the appeals committee. Stage 1 is called the 'factual stage'; stage 2 is the 'balancing stage'.

STAGE 1

The first stage relates to parental preference. As stated in 3d 'Getting a Place', a LEA or school MUST comply with parental preference unless it can show that one of the exceptions in the 1980 Act applies. If the school or LEA cannot show that one of these three exceptions exists, then the parents have won. The appeals committee is bound by law to allow the parents' appeal, and they can go home and celebrate. If the school or LEA CAN show that one of the three sets of circumstances prevails, then the appeal moves to the second stage.

STAGE 2

It is not enough for the school or authority simply to assert that efficient education will be prejudiced or that the character of a school might be affected by accepting a particular child. To win the case they must also balance the extent of this prejudicial or character-changing effect against the arguments and individual circumstances of the parents.

Parents must be told in writing of the appeals committee's decision and the grounds on which it was made. Unsuccessful candidates must be told how the two-stage process operated. This includes spelling out the reasons why giving that child a place would have prejudiced efficient education, and why the individual circumstances of the parents' case were not enough to outweigh the arguments of the LEA or the school governors.

LARGE-SCALE APPEALS

Matters become even more complex if large numbers of parents are all appealing for entry into one school. In such circumstances appeals committees have to adjudicate between individual cases. Large-scale appeals can be heard in the following two ways:

1 GROUPED APPEALS: where the school or LEA presents its evidence to all the affected parents at one go. Unless they object, appeals by parents can be heard in the presence of other parents. Councils are advised in their guidance notes not to take this form of appeal hearing because it can intimidate parents.

2 INDIVIDUAL APPEALS: where each case is heard individually. The clerk must, however, ensure that the school or the LEA does not

introduce new evidence in later cases that could adversely affect the prospects of parents who put their case earlier.

GRANT-MAINTAINED SCHOOLS

In grant-maintained schools the appeals committee must consist of three, five or seven members chosen by the school's governing body. These comprise governors not directly involved with admissions, and other independent members. To be defined as an independent member you cannot be:

a) a member or former member of the governing body.

b) an employee of the school.

c) a parent of a pupil registered at the school.

All those appointed must have some knowledge of education and be acquainted with local conditions. Appeals panels can be set up under joint arrangements to cover one or more grant-maintained schools.

Parents must give written notice of their appeal to the clerk to the appeals committee, setting out the grounds on which it is made. Once

WHO CAN YOU TURN TO?

STEP 1
If you don't get the school of your choice, you should appeal to:

- THE LOCAL EDUCATION AUTHORITY if it is an LEA school.
- THE SCHOOL ITSELF if it is grant-maintained.

STEP 2
If you believe there were irregularities in the way the case was handled, you can appeal further to:

- THE LOCAL GOVERNMENT OMBUDSMAN (for LEA schools).
- THE EDUCATION SECRETARY (for grant-maintained schools).

You can also apply for a JUDICIAL REVIEW to test the law, but would be advised to take legal advice first.

THE EDUCATION SECRETARY also has powers to intervene in LEA appeals if the constitution of committees and the presentation of the LEA's case is considered improper or unfair.

the clerk receives the written appeal, the parents will be invited to give evidence in person. The procedure is almost identical to appeals against schools run by local education authorities, and the same advice applies.

TAKING IT FURTHER

If you feel the appeal process was not handled properly you can complain to the local government ombudsman (see panel opposite), if the school is run by a local education authority. It is the ombudsman's job to investigate maladministration and unfair practices by local government. If the school is grant-maintained you can complain to the Education Secretary at the Department for Education.

Remember, it's not enough just to dislike the decision or feel it is unfair. You must have a case. If in doubt seek legal advice. In extreme cases lawyers may decide to seek a judicial review.

Department for Education (DFE)
Sanctuary Buildings
Great Smith Street
London SW1P 3BT

General enquiries: 071-925 5000

Advisory Centre for Education (ACE)
1b Aberdeen Studios
22 Highbury Grove
London N5 2EA

(Free telephone advice line 2–5 pm each weekday 071-354 8321)

Commission for Local Administration (The Local Government Ombudsman)

ENGLAND
21 Queen Anne's Gate
London SW1H 9BN

Tel: 071-222 5622

WALES
Derwen House
Court Road
Bridgend
Mid Glamorgan
CF31 1BN

Tel: 0656 61325

HOME ALONE

TEACHING YOUR CHILD AT HOME

There is no law that says you must send your child to school. What the law does say is that he or she must be provided with an education suitable for his or her 'age, ability and aptitude'. Section 36 of the 1944 Education Act says this can be delivered in a school or 'otherwise', which includes at home. Local education authorities are responsible for ensuring that each child in their area receives a suitable education. They can serve attendance orders to put children back into school if the education being provided is considered inadequate.

Estimates of how many parents teach their own children at home vary between 10,000 and 20,000. Parents of all backgrounds who have taken the step insist, however, that it is not to be taken lightly. Time, patience, sacrifice and a sense of humour are vital, but the rewards can also be great.

Probably the biggest grouping of home educators took the name of its organisation from the 1944 Act to call itself 'Education Otherwise'. It has about 2,400 member families and acts as an advice and support group for them.

THE LAW SAYS:

- Parents are responsible for ensuring their children are adequately educated.

- Children can be educated at school or otherwise, which includes at home.

- Local education authorities are responsible for ensuring all children in their area receive an adequate education.

WHY PARENTS CHOOSE HOME EDUCATION

1 Philosophical reasons – parents have a conviction that it is best for their child.

2 Dissatisfaction with schools in the state or independent sector.

3 Bullying, school phobia or other problems.

4 Pupils' special needs not being met.

5 Parents can't secure the school of their choice.

HOW DO YOU EDUCATE AT HOME?

If your child is already at school you must first de-register him or her from the local education authority's register. The council will want to satisfy itself that the child is being properly educated, which will involve a visit from an inspector, but the process should not be over-complex. If your child has yet to be registered at school, you don't really have to do anything, though you might be advised to alert the council out of courtesy before they track you down, which they will.

Home educator Jo Rust, who taught her sons Thomas and William at home in their 300 year-old thatched cottage in Gamlingay near Cambridge, has experienced both situations. 'It is the parents' responsibility to ensure their children are educated according to their age, aptitude and ability. If they hand over that responsibility, as they do when they register their child at state school, the local education authority or the school is responsible.'

William, then nine and a half, was attending a local middle school, but his parents weren't happy with the kind of education he was receiving. 'I wrote simultaneously to the head of the school and the chief education officer of the county, declaring my intention to home-educate under Section 36 of the 1944 Education Act,' said Mrs Rust. 'I asked them to de-register William from the school he was attending as of a specified date, and named the school.' She added 'You don't have to explain the reason why you want to de-register your child. But you will get a visit from an inspector.'

Her younger son Thomas was four when they decided not to send him to school eight years ago. 'I sent a letter to the local primary school alerting them that we would not be registering him. We didn't have to. But it was probably no bad thing to keep out of trouble with social workers.'

DEALING WITH THE SYSTEM

Mrs Rust, a former teacher of mentally handicapped children whose husband Graham is a creative director in an advertising company, said a visit by the education authority inspector can be intimidating if parents are not clear on the law and their rights.

'Sometimes they ask for details of a full curriculum or evidence of a home tutor. This is what freaks people out; parents are not usually going to employ tutors. So you ignore that, and send them back instead some statement of what you intend to achieve for the next term or year. The more detailed the better, because it tends to flummox them.'

She urged parents to be creative in their approach to teaching their child, and not just to think in terms of doing lessons. 'You should remember that you are not required to replicate school conditions, or specify times when your child will be taught. Nor do you have to follow the National Curriculum. The beauty of teaching at home is that nature walks and trips to explore new concepts are much easier to organise. You can do lots of practical work. You can learn in the garden or further afield. You don't have to stay indoors,' she said.

Mrs Rust said many local council officials find it hard to get to grips with the idea of pupils learning at home, so they sometimes make unreasonable – and legally unenforceable – demands about what should be taught and for how long. 'It's rubbish,' she said. 'If a local education authority claims that a child must be in intensive home education between 9 am and 3 pm, ignore it. It would not hold up in court. But they prey on your insecurities.'

Indeed, guidelines suggest that a child up to the age of eight should have a maximum of one and a half hours' tuition per day. At age eight this should rise to two and a half hours. This is because children learn much more intensively with one-to-one tuition.

Getting an organisation like Education Otherwise to steer you through the pitfalls (address on page 134) can help enormously. 'Without it, you feel out of your depth.'

HOW DO YOU COPE?

Learning can be organised using the rich variety of commercially-produced material from bookshops. 'Keep your eyes peeled for resources. You can even make use of adult education courses.' Some parents use correspondence courses, which are particularly useful for qualifications such as GCSE and A-level. But Mrs Rust advises that revision notes be avoided as they presume the work has already been covered once.

The family converted the garage into a study-room to help create an atmosphere for learning, which takes place all the year round, and which does not stop for the long summer breaks enjoyed by school pupils.

Home educators cannot, as the law stands, opt in and out of school for certain subjects or lessons. It is all or nothing.

Mrs Jo Rust teaches her sons Thomas and William at their home in Gamlingay

Picture by
Mark Richards,
courtesy Daily Mail

WILL MY CHILDREN MIX?

One of the major worries parents have about educating their children at home is the fear that they will not have the opportunity to mix with other children or develop social skills. Mrs Rust says this has not been a problem for her children, as their house is always full of other people's children. But other parents may well find that this is something to watch out for. Joining in with local youth, sports or special interest groups can help your children make the social contacts they need.

HOW TOUGH IS IT?

Mrs Rust says 'Before you do it, talk to people who already have. Write down all the pros and cons. It is a real test. It is pretty tough on your family, particularly in the beginning.' Jane Lowe from Welwyn Garden City who has taught her children aged seven and eight at home in their four-bedroom, former council house, said 'It is hard work and one hell of a commitment, usually long term. A sense of humour is essential. Both she and her husband Paul, a business systems analyst, went to grammar schools.

133

WHAT DOES IT COST TO EDUCATE AT HOME?

It can cost as much or as little as you like, depending on whether you buy books, or borrow them from the library, or splash out on extra tuition in some subjects.

Mother Lynne Fox, also from Welwyn Garden City, calculated the comparative costs of educating her 11 year-old son, Elliott, at primary school and at home for Education Otherwise. She decided it was cheaper at home.

Education Otherwise
PO Box 120
Leamington Spa
CV32 7ER

Tel: 0926 886828

Living room school

Former comprehensive teacher Lynn Alcock was so fed up with the way her gifted son was taught at school that she set up a classroom of her own in her living room. The venture proved so successful that she went on to teach 17 local children and the school took over her home. Back went the sofa, out went the dining-table, and in came the desks before lessons began at Mrs Alcock's modern four-bedroom home in Coventry.

At age nine, Christopher did not find it strange to have his mum teaching him. 'When she's being mum, she's a good mum. And when she's being teacher, she's a good teacher,' he said.

After washing up the breakfast dishes she would await the arrival of the first pupils and two teacher helpers at 9.15 am. Lessons were held in the living-room, dining-room and garage, with the garden used for games, breaks and special projects.

'I have a reading scheme that I developed myself from three or four graded schemes blended together. It is structured so I can measure how the children are doing.' Other lessons include gardening, cookery, French, English, science and art. The television was used to show educational videos. School finished at 3.30 pm and at 4.30 pm Mrs Alcock began tutoring local 7 to 11 year-olds before tea-time at 5.30 pm. Setting up school in her home meant obtaining planning permission, obeying building regulations, being vetted by social services and paying the business rate towards local taxes.

★ SARAH GREENE ★

OCCUPATION
Broadcaster and former 'Going Live' presenter

SCHOOLS
Robinsfield Infants, Gospel Oak Junior, Grey Coat Hospital Grammar (direct grant), all in London

SCHOOL REPORT
Games report: 'Sarah must learn that vivacity is no substitute for hard work.' Observant, but so wrong.

TEACHER WHO MADE A BIG IMPRESSION
For better, English A-level teacher Mrs Roberts. For worse, Mrs Edwards at junior school for berating my left-handedness and hitting us with a ruler.

MOST IMPORTANT LESSON LEARNED AT SCHOOL
Make people laugh whenever you can.

BEST MOMENT AT SCHOOL
The day I left. Freedom at last.

WORST MOMENT AT SCHOOL
The day I left. Eeek, now for the real world.

SWOT POINTS
Senior prefect in charge of voluntary service scheme at St Thomas's Hospital, plus a few prizes.

EMBARRASSING MOMENT
Caught out having buried our form's Christmas party alcohol supply in the geography room sand-pit, aged 16.

QUALIFICATIONS
9 O-levels, 3 A-levels, 1 S-level, BA (Hons) degree from Hull University

POINTS TO CONSIDER WHEN CHOOSING A SCHOOL
The school should suit the individual needs of the child.

GOLD STAR CELEBRITIES

Picture by David Crump, courtesy Daily Mail

4 INFORMATION

THE INFORMATION REVOLUTION

There has been an information revolution in schools. It will continue for some time yet. In the past, parents were pretty much in the dark when it came to unearthing hard facts about pupil performance. I am not alone in having telephoned what seemed like innumerable LEAs to ask which were considered the best schools in their patch. 'All our schools are good,' was the inevitably defensive reply from the schools' chiefs. 'Well where do you send your children?' was my next question, knowing full well that they had access to the secret council 'league tables' which highlighted the high-flying and the horror schools. I was condemned, of course, for gross intrusion of privacy and told to mind my own business. But it is my business. And it's yours. Now all

Publish and be judged, 7-plus schools are told

that kind of information must be made public, and displayed in a form by which comparisons can be made.

HI-FI VERSUS HIGH SCHOOL

The amount of information about schools now available to parents has grown dramatically in recent years. This is mainly a result of the government's education reforms, but is also due in part to schools themselves responding to the greater demand from parents. The crucial skill for you, as a parent, to master is how best to interpret and use the information, some of it the subject of intense controversy, to find the school which best matches the ability, interests and nature of your child. As Graham Locke, Head of Audenshaw High School in Greater Manchester, told me: 'Parents are realistic. They know the strengths and weaknesses of their child. With that in mind, they will want a school that will give their child the best opportunity available.'

Sensible use of information from a wide variety of sources is a necessary skill to master in the modern world. If you want to buy a stereo, a fridge or a washing machine, you don't just take the one you are first offered by the shop assistant; you shop around to see what is available on the market. You won't necessarily buy the biggest stereo, the one with the most gadgets, or the most expensive one. You will go for the one that best suits your needs. Choosing a school for your child is infinitely more important than buying a stereo or washing machine, but the same principle applies: you have to match what is on offer to your family's needs. You will therefore be seeking a school where you believe your child will succeed and be happy.

SIX KEY DOCUMENTS

There are six key documents you are entitled to receive as a parent:

1 An annual report on your own child's progress.

2 Reports on each school's standards by independent inspectors.

3 Performance 'league tables' showing test and exam results and truancy rates.

4 A school prospectus.

5 The school governors' annual report.

6 A summary of the inspector's report on your child's school.

PUPILS' EDUCATIONAL RECORDS

Governing bodies of state schools must, by law, keep a formal record of each pupil's academic achievements, skills, abilities and general progress in school, which must be updated each year. As a parent you have a right to see, and if necessary challenge, this information record, provided your child is below the age of 18. Other material which may be recorded includes details of the child's behaviour and family background, although this is not compulsory. The pupil's education record does not include notes made by a teacher for his or her own use. Governing bodies must make the record available WITHIN 15 days of the request to:

• parents of a pupil aged under 17

• pupils aged 16 and 17.

Once a pupil reaches 18, only he or she may demand to see the record. Parents no longer have that automatic right. People in other educational establishments may have access to it.

They include:

- the head of an independent school interested in that pupil's record

- the governing body of any other school that has an interest in that pupil's record

- the head of a further or higher education college to which a pupil might apply for a place.

Schools may not pass on a child's assessment results to other schools until AFTER the pupil has been admitted. This is to stop underhand selection taking place in non-selective schools.

Schools are only obliged to release information dating from 31 August 1989, though they can release earlier documents if they wish.

CHARGING FOR COPIES

Schools must keep a statement about charging arrangements which parents are allowed to inspect free of charge. Schools can only charge parents the cost of providing copies of the statement or the record.

❛ If information is misleading, the answer in an open society is not suppression but the publication of further information so as to dispel any misperceptions. ❜

Dr John Marks, Standards in Schools, *The Social Market Foundation*

THE PHONE TEST

It is only a rule of thumb, but I have found it to be pretty reliable as an indicator of a council's efficiency. How many rings does it take for the switchboard to answer? In general, the longer the delay, the less efficient the council and the greater the likelihood of an unhelpful response. Many organisations in the commercial sector, and some councils too, have woken up to this. They insist on calls being picked up by the third ring. In business, a lost call could be a lost order or, at the very least, a disgruntled customer. Unfortunately local government does not always show the same concern and you may have to fight to be heard.

PUPIL REPORTS

If one document can be guaranteed to send shivers down the spines of generations of pupils, it must be the school report. Those dreaded words 'must do better' and the family rows that begin in their wake have become the stuff of legend, cartoons, jokes, drama and even literature. Most people think they know what a school report looks like: 'English – B. Must pay more attention to spelling' or 'Maths – D. Not enough effort'. Yet in recent years there has been growing alarm about the fate of the school report.

Good schools have, of course, continued the practice of sending parents a detailed summary of their children's performance. But others just haven't bothered at all, particularly primary schools. Now schools must issue all parents with annual reports so that they can keep track of their children's progress. Though each must conform to certain minimum requirements, they can still vary enormously in their detail and usefulness.

I received one outraged letter from a mother who had received a report on her child's progress. It was a computer print-out that listed all the things which the National Curriculum Orders say a child must cover between the ages of five and seven. 'Your child can now...' it said before launching into a long list of skills described in dense educational mumbo-jumbo. It certainly complied with the letter of the law, but it told the parents nothing meaningful.

WHAT YOU ARE ENTITLED TO

All parents must now receive a written school report on their child's progress at least once a year.

'PASSPORT FOR LIFE'

School-leavers now have their performance permanently logged in a compulsory 'passport for life'. The burgundy document is called the National Record of Achievement, and is designed to give universities, colleges and companies an instant background briefing on the academic and personal achievements of the prospective student or employee.

Head-teacher of Didcot Girls' School, Oxfordshire, Jeanette Hebbert, said: 'We were one of the first schools in the country to use this scheme and cannot praise it enough'.

It will show your child's:
- performance in all National Curriculum subjects.
- results from national tests at age 7, 11 and 14.
- assessments in other subjects and activities.
- GCSE, A-level results and any vocational qualifications achieved.

You must be told how your child's results in exams and national tests compare with those of other children of the same age. The bench-mark figures against which to judge your child's achievement will be the national average, the school average and the area average.

General comments from the class teacher or head-teacher about your child's progress will be given. You will receive details of your child's attendance record. Schools must now also produce their overall truancy rates, which will be compiled in school-by-school 'league table' form along with test and exam results.

You will be told who to talk to in school about your child's report, and how to fix an appointment time to do so. Schools also keep their own records about your child's behaviour, academic record and other achievements, which you are entitled to see, if you ask.

Keeping the status quo

Former head-teacher Peter Dawson admits that the school reports he wrote were not always spot-on. For one 15 year-old boy intent on being a rock star, he wrote: 'He has made no provision whatsoever for the possibility of failure in this direction. He must ask himself if this is the attitude of a sensible and mature young man.' The pupil in question was Francis Rossi who went on to become the multi-millionaire leader of the rock group Status Quo. Mr Dawson went on to expel another boy, George O'Dowd – who later found pop fame as Boy George.

Mr Dawson was the role model for the central character in the hilarious film 'Clockwise', in which John Cleese plays a head with an obsession for punctuality, who spies on pupils with a pair of binoculars. The wife of the film's screenplay writer Michael Frayn worked at Mr Dawson's school. Mr Dawson, a former general secretary of the no-strike Professional Association of Teachers said 'We went to see 'Clockwise' at the cinema and my wife suddenly nudged me and said, "It's you, it is!"'

4c INSPECTORS' REPORTS

An extremely important source of information for parents about standards in individual schools is the new inspection reports. Every state school must now be thoroughly inspected every four years. A controversial new system of licensed private inspection teams will check 6,000 primary and secondary schools each year.

Each independent and properly vetted team must, by law, include a 'lay' inspector – someone not already working in education, to give a 'commonsense' view. The inspectors' reports must be made public under the system, which is administered by the Office for Standards in Education.

SEE ALSO:
An Inspector Calls

BEFORE THE INSPECTION: PARENTS AIR THEIR VIEWS

Before each inspection, inspectors will hold an open meeting for parents to air their views. You should be given three weeks' notice of the meeting. 'Pupil post' can be used to notify parents.

The final report should, however, note whether any criticisms raised by parents are justified. It must be written within five weeks of the inspection, which should take no longer than a week. Copies are then sent to OFSTED, the local education authority (if the school is council-run) and the school's board of governors.

FREE REPORTS

As a parent with a child at school, you will automatically be sent via the school a FREE summary of the report, prepared by the inspectors. It will set out the school's strengths and weaknesses, and suggest where and how improvements can be made. You may also send for a copy of the full report, for which you may be charged (see page 143).

The school must ensure that the report is widely publicised by sending FREE copies to:

- one or more local libraries

- local newspapers and radio stations.

Schools must, by law, make the inspectors' full report and summary available to any person who asks to see them.

OFSTED insists that the reports must be in 'clear, accessible language' so that parents have no difficulty in understanding them. Schools are also asked to consider translating the report, summary, or both, into other languages.

CHARGES

Single copies of the summary report must be provided free of charge. The school may, however, charge for providing several copies of the summary, and for supplying copies of the full report. The maximum rate is 10p per sheet. Governing bodies may, however, decide to waive any fee and provide all documents free of charge. They are 'encouraged' to charge less than 10p if the cost of production is less than this figure.

> ❝Head-teachers, staff and governors do not attend such meetings unless they are also parents of pupils currently attending the school. All findings and comments are in strict confidence and cannot be used publicly or as part of the report. No individual member of staff, governor or pupil may be named in the meeting.❞

OFSTED, setting out details for private inspection teams when organising parents' meetings

Resist temptation? Cripes mate, that's abnormal!
Courtesy Mahood of the Daily Mail

ACTION PLAN

You will also be sent an action plan prepared by the school governors, in which they set out how they plan to tackle problem areas.

Copies must be made available for inspection by any member of the public. A single copy must be provided free of charge to ANYONE who wants

143

THE STANDARD REPORT FORMULA

PART A

1 Introduction:

- Basic information about the school
- Intake of pupils and area served by school
- School facts, figures, results
- How the evidence was collected.

2 Main findings:

- Standards, quality, efficiency and ethos
- Key issues for action.

3 Standards and quality achieved

4 Efficiency of the school

5 Quality of the school as a community:

- Behaviour and discipline
- Attendance

- Pupils' spiritual and moral development
- Pupils' social and cultural development.

6 Factors contributing to these findings including:

- Quality of teaching
- Management and planning
- Quality of the curriculum
- Organisation and administration
- Management of resources
- Pupil support and guidance
- Community links.

PART B sets out how the individual curriculum subjects, such as maths, English and science, are being taught.

one, provided they live within three miles of the school. Anyone else can be charged for copies on the same conditions as for an inspection report.

SCHOOLS 'AT RISK'

If the inspectors consider a school is in such difficulties that it is 'at risk' of failing, the report will tell you. A rescue plan then swings into action,

details of which can be found in Chapter 2d 'An Inspector Calls'.

NEXT STEPS

The full report and the action plan will be discussed at the annual meeting that governors hold with parents. A summary of the report and action taken will be published in the school prospectus.

> ❝ Parents should be able to tell how well their children's school is doing in comparison with others because they will already have statistical information available to them on such matters as examination and National Curriculum assessment results.
> The report of each inspection will seek to explain all the available statistical information by exploring why a school is doing better or worse than average, or than it should be, and will point to the action that is needed. ❞

OFSTED briefing paper, October 1992

SAMPLE REPORTS – SEE FOR YOURSELF

Examples of the new school inspection reports can be obtained free of charge by telephoning OFSTED Publications on 081-985 7757.

SEE ALSO:
An Inspector Calls
Becoming a Governor or Lay Inspector

'LEAGUE TABLES'

BACKGROUND TO THE CONTROVERSY

Few government policies have provoked so much interest and controversy as the decision to publish school examination results. Parents are generally fascinated by them while many educational professionals view them with undisguised contempt, condemning them as unfair, misleading and divisive. In autumn 1993 the government performed a significant U-turn by scrapping 'league tables' of test results for pupils aged 7 and 14. But it insisted that they should remain for pupils at age 11, and those taking GCSEs and A-levels.

Each year the government publishes information tables showing the comparative performance of all secondary schools and LEAs. Booklets for each area are produced in a standard form, allowing parents in different areas to compare results. Parents can also measure each school's results against national and local bench-mark averages. Newspapers and other interested parties are also able to compile local or national 'league tables' in which all schools can be ranked. The first official tables were published in November 1992, although a number of newspapers had already compiled their own unofficial tables before then. GCSE and A-level exam results have been phased into the tables.

PERFORMING BY THE BOOK

The results, in alphabetical order, are available in 108 booklets, each covering one education authority in England. They can be consulted in libraries and schools and obtained free of charge from the Department for Education. The governing bodies of primary and middle schools must, by law, obtain copies of the document, which contains comparative information on the performance of local secondary schools in public exams. They must then send copies to all the parents of pupils in the oldest age group, before the children go on to secondary school. Summaries, which are often pretty comprehensive, are usually published in local or national newspapers as soon as the information is made available.

NEW FROM 1993

From 1993 government 'league tables' that survive also include information on National Curriculum tests, truancy rates and vocational qualifications. Tables of GCSE results will be simplified to show only:

- the % of pupils gaining five or more A–C grades
- the % of pupils with one or more and five or more A–G grades.

Ministers say that the publication of National Curriculum test results at age 11 will allow parents to measure the 'added value' of a school by the time pupils sit their GCSEs. By this they mean the extent to which the school has enabled a pupil to achieve more than seemed possible in the past. This, they argue, overcomes the criticism that 'league tables' measure only what you get out, not what you put in. But the government has rejected any notion of allowing for 'social factors', such as a school being in a deprived area. 'Beacons of excellence' can thrive even in the heart of the most disadvantaged areas, ministers insist. Teachers contest this view. Their boycott of the 1993 tests forced the government to abandon planned 'league tables' at ages 7 and 14 as a compromise to safeguard the rest of their reforms.

'OUR HANDS ARE CLEAN'

Ministers point out correctly, if a little disingenuously, that the government does not actually produce 'league tables'. It simply lists all schools, whether council-run, grant-maintained or independent, in alphabetical order. Newspapers and anyone else who is interested can choose to manipulate the exam

TOP SCHOOL 92
The list no parent can afford to miss

BRADFORD

School					
Bradford Grammar School	I	G	b	95.0	23.5
Shaw House School	I	G	M	69.0	0.0
Ilkley Grammar School	v	C	M	58.0	21.7
St Josephs College	V	C	G	45.0	14.3
Bingley Grammar School	GM	C	M	40.0	14.3
Salt Grammar School	LA	C	M	31.0	16.0
Rhodesway School	LA	C	M	31.0	12.8
Queensbury School	LA	C	M	30.0	9.4
Beckfoot Grammar School	LA	C	M	29.0	9.2
Nab Wood Grammar School	LA	C	M	27.0	11.8
Yorkshire Martyrs Coll. Sch.	V	C	M	27.0	11.5
The Holy Family RC School	V	C	M	26.0	11.5
Thornton School	LA	C	M	25.0	12.4
St Bede's Grammar	V	C	B	24.0	18.7
Hanson School	LA	C	M	24.0	17.0
Oakbank School	LA	C	M	23.0	11.4
Temple Bank School	S		M	20.0	0.0
Tong Upper School	LA	C	M	17.0	10.0

scores into rank order and create the 'league tables'. One senior civil servant was severely reprimanded by a superior for calling the government's booklets 'league tables' instead of the Whitehall-approved name of 'performance tables'. This does not disguise the fact that it suits ministerial purposes for the schools to be ranked.

RELEGATING 'LEAGUE TABLES'

One of the main objections raised by the teaching professionals is that parents are simply unable to interpret the 'raw' data. They say that a school's performance depends upon a complex cocktail of factors including the intelligence of the pupils when they arrive, the social class of the area, its crime rate and the level of school funding. Opponents of the tables, including teachers' leaders and the Labour Party, argue that schools are not football teams or pop stars in the charts, and that it is unfair to use 'raw' statistics for comparison. They do not tell the whole story and are therefore misleading.

PROMOTING 'LEAGUE TABLES'

Ministers, on the other hand, insist that teachers are arguing from the wrong premise. The government wants parents to have as much information as possible from which to make sound judgements about their children's schooling. Performance tables are just one part of that information, which parents will weigh alongside other factors, such as inspectors' reports, visits to the school, chats with the head-teacher and school-gate gossip. They say that the tables allow parents, for the first time, to make direct comparisons between schools. The government has hailed the publication of GCSE and A-level results from all 4,400 state secondary schools as a 'triumph' for parental choice and another step towards raising standards. From 1993 publication also became compulsory for all independent schools.

The government says that the exercise has put into practice Prime Minister John Major's Parents' Charter pledge to help people make decisions on the basis of hard facts and intelligent

> ❝We know parents are not daft... They are not so silly as to look at the raw-end results. I'm not worried about league tables. They can be horrendous. But don't let's worry about them. Parents use them sensibly.❞
>
> *Michael Marland, Head-teacher of North Westminster Community School*

interpretation, rather than relying on 'the grapevine'.

Supporters of the tables say that parents, as consumers, have a right to information which, until now, has been kept secret. They accuse teachers of a 'patronising' attitude towards parents and insist that the figures should speak for themselves without being 'cooked' by introducing other factors.

LEARNING TO LIVE WITH 'LEAGUE TABLES'

The concept of 'league tables' is obviously not new to the British public. We have them in football, the music charts, and, thanks to *Which?* magazine, they have been compiled for innumerable consumer goods.

Education authorities and head-teachers have been compiling their own exam 'league tables' for internal use for years. It does seem only logical to make such tables available for something much more important than consumer durables.

And just as no one in their right mind would buy a car on the basis of motor magazine performance tables alone, so parents are well advised to do the same with schools. Ask for a prospectus, look at inspection reports, talk to other parents and pupils, visit the school and talk to staff.

LEAGUE DIVISIONS

Below is a summary of why government and teachers are at loggerheads over 'league tables'.

THE GOVERNMENT SAYS:

- Parents have a right to see each school's 'raw' exam and National Curriculum test results in a form that allows comparison between schools.

- Parents are sensible and intelligent enough to use those 'raw' results in conjunction with other information, such as inspectors' reports and local knowledge, to form a rounded view of a school.

- It would be wrong to suppress or censor such information.

- The 'raw' results cannot lie. They are the marks actually achieved. Building in allowances for 'social factors' would simply distort the true results.

- The publication of performance tables will give all schools an incentive to do better.

- The government doesn't actually produce 'league tables'. It produces performance tables that list schools, area by area, in alphabetical order. Newspapers and others rank the schools by test and exam results.

- Early performance tables showed that the social background of pupils was no guarantee of success or failure. Some inner-city schools in deprived areas did much better than expected, and a number of schools in middle-class 'leafy suburbs' performed much worse.

- Parents can see the 'added value' of a school by checking how well pupils do in tests at age 11 against GCSE results at age 16. Has the school boosted pupils' achievements beyond expectation?

- Teachers who oppose publication of 'league table' results prefer to keep parents in the dark about how their schools are performing.

- Opposition to the tables is symptomatic of the 'anti-competitive' attitudes held by some teachers and educationists.

- Competition is a fact of life in the world outside school.

TEACHERS SAY:

- 'League tables' are unfair, divisive, over-simplistic.

- They set school against school.

- They do not tell the whole story.

- They do not take account of the fact that different schools start with pupils of widely differing

'But league tables are distorting and misleading!'
Courtesy Mahood of the Daily Mail

abilities. They therefore fail to measure the 'added value' of a school.

- 'League tables' do not take account of the social background of pupils.

- A school that might appear to be performing badly, judging by its poor showing in the tables, might actually be stretching its pupils more than another school whose results put it much higher.

- Parents do not have the professional judgement and experience that teachers can employ to interpret the 'league tables'.

- Parents may simply decide to send their children to the schools with the best results, without taking account of other factors, such as the quality of the intake. This could lead those schools with the worst results to flounder, to risk becoming 'sink' schools, or even to close.

- Schools work better when they co-operate, rather than compete, with one another.

- Parents are more interested in knowing how their own child is performing than in comparing school with school in such a crude manner.

- The government will use the tables to monitor teachers' performance and link the results to pay.

HOW TO READ THE TABLES

Ministers themselves are at pains to stress that while comparative exam information is an extremely important indicator of school performance, it is not the only one. What most parents need, more than anything else, is

> **6** I think the publication of results is one thing. The arrangement of them into "league tables" is horrendous. But it is going to happen and schools have got to learn to live with this pressure. **9**

John Trevis, Head of fee-paying school advisers Gabbitas, Truman and Thring

guidance to help them understand and interpret the tables. So how should a sensible parent approach them? I suggest you proceed with an open mind, a degree of scepticism and a sense of proportion.

CHECK THE DETAILS OF THE SCHOOL

When viewing any local 'league table', don't just look at the name of the school and its results. Consider the location of the school and examine the pupil intake carefully. There is intense debate about the extent to which 'social factors' influence a school's performance. Teachers' leaders claim that they do, suggesting that a child reared in a poor home in a crime-ridden area is less likely to reach his or her potential than a pupil raised in a prosperous middle-class suburb. Ministers are less convinced by this argument, believing that the quality of teaching is the key issue and accusing some teachers of using 'social factors' as an excuse for pitching their expectations too low.

Tips for using 'league tables'

- Schools that attract lots of bright pupils may appear to do well even if pupils are performing below their potential.

- A state grammar school, by definition, selects only the brightest pupils, so you would expect it to do well. But is it doing as well as it could be?

- Many, but not all, independent schools are likewise highly selective. But are you getting real value for money by sending your child there at great personal expense and financial sacrifice?

- Schools with less-able children may appear to do badly, even if excellent teaching has stretched them to achieve levels way beyond expectations.

> 6 I am not going to choose a school for my ten year-old son on the basis of league tables. I am going to compare the schools on the basis of the total education they provide and the atmosphere there, and how happy my child is going to be there. 9

Labour MP Anne Taylor, Shadow Education spokeswoman

- Comprehensive schools take pupils from all ability ranges, so are unlikely to beat the selective schools in the performance tables. But some do get better results, especially at A-level. This is because school sixth forms are largely 'self-selecting', with only the brightest staying on.

- Just because a school is in the middle of a rough area doesn't mean it isn't doing a great job for its pupils. Investigate further.

- Is the local fee-paying independent school being given a run for its money by a grant-maintained or council-run comprehensive? It's worth making the comparison.

- Is the school in the middle-class suburb really doing as well as it ought to be for its pupils? Look into it.

- One year's results in isolation can be misleading. Schools can have freak or untypical years. Parents should consider average results over several years.

The 'milk test'

David Woodhead, National Director of the Independent Schools' Information Service says parents should apply what he terms 'the milk test' to schools. To explain the approach, he gives an example:

'School A takes only the academic cream. Rigorous selection procedures ensure it recruits those pupils whose abilities match the highest expectations. It whips the cream into shape and, with apparently effortless ease, secures giddily high pass marks and grades.'

'School B takes silver and red rather than gold top. There is some cream, but it is mostly pretty average milk with some distinctly watery stuff lower down. The cream get excellent results, as good as their peers in school A. Much of the milk and water do better than expected. And school B is as proud of them as the high-flyers. But the overall pass and grade rates are pulled down by the predictably poor performers. Which is the better school?'

6 However you present the results, parents are going to compare one school with another in order that they can make decisions about the school to which to send their children. 9

Tory MP Dr Robert Spink, House of Commons Education Select Committee

BOTTOM OF THE LEAGUE

Fed up with newspapers running 'league tables' which ranked their schools in order, the heads of Britain's top independent schools decided to get their own back. They ran their own tongue-in-cheek

'Thanks to all you lazy morons, we are near to the bottom of the lig tibble of ed... edu... educashunal... er, ... big word starting with 'A'...'
Courtesy Mac of the Daily Mail

4d

'league table' of education correspondents from national newspapers. I came bottom – the only honourable position for a journalist to hold. The reason, I suspect, was my wicked habit of pointing out how many state comprehensives, grant–maintained and grammar schools were achieving better exam results and 'league' positions than independent schools charging up to £12,000 a year.

Get free school performance tables from:

• your local library, or

• your local schools.

Or write for free copies to:

Department for Education (DFE)
Publications Centre
PO Box 2193
London E15 2EU

Do state the area of the country for which you want information. A summary of the tables is also published in local and national newpapers when the results are announced.

PROSPECTUSES AND PR

School prospectuses or brochures come in a variety of forms, styles and degrees of professional display. Some may be so slick that you wonder whether some multinational corporation hasn't had a hand in them. Sometimes, depending who is on the board of governors or is a school sponsor, they have. Schools must, by law, produce them for parents or prospective parents, and even in their most basic form they must give certain information. This includes exam and National Curriculum results for the school as a whole, as well as local and national figures. This allows parents to compare the performance of their school against local and national bench-mark averages.

The total number of pupils in each year group must also be stated. This is to stop the practice of schools unfairly boosting their performance by leaving out of the equation pupils who were unlikely to perform well. These pupils might simply not be entered for the exam, or entered elsewhere. But the results of individual pupils will not be disclosed.

Anybody can ask for a prospectus, free, from any school.

THE SIN OF OMISSION

Watch out for schools that produce a general prospectus with a pouch at the back in which to insert updated facts, figures and exam results. In the vast majority of cases this is not a problem. It is very easy, however, for these additional, but vital, bits of information to be inadvertently left out. And you might not notice. This little tip came from a wily head who noticed that parents seeking prospectuses from a rival school were getting the glossy brochure, but without the all-important exam results in the back. His own school published a conventional prospectus in which the results were published as an integral part of the document.

THE SCHOOL PROSPECTUS MUST INCLUDE:

- the school's name, address and telephone number

- the names of the head and the chairperson of governors

- the type of school and any religious affinity

- how parents can visit the school before choosing

- how teaching is organised –

155

Oakham School, Rutland

*Brookfield School Prospectus,
Knowsley Metropolitan Borough,
Merseyside*

*Weaverham High School,
Cheshire*

particularly whether pupils are taught in separate ability groups

- homework policy

- arrangements for children with special needs

- pastoral care arrangements

- discipline policy, including how parents are informed if their children misbehave

- school uniform policy, dress code and rules

- policy on charging

- school societies and activities

- how parents and others may see and acquire documents that the head must make available for inspection at the school. As well as the school prospectus, these include:

  - schemes of work
  - syllabuses
  - the governing body's annual report

- reports by independent inspectors.
- Education Department circulars
- copies of Statutory Instruments.

The school may make a charge for providing personal copies of some documents.

The school prospectus must contain information about the curriculum, including:

- details of overall exam results in National Curriculum tests, GCSEs and A-levels, subject by subject, as national and local averages

- a list of the exam boards and syllabuses used by the school

- sex education and careers advice

- details of complaints procedures relating to the curriculum.

NEW FROM 1993

The government announced that, from 1993, the responsibility for publishing prospectuses for LEA-run schools was to shift from councils to the schools themselves. Such responsibility already rests with the governors of grant-maintained and voluntary-aided schools.

Ministers now want school prospectuses to include information about:

- classroom organisation and teaching methods

> 6 Schools shouldn't be marketed like a packet of biscuits or baked beans.9

Jon Berry, National Union of Teachers, Hertfordshire

- special needs policy (in the light of the 1993 Education Act)

- a statement about the moral, spiritual, social and cultural development of pupils at the school

- details of the admissions policy

- information about the number of applications for admission received in the previous year, alongside the number of available places

- comparable GCSE figures for the previous year

- comparable attendance figures (truancy rates) for the previous year

- information about what happens to pupils after age 16, eg how many stay on at school, go to sixth-form college or drop out.

PROPAGANDA WARS – USING PR

Schools are increasingly having to 'sell' themselves to parents as their budgets are determined largely by the number of pupils on the roll.

And as parents become ever more sophisticated, schools are having to treat the matter of their 'image' with an unprecedented degree of professionalism. In addition, the government has made the publication of so much information compulsory; so PR isn't the choice of the few but a necessary development for all schools.

FORMS OF MARKETING

- Glossy leaflets and prospectuses

- Adverts in newspapers, on radio and even on television

- Cultivating media links to promote 'good news' stories likely to be read by parents

- Creating links with local industries for work-shadowing

- Sponsorship from local or national firms

- Leaflet drops to local homes

GOOD PR MEANS:

- schools explain themselves

- parents are better informed

- a professional approach

- schools pay more attention to their weaknesses knowing that they will be put under public scrutiny

- schools extol their strengths, which may have been hidden

- rival schools, faced with competition, try to improve their standards.

THE DRAWBACKS OF PR

- Some schools may go 'over the top' in marketing themselves.

- Style may detract attention from content and so disguise problems.

- A school could give a deliberately misleading impression to parents.

- Rival schools might start marketing wars.

Radio waves

Grant-maintained Colyton Grammar School in Devon angered rival schools when it ran 15 adverts, costing a total of £800, on a local radio station. They informed parents about the eleven-plus exam that pupils had to pass to win a place. Head-teacher Barry Sindall insisted, 'We were not trying to filch pupils.'

A consortium of local comprehensives hit back by spending £200 to distribute 1,000 leaflets entitled *Access to Excellence*.

ADVERTISING WARS

David Hart, General Secretary of the National Association of Head Teachers, said advertising was the legitimate tool of a school trying to get its message across. 'As long as it is truthful and accurate, there is no reason why schools should not do it...' But the NAHT does have guidelines for its 33,000 heads and deputies to stop things getting out of hand. And the union is strongly opposed to what the advertising world dubs 'knocking copy'. This is where a school, instead of advertising its strengths, exposes the alleged weaknesses of its rivals. It's the sort of strategy you get in party political broadcasts. So an advert along the lines of 'Don't send your child to St Trinian's because the exam results are awful, it's rife with bullying and the headmaster is having an affair with the gym mistress' might come in for some criticism.

CORPORATE TAKEOVERS?

Many local and national companies are now targeting schools. Sometimes they offer small-scale sponsorship deals. Sometimes they launch national campaigns offering free computers or books for schools, such as those undertaken by Tesco Supermarkets and WH Smith. In

> ❝ State schools collectively in Britain have had an awful public image. It is getting better, but they still have a long way to go. ❞

Tim Devlin, education marketing consultant

many cases the arrangements work well and to the benefit of all parties. But sometimes they cause controversy. Schools must judge carefully the benefit they receive from entering into such arrangements, and the cost to their reputation.

MEDIA HYPE

Efficient schools have set up systems for dealing with the media. While schools may seek to cultivate the media to put across the 'good news', they must also expect attention when bad news or scandal comes their way, and know how best to deal with it.

I have given media seminars to literally hundreds of head-teachers and senior staff. They have needed to know how to avoid turning a drama into a crisis when the police do a drugs raid at the school, find one of their staff is on the fiddle, or some other event causes intense media interest. The worst thing they can do – and it is surprising how many do it

Bus advert is just the ticket

Sir John Newsom School in Welwyn Garden City, Hertfordshire, has spent £1,500 to spread its message around the county on the back of a bus.

Courtesy Fairley of Luton and the Daily Mail

Sir John Newsom School in Welwyn Garden City spent £1,500 putting its message on the back of a bus. As the vehicle criss-crossed Hertfordshire

picking up passengers, it proclaimed the message 'SJN Cares' and spelled out the school's aims in helping each of its pupils achieve their potential. Head-teacher Vic Lindsey said, 'It is antediluvian to criticise such advertising. We are trying to overcome the talk at the school gate or in the local shop which might be 20 years out of date.'

– is to bury their heads in the sand and shout 'no comment'. The expert schools will learn to use some of public relations 'black arts' to limit damage, or turn a potentially nasty situation to their own advantage. Schools' marketing expert Tim Devlin said: 'State schools have taken to marketing in a big way, but they have only done so in the past five years. They still have a long way to

go.' He noted that some schools, in their innocence, still commit classic howlers which do nothing to attract parents or pupils. 'There was a primary school in Devon which used its prospectus to tell people not to go too close to the local prison. Then there was the East London school which sent out regulations about head-lice when there was no known problem at the school.'

GOVERNORS' ANNUAL REPORTS

The governors' report is produced for discussion at their annual meeting with parents. When you are sent your copy of the report, you will also receive your invitation to the meeting. Good schools will make the report easy to read. Many reports will, however, look as dull as ditch-water, even though they may contain some real gems. The problem is that you will have to go digging.

CONTENTS

The report must include:

- the date, time and place of the annual parents' meeting, its agenda and a brief description of the meeting's purpose

- details of the governing body membership and their terms of office

- the name and address of the chairperson of governors and the clerk to the governors

- how and when to elect parent governors

- the school budget

- overall school exam results

- information about standards, truancy and school-leaver destinations

- details of governors' work to strengthen school links with the community, including the police

- a summary of changes to information in the school prospectus since it was last published

- dates of the beginning and end of each term and half-term for the next school year.

Generally, the report should give parents a fair picture of how the school is doing, and explain how the governors' plans and policies are being put into practice.

SEE ALSO:
Annual Parents'
Meetings
Becoming a
Governor or Lay
Inspector

NEW FROM 1993

Ministers have decided that information that in the past has been published alongside governors' annual reports should, from July 1993, be published in the body of the report itself. This includes details of examination and National Curriculum test results.

ANNUAL PARENTS' MEETINGS

Once a year parents have the chance to air their views formally at their school's annual parents' meeting. The meeting is a legal requirement and all parents of pupils on the school roll must be invited. The government stresses, however, that it should not be an overly formal occasion. In fact, the school should go out of its way to ensure that parents are encouraged to attend, are not intimidated and will take part in useful discussion.

Governors with a little imagination have tried to combine the annual parents' meeting with a social event. Never mind the wine and cheese, I heard of one school putting on a

❝ Parents see their role more often as individuals concerned only with the progress of their children, particularly if they are not inclined to join an organised group such as the parent/teacher association. ❞

Annual Parents' Meeting Project report, University of Birmingham

fully fledged bar. So once the official business was over, the governors and parents could relax over a drink and watch the school's fund-raising go into overdrive.

More simply, it is good practice to arrange the seating in a 'non-threatening' manner, or have someone on the door to greet parents and put them at their ease. Not everyone has happy memories of their own schooling and for some the return to classrooms and corridors may be off-putting. Still, the atmosphere, formality and usefulness of the annual meeting varies enormously from school to school. So do levels of attendance.

However your own school's meeting is organised, you should remember that this is your chance to hear what the school has to say for itself, and to air your own views. If you are unhappy about the style or format of the meeting, raise the matter yourself when you get there. You have as much right as any other parent or governor to be heard. That is why you are there.

SETTING THE SCENE

The main purpose of the meeting is to discuss the governors' annual report to parents. It also gives parents a chance to talk about what has been happening at the school over the previous 12 months. This may include decisions or actions taken by the head, governors or, where relevant, the local education authority.

The exact timing, location, length and tone of the meeting is up to the school's governing body. The meeting usually takes place in the school itself after normal working hours. It might run for an hour or two, or longer. Governors may choose the hall or, with a bit of imagination, a less imposing and more friendly venue. The governors also draw up the agenda of matters to be tackled at the meeting.

> 6 Anyone who has had the depressing experience of attending the annual meeting for parents will need some convincing of the desire of the vast majority of parents to interest themselves, quite properly, in anything but the progress of their own children. 9

John Rowland, President of the National Association of Schoolmasters / Union of Women Teachers 1993 – 94

The head may also attend, whether or not he or she has chosen to take up a place on the governing body. Governors may, if they wish, invite other people to be present. The meeting is usually chaired by a governor. A good chairperson is important to stimulate discussion, ensure everyone has their say, draw proceedings to a satisfactory conclusion, and keep order if debates become heated.

PARENT RESOLUTIONS

Parents may raise matters concerning the way the governors, the head or the local education authority have carried out their responsibilities. If enough parents are present, they can pass a resolution on a topic. To be valid, the number of parents present must be equal to at least 20% of the number of registered pupils. In a school of 1,000 pupils, that means 200 parents must be present. Resolutions must be considered either by the governing body or passed on to the head-teacher or local education authority, if more appropriate. The following year's report should comment on any resolutions so passed.

DANGER SIGNS

As I have suggested, the success of any annual meeting depends on the skill of the governors in turning it into a productive event. It is a useful rule of thumb that parents' meetings are at their busiest when there is a crisis. Passions and interest then run particularly high. There may be a parents' revolt against the ruling governors, head or teachers over any number of issues. It's great spectator sport, but can be heartbreaking if you are caught up in the middle of it.

When things are running smoothly, the annual meeting gives parents a good chance to help shape the future of their children's school. However, the last thing most sensible parents want is to get bogged down in an over-lengthy and boring debate about motions and amendments. Schools should therefore nip in the bud any tendency for meetings to be dominated by small cliques of busybodies or parish worthies. The result of such meetings is that others who want to make constructive or imaginative points get drowned out. Parents feel intimidated and, rather than risk being humiliated or insulted, stay at home.

NEW FROM 1993

The 1993 Education Act says that governing bodies must now discuss, at least once a year, whether or not the school should seek to opt out of local authority control to become grant-maintained with funding from Whitehall. The governors must state their reasons for their decision in the annual report. Whatever the decision, it cannot be implemented without a ballot of parents.

HOW TO IMPROVE THE ANNUAL MEETING

Academics at Birmingham University researched the effectiveness of these meetings for the Department for Education (1992). Among the tips they gave are the following.

DO:

- send an informal invitation emphasising the brevity of the meeting

- use a return slip, which commits parents to attending

- provide a crèche

- provide refreshments

- ask governors to introduce themselves

- allow speakers to remain seated

- encourage lots of questions.

DON'T:

- make it bureaucratic

- read out the whole report. A summary will do.

★ LORRAINE KELLY ★

OCCUPATION

Breakfast TV presenter (GMTV)

SCHOOLS

Strathclyde Primary, John Street Secondary School, Glasgow and Claremont High in East Kilbride

SCHOOL REPORT

I was called 'sensitive' and 'university material' at primary school, and was told to 'concentrate more' at secondary school.

TEACHERS WHO MADE A BIG IMPRESSION

Miss McPhedrin at Claremont High. A real teacher of the 'old school' who gave me my love of Shakespeare and taught me basic grammar and spelling. Miss Spiers at Strathclyde Primary, for her enthusiasm and genuine interest in bringing out creative talent.

MOST IMPORTANT LESSON LEARNED AT SCHOOL

How to get on with people from all walks of life

THINGS I WISH I'D DONE DIFFERENTLY AT SCHOOL

I wish I'd tried harder, studied more and carried on with sport.

BEST MOMENT AT SCHOOL

Being made house captain

WORST MOMENT AT SCHOOL

Leaving. I'd loved school.

SWOT POINTS

Top girl in primary school, head of sixth form, netball team member

EMBARRASSING MOMENTS

Belted for talking in primary school. Belted for not doing maths homework at secondary school.

QUALIFICATIONS

9 Scottish O-grades, 4 Scottish Highers, including Russian, Sixth Year Studies in English

MY VIEW OF TODAY'S EDUCATION SYSTEM

I'm shocked by the low morale of teachers and the lack of money, which means children sharing books and working from photocopies. More money and discipline is needed to improve standards.

★ GOLD STAR CELEBRITIES ★

5 EXAMS

GCSEs AND A-LEVELS

GCSE – THE TROUBLESOME TEST

It has been said that the General Certificate of Secondary Education, the GCSE, had a difficult birth, a fraught childhood and an even more troublesome adolescence. Even as it grew to maturity, controversy continued to dog the exam, which replaced the old O-level and CSE examinations from 1988. The watershed came in the summer of 1992 when the exam boards and hundreds of thousands of pupils celebrated record GCSE results. However, following sceptical media attention, ministers, government advisers and inspectors became suspicious of the bonanza. There were worries that 'grade inflation' had begun to creep in to devalue the grades. In short, people began to worry that the GCSEs were simply easier than the previous exams.

As a result of this widespread concern, ministers have introduced a strict code of conduct for the exam boards. In place from summer 1993, the code covers the setting of question papers, mark schemes, coursework assessment and moderation, and the setting of grade standards. Nevertheless, many parents and pupils are still confused by the numerous changes that have and which continue to take place.

What parents really want is the confidence that a grade means what it says, year after year. Otherwise the system loses its value. However, one father, who celebrated his own daughter's top grades in 1992, told me, 'If that was an easier year, I'm glad she took them then rather than when they tighten up'.

A STAR IS BORN: ENTER THE 'SUPER-A'

From the school year 1993–94 the method of grading the GCSE is being changed to make it more rigorous. Up to now, grades have run from A down to G, where A was the top grade, but there was concern that the exam was not recognising the efforts of the very brightest pupils. So now there is an even tougher top grade, the A★, or, as it has been dubbed, 'the Super-A'. At the other end of the scale, pupils who fail to achieve grade G are deemed not to have reached minimum standards. They are considered 'unclassified' and will not receive a certificate. The introduction of the A★ grade was very

SEE ALSO:
Vocational
Qualifications
Appealing
against Poor
Grades

167

much a last-minute decision by the government's exam advisers. Originally, the A–G grading scale was to have been replaced with one running down from ten at the top to four at the bottom. The new grade 10 would have been tougher than the previous grade A, and equivalent to the new A★. The numbers were designed to bring the GCSE grades into line with the ten-level National Curriculum scale, against which all pupils are supposed to be measured in tests and teacher assessments throughout their school lives from age 5 to 16.

SPOT THE DIFFERENTIATION

As with the National Curriculum tests, papers in many subjects will be 'differentiated'. This means different papers will be set for pupils of different abilities. The level of the papers will overlap, to reduce the risk of any child not being able to show his or her maximum potential

Courtesy Mahood of the Daily Mail

And now for something completely different…

Ranking Monty Python's *Life of Brian* and the TV comedy "Allo 'Allo alongside the works of Shakespeare in a GCSE English syllabus did not impress ministers. The groans were audible when it emerged that TV soaps like 'Neighbours', 'Brookside' and 'Coronation Street' would be studied alongside the works of Wordsworth and Dickens on the two-year course for 180,000 pupils. The controversial syllabus was published by the Northern Examination and Assessment Board.

in the exam. Differentiated papers were introduced to cope with the wide variation in the ability range of pupils sitting the all-embracing GCSE. Some critics claim that differentiated papers are a return to the old two-tier O-level and CSE system. Supporters of the idea say it simply gives pupils of all abilities a better chance to show what they can do.

WHICH GCSES MUST MY CHILD TAKE?

The law lays down which subjects your child must study and be tested on. At age 16, the GCSE exam is now compulsory in the three core subjects, of English, maths and science, for all students except those considered unlikely to achieve a grade G. It is intended that 'technology' will join this list of compulsory exams at the end of the two-year GCSE courses beginning in September 1993, with other subjects coming on-stream in subsequent years. The government's review of the National Curriculum and testing could, however, change these plans. Most pupils will normally take GCSEs in the subjects they already have to study as part of the National Curriculum. This can leave little flexibility for choosing other subjects in which your child might have a particular interest, such as an additional foreign language, Latin or economics. The government's review of the

RISING STANDARDS OR 'GRADE INFLATION'? HOW GRADES HAVE IMPROVED OVER THE YEARS			
GCSE/O-level/CSE		1984–85	26.8
Academic year	% of pupils achieving 5 of more passes	1985–86	26.7
		1986–87	26.4
1979–80	24	1987–88 (first year of GCSE)	29.9
1980–81	25	1988–89	31.9
1981–82	26.1	1989–90	35.2
1982–83	26.2	1990–91	37.8
1983–84	26.7	1991–92	38.1

- The percentages of pupils achieving the equivalent of five or more GCSE grades A to C, O-level pass grades A to C, or CSE grade 1.

Chris Potter, Headmaster of grant-maintained Old Swinford Hospital School in Stourbridge, West Midlands, celebrates record GCSE results with some of his star pupils.

Picture by Peter Lea, courtesy Daily Mail

National Curriculum will look closely at this matter.

GCSE AND O-LEVEL PUT TO THE TEST

In 1992, with the support of their schools, I put two anonymous groups of pupils, under exam conditions, through some old O-level papers that covered broadly what they had learned on their GCSE courses. The results in maths and history, marked by senior O-level and GCSE examiners, showed that while the brightest pupils did well whatever the exam, the weaker pupils appeared to be getting better grades at GCSE than they might have managed at O-level. Part of the

reason was in the different nature of the two exams. O-levels tended to measure the knowledge that a pupil had learned and understood, while the GCSE puts more emphasis on the 'skills' that pupils can demonstrate and apply. The history teacher at one of the guinea-pig secondary schools noted, 'There has been an ideological battle between the more traditional approach...and the GCSE.'

COURSEWORK

The role of coursework and the extent to which it should be used to assess pupils at GCSE level has been a cause of great debate since continuous assessment was introduced. Coursework can help

COURSEWORK LIMITS FOR KEY STAGE 4

Course beginning	Subject	Coursework limit
September 1992	Maths	20%
	Science	30%
	English	40%
September 1993	Biology	30%
	Chemistry	30%
	Physics	30%
	Welsh	40%
	Welsh (second language)	40%
	Technology	60%
September 1994	History	25%
	Geography	25%
September 1995	Modern foreign languages (provisional)	30%

children who might not shine in an end-of-year exam. This may be because of nerves, or simply because they prefer applying their knowledge in the way that course-work demands, rather than having to regurgitate as many facts and figures as they can remember in the examination hall. Some pupils are simply better suited to showing their ability over time in a sustained project. Others like nothing better than the adrenalin-pumping excitement that the prospect of answering tough exam questions can bring.

Many experts felt that it was unfair that a student who had achieved good classroom results by working steadily throughout the year, but gone to pieces on exam day, could be beaten by another pupil who might have done the bare minimum in class, yet mugged up on key questions the night before and turned in a sparkling paper just when it counted. However, ministers became alarmed when they saw that some GCSE courses had 100% coursework assessment and no final exam. Inspectors and, it has to be

Those were the Krays

Schoolboy Andrew Ball studied for a GCSE with a difference – on the Kray twins. The 16 year-old was given permission to study the life and crimes of the 60s' underworld villains as part of his English language studies. Andrew, a pupil at Millfield High School in Cleveleys near Blackpool, Lancashire, wrote to Ronnie and Reggie Kray for their assistance. The school said 'Crime and punishment is always in the public eye and that is why it is a legitimate subject for someone to tackle in a serious manner.'

said, some teachers too, raised the alarm about 'cheating'. Some parents were helping out just a little too much, it was claimed. Pupils from wealthier or better-educated households were at a distinct advantage in this respect. A lot of work, assessed by the teacher, would be handed back to the child for 'polishing'. The final product might bear no relation to the child's original work. Against this background, ministers introduced new limits on the amount of coursework in GCSE exams, and placed more emphasis on a 'vigorous terminal examination'.

A-LEVELS

The A-level has been described as the 'gold-standard' exam. It was designed for the top 30% of the ability range at 18, and is the passport to higher education in England and Wales. The casualty rate is, however, quite high. The intellectually demanding two-year courses tackle specialist work that in some other countries would be considered university degree standard. Whereas students abroad may study a broader range of subjects less intensively up to the age of 18, it is usual for students in Britain to study only three 'Advanced Level' subjects in a school sixth form, a sixth-form college or a college of further education.

Students in Britain usually concentrate on either arts or science subjects. There has been an attempt to broaden the range of study for 16–18 year-olds with the introduction of the 'leaner' AS courses. But as universities are usually quite specific about the subjects and grades they require for entry, it is worth checking this out well in advance of choosing A-level courses. Students should also try to be realistic about their chances of getting the A-level grades and plan their strategy accordingly. Aim high, by all means, but pack a reserve parachute. If, on the other hand, A-levels really don't appeal, it is worth considering GNVQ courses. These are supposed to be equally valued by higher education institutions.

QUALIFYING FOR A-LEVEL COURSES

Schools and colleges usually require students to have five or more GCSEs at grade C or above to begin a course, though this is not set in stone. The jump from GCSE to A-level study is a difficult one. The difference in approach became even more marked with the replacement of the old O-level with GCSEs. This is because the O-level was a 'traditional' exam which required pupils to absorb and show mastery of a body of knowledge, a style more in keeping with the A-level. The GCSE, by contrast, puts more emphasis on being able to demonstrate the application of knowledge. The result, many teachers and pupils have noted, is that the work required for A-level study can come as a shock.

NO TARNISHED 'GOLD STANDARD'

Various attempts have been made to scrap A-levels as they currently stand. One of the most controversial came in the 1988 Higginson Report. It concluded that English and Welsh students specialised too early so that their sixth-form study lacked breadth when compared to the equivalent *Abitur* in Germany or the French Baccalaureate. The report proposed replacing the existing pattern of three A-levels with five less extensive but no less rigorous exams. Ministers responded that the A-level has a proven worth and rejected the move on the grounds that if something isn't broken, why mend it? They were also mindful of the controversy that surrounded the replacing of the O-level by GCSEs and did not want to be accused of diluting standards.

AS QUALIFICATIONS

Despite rejecting the Higginson proposal, ministers did sanction the creation of a new exam called the Advanced Supplementary or AS. AS courses cover half the content of an A-level, but are assessed at the same academic level. Studied over two years, AS was introduced to encourage pupils to broaden their sixth-form course by increasing the number of subjects studied, possibly taking a mix of arts and science subjects – usually two A-levels and two ASs. Though the exam was meant to supplement A-levels, it is sometimes mistaken as an alternative for less able candidates. Take-up of the exam has been sluggish because few sixth-formers and teachers believe it matches the A-level in prestige.

SEE ALSO:
Vocational
Qualifications

Sixth-form fact file

- Tax-payers spend £2 billion a year funding educational and vocational courses for 16–19 year-olds.

- Each A-level course costs tax-payers on average £3,000 per student, though the sum for individual courses can vary between £1,000 and £7,000.

- Of the 600,000 pupils who reach the age of 16 per year:

  – 35% remain at school.

  – 32% transfer to sixth-form or further education colleges.

- About 160,000 students sit A-levels each year.

- About 23,000 students sit AS exams each year.

- About 13% of students drop out before completing A-level courses.

- The cost of courses taken by students who either drop out or fail is about £500 million a year.

- Research by the Audit Commission shows that student performance in three A-levels can drop an average of one grade per subject, depending on the quality of teaching at the school or college.

MODULAR A-LEVEL AND AS COURSES

A-levels have traditionally involved two years of study followed by a final examination. The government has, however, been working towards the creation of 'modular' A-levels and AS courses. This involves putting together individual elements of a course like building blocks. It means that students get credit for all the 'modules' they complete, even if they do not finish the whole course. Many university and college courses work on a similar principle. In April 1993 the government's exam advisers set out their ground rules for any such modular courses drawn up by exam boards. They stress that not all subjects will be suitable for the modular approach.

GOVERNMENT GROUND RULES FOR
MODULAR A-LEVELS STATE THAT:

- each course can have up to six modules

- each module must be up to A-level standard.

CHOOSE WITH CARE WHERE YOU SIT YOUR A-LEVELS

Sixth-formers must take care when choosing where they sit their A-levels. Wide variations in the quality of school and college courses mean that students have the potential for achieving results at least one grade higher in each subject at one institution rather than another. Given the point-scoring system for entry into higher education, that could mean the difference between securing or losing a place at university.

A disturbing report in 1993 by the Audit Commission and OFSTED said that thousands of sixth-formers are getting lower A-level grades than they should because of poor teaching. The watchdogs even witnessed worrying differences in the

performance of different classes within the same institution, and highlighted wasteful inefficiencies in the system which are costing tax-payers £330 million a year. The report discussed one unnamed college where the pass rate in an English class was twice that of another in the same building. The report noted: 'The differences between the best and the worst are significant. The degree of success for courses is uneven. On some courses, the lack of success is alarming.' Reassuringly, the report noted that it makes very little difference to performance whether pupils are at one type of college or another, eg an FE college as opposed to a school sixth form.

6 A-levels have established themselves as the "gold standard" of post-16 education in this country. Their standards of academic excellence allow students to cover subjects in depth, so that they are genuinely an advanced level of study.9

Lord Griffiths, Chairman of the now defunct School Examinations and Assessment Council

APPEALING AGAINST
POOR GRADES

Waiting for exam results can be one of the most traumatic times in the life of a teenager – and a parent. When the GCSE or A-level grades come out, you must brace yourself for your young loved one to rise to heights of dizzy joy, or sink to the depths of despair. Sometimes it's a mixture of both emotions. The stakes are obviously much higher for A-levels, which determine entry to university and college. Often the cry will be, 'I just don't believe it! There must have been a mistake.' The A-level results were worse than expected. They are convinced that laziness or poor performance on the day was not to blame. And now their disappointment has turned to anger against the system which, they believe, has failed them. The examiners, not themselves, must have made the mistake. But what can they do? The answer is, they can appeal.

WHAT ARE THE CHANCES OF SUCCESS?

Every year, the exam boards receive more than 15,000 appeals against A-level grades. Less than 5% of

challenges result in an upgrade. But such low odds do little to deter pupils and parents who are convinced of their case. In the past, these challenges began and ended with the exam boards, but now they can go higher to an independent 'court of appeal'. In 1991, out of 4,700 appeals to the Associated Examining Board, one of the biggest in the country, about 430 resulted in upgrades, proving that the examiners can make mistakes.

In March 1993 the Northern Examination and Assessment Board upgraded 1,667 chemistry students who had been wrongly given B and C grades. The board's internal appeals panel decided that they had been 'too harsh' and lowered the A grade boundary by 2% and the B grade boundary by 1%.

CONTACT THE SCHOOL

If your child is unhappy with his or her grades, your first contact should be with the school. See the teacher of the subject concerned and see if he or she agrees with your son or daughter's view. Candidates need the backing of their head-teacher or college to proceed with an appeal. George Turnbull, of the Associated Examining Board, said: 'The schools are in a better position to judge a candidate's performance. If they feel there is a case which needs to be investigated, they will raise an enquiry with us.'

Once you have the school's backing, a sliding scale of options is available.

CLERICAL RECHECK

The first step is a clerical recheck, which involves totting up the marks awarded on the answer paper and making sure the final tally is correct. This costs about £2 per candidate per subject. It does not involve re-marking the work.

CHECK, RE-MARK AND STATEMENT

A clerical check and a re-mark costs between about £18 and £24. The marks are totalled up, but the work is also re-marked as if for the first time. If, in addition, the candidate receives a statement of the marks and a brief report, the cost will be about £39 per subject.

The process, however, is slow. And candidates who appeal are likely to lose their course place before the final outcome is known. Mr Turnbull said 'It takes about four weeks to do a recheck and a re-mark, so candidates

are advised to apply as soon as possible. The deadline for A-level appeals is usually 30 September, and for GCSEs 1 October, but do check to make sure.'

GROUP APPEALS

Sometimes a group of candidates from one school may appeal together, in which case the cost is £96 for a group of four and £22 for each additional candidate.

TAKING IT FURTHER

If the examiners reject their challenge, candidates can then appeal to the secretary of the exam board through their school. If the secretary rejects the challenge, the next stage is the board's education committee.

> 6 Examining is not an exact science. The school examination system is of great complexity and rests on many decisions and judgements on the part of many people. But candidates and their parents wish to be satisfied that the grades awarded are fair, particularly as downgrading by one or two grades may affect a candidate's future, especially at A-level. 9

Lady Anson, Chairwoman of the Independent Appeals Authority for School Examinations

177

Case 1

THE PARTIES

Woking College and Rainham Mark Grammar School against the Associated Examining Board, A-level English Literature syllabus (652) 1991.

THE SCHOOLS' EVIDENCE

They complained that the exam had failed to discriminate between candidates of 'widely differing abilities'. Ten Woking candidates were awarded marks two grades lower than expected, while gaining high results in other subjects. They blamed a failure in marking policy.

THE EXAM BOARD'S EVIDENCE

The board contended that it was not unusual for pass rates to differ between different syllabuses in the same subject.

THE JUDGEMENT

Grade boundaries had been set at very different levels compared with the previous year. This particularly affected grades A and B, and seemed to mean that an extra 47 marks were required to gain grade A. A mark which would have gained a grade C in 1991 could have earned an A in 1990.

THE OUTCOME

The Independent Appeals Authority asked the AEB to reconsider the grades.

Case 2

THE PARTIES

Hazlewick School in Crawley against London and East Anglian Group GCSE Chemistry (Nuffield) 1990.

THE SCHOOL'S EVIDENCE

Some 115 candidates sat the tougher paper for more able pupils. But only 26% gained A–C grades, compared to 47% on another syllabus the previous year. Two other schools reported a similar fall in results.

THE EXAM BOARD'S EVIDENCE

The school was 'unfamiliar' with the new syllabus.

THE JUDGEMENT

The case left 'the greater doubt in the Authority's mind about possible injustice to the school's candidates and maybe to others including future candidates if the practices which came to light in this case went unchallenged.'

THE OUTCOME

Grade boundaries changed. Grades of 730 candidates including 26 from Hazlewick School were raised.

SEE ALSO:
Vocational
Qualifications

GCSEs and
A-Levels

'COURT OF APPEAL'

If all else fails, the very last chance is the Independent Appeals Authority for School Examinations, headed by legal adjudicator and qualified barrister Lady Anson. The body was set up by the government in November 1990 in answer to criticism that exam boards were sitting as judge and jury in cases where they were also the accused. In 1991, out of 20 appeals heard, nine were upheld; five for A-level and four for GCSE.

At the Appeals Authority, both the examiners and the plaintiff have a chance to put their case in a formal public hearing, which also sanctions a form of cross-examination. Schools or parents are required to send a £50 deposit when they approach the Appeals Authority. This is returned if the appeal is heard, even if it is rejected, as long as the authority believes the request was a 'reasonable course of action'.

There have been calls for the watchdog authority to be given more 'teeth', for it has no power to enforce the boards to change grades. In an annual report Lady Anson noted 'While there are grounds for confidence in the working of the system, it may be that individuals and groups of candidates and their schools come to grief; the accounts of the hearings to date leave no doubt that the system is imperfect.'

Independent Appeals Authority for School Examinations
Newcombe House
45 Notting Hill Gate
London W11 3JB

Tel: 071-299 1234
Fax: 071-229 8526

> ❛One mark can make the difference between a grade A and a grade B. But the system has checks and rechecks to ensure that the grades we issue are the true grades based on the evidence we have seen. And in borderline cases, we do give students the benefit of the doubt.❜
>
> *George Turnbull, Associated Examining Board*

VOCATIONAL QUALIFICATIONS

Not everyone is suited to taking traditional academic qualifications. Some pupils may struggle to gain decent GCSE grades or A-levels in exams, yet know they have an untapped talent for more practical or work-related activities. It is for them that a new range of vocational courses – GNVQs – is now being developed. The government has made it clear that it wants such courses to be alternatives to GCSEs as well as to A-levels, so pupils may start them at age 14. A 'twin-track' approach is envisaged, by which students can take a mixture of 'academic' and 'vocational' courses. That is why the new GNVQ level 3 has been dubbed a 'vocational A-level'. Ministers hope that parents, pupils, schools and employers will eventually attach the same importance to these qualifications as they do to GCSE and A-level. This would give the vocational qualifications what experts term 'parity of esteem'.

Hopes are high, but let's be realistic. Britain is struggling to overcome an unfortunate national trait that has cost this country dear since the last war. This is the tendency to look down one's nose at 'trade' and to undervalue work-related qualifications. One need only look at Germany where an engineer is seen as an aristocrat of industry, and viewed in the same professional light as a doctor or lawyer. In Britain, by contrast, engineers are seen as spanner-wielding labourers. To catch up with economic rivals like Germany, Japan, France and the USA, it is vital that the status of vocational qualifications is raised. Saying it is one thing. Making it happen is another.

GNVQS

The government wants as many as half the country's 16–19 year-olds to study for General National Vocational Qualifications (GNVQs), which it hopes will gain support from universities and employers. In 1993 the government said it wanted GNVQs to be available in at least two subjects in more than 1,500 schools and colleges within three years, catering for a quarter of 16 year-olds.

There are five levels of GNVQ, but levels 2 and 3 have taken off first. At

A GUIDE TO VOCATIONAL QUALIFICATIONS

NATIONAL COUNCIL FOR VOCATIONAL QUALIFICATIONS

The main independent body. It gives its stamp of approval to vocational qualifications and courses produced and awarded by a number of commercial organisations. The main organisations are:

- BTEC (Business & Technology Education Council)
- City and Guilds
- RSA (Royal Society of Arts Examinations Board).

GENERAL NATIONAL VOCATIONAL QUALIFICATIONS

Broad-based courses offered by the main vocational training bodies but delivered in schools and colleges. Intermediate level is equivalent to four or five good GCSEs. Advanced level is equivalent to two A-levels. Although more are planned, qualifications are currently awarded in five main areas:

- art and design
- business
- health and social care
- leisure and tourism
- manufacturing.

GNVQs are designed to equip young people with the knowledge, skills and attitudes valued by industry.

National Vocational Qualifications

These are specific to particular job areas and their content is determined largely by employers.

Level 1: Requires basic competence in routine and predictable work activities and is equivalent to a low grade GCSE.

Level 2: Basic craft level, broadly equivalent to four or more GCSEs at grades A to C.

Level 3: Technician, advanced craft and supervisor level, broadly equivalent to two or more A-levels.

Level 4: Higher technicians and junior management level.

Level 5: Professional and middle management level, the work-related equivalent to a university degree.

It is intended that in time GNVQs and NVQs will replace the wide range of vocational qualifications currrently available.

HOW THE QUALIFICATIONS MATCH UP

5c

HIGHER DEGREE		NVQ5
DEGREE	GNVQ4	NVQ4
A/AS LEVEL	GNVQ ADVANCED LEVEL	NVQ3
GCSE	GNVQ INTERMEDIATE LEVEL	NVQ2
	GNVQ FOUNDATION LEVEL	NVQ1

AGE 16

National qualifications framework showing equivalences of qualifications
Progression chart courtesy of City and Guilds

GNVQ level 3, 'Advanced' level, students study for two years and are assessed on exams totalling 12 hours, as well as on coursework. A pupil would normally need five GCSEs with grades A to C to begin the course. Level 2, or 'Intermediate' level, takes one year of study and is equal to four or five good GCSEs. Level 1, or 'Foundation' level, is pre-GCSE and has no entry requirements.

From September 1993 the first GNVQs at levels 2 and 3 became generally available in 1,000 schools and colleges. These courses, validated by BTEC, City and Guilds and RSA examination boards, were in art and design, business, health and social care, leisure and tourism, and manufacturing. Further GNVQs are being developed in science, construction, catering, engineering,

Famous five

Five 16 year-olds from Barnfield College in Luton were awarded the first GNVQs in May 1993 after taking part in a pilot business course. Gary Brogan, Nathan Bright, Kevin Cushing, Scott Drummond and Greig Bescoby completed RSA's 'Intermediate' level GNVQ in business and are progressing to 'Advanced' level. The college's Head of Faculty Alan Euinton said, 'GNVQs will provide students with a genuine alternative to A-levels'. Martin Cross, Chief Executive of RSA Examinations which organised the course, said: 'This is undoubtedly a turning point in modern educational history.'

information technology, performing arts, agriculture, distribution and management.

Since September 1993, vocational bodies have also been allowed to compete with existing exam boards to award GCSEs in work-related courses at school. The new courses include technology, design technology and information systems.

National Council for Vocational Qualifications
222 Euston Road
London NW1 2BZ

Tel: 071-387 9898
Fax: 071-387 0978

BTEC
Central House
Upper Woburn Place
London WC1H 0HH

Tel: 071-413 8400
Fax: 071-387 6068

City and Guilds
326 City Road
London EC1V 2PT

Tel: 071-278 2468
Fax: 071-753 5280

RSA Examination Board
Westwood Way
Coventry CV4 8HS

Tel: 0203 470033
Fax: 0203 468080

SEE ALSO:
GCSEs and
A-Levels

★ GOLD STAR CELEBRITIES ★

★ SIÂN LLOYD ★

OCCUPATION

TV weather presenter/journalist

SCHOOLS

Neath Welsh School (Junior), Ystalytera Bilingual Comprehensive

It was very different from most comprehensives, run along the old grammar school lines. Because it was bilingual, I have no hang ups about languages.

SCHOOL REPORT

'She is a giggler and is often late for class.' Both these traits remain.

TEACHER WHO MADE A BIG IMPRESSION

My domestic science teacher Mrs Lillian Powell, who insisted on good manners and politeness, and taught us how to lay the table correctly. To this day my favourite sandwich filling is one of hers – egg, onion and mayonnaise. Also my mum Barbara, a Past President of the National Union of Teachers.

MOST IMPORTANT LESSON LEARNED AT SCHOOL

To communicate and participate. Ours was a school boasting debating societies, public-speaking teams and choirs galore.

SOMETHING I WISH I'D DONE DIFFERENTLY AT SCHOOL

I wish I'd been less creative with my school uniform. My micro-mini coupled with over-the-knee socks must have looked ridiculous.

BEST MOMENTS AT SCHOOL

Winning the Royal National Eisteddfod crown. Being asked out by the biggest 'catch' in the school.

WORST MOMENT AT SCHOOL

Being told that he was two-timing me while away at holiday camp. But I got my revenge.

SWOT POINTS

Head girl, captain of the swimming and netball teams

EMBARRASSING MOMENT

Having to wear a leg plaster for a couple of months after a vicious tackle in a girls vs boys rugby match

QUALIFICATIONS

10 O-levels, 3 A-levels, English 'S' paper, BA Hons (First Class), Met. Office College exam, A-grade

★ LADY OLGA MAITLAND ★

OCCUPATION

MP for Sutton, South London

SCHOOLS

Queen's Gate School, London, School of St Mary and St Anne Abbots, Bromley and Lycée Française de Londres

SCHOOL REPORT

'She perseveres!'

TEACHER WHO MADE A BIG IMPRESSION

English teacher Miss Borchend. As an eight year-old I was much struck by this hugely tall athletic woman with brown hair tied up in a plait over her head. She always wore the same brown cardigan and tweed skirt. In short, the classic English teacher.

MOST IMPORTANT LESSON LEARNED AT SCHOOL

Discipline, academic and personal

SOMETHING I WISH I'D DONE DIFFERENTLY AT SCHOOL

I wish I had insisted on proper, full-strength glasses so I could play ball games. As I never could see the ball, this was always impossible.

BEST MOMENT AT SCHOOL

Winning the cup for high jump and joining the school diving team.

SWOT POINTS

Very undistinguished career. I just made it to deputy house prefect.

EMBARRASSING MOMENT

Told to pull down a simply marvellous tree house I had built with another girl's help. Such a shame. From our refuge very high up in the trees we could escape the iniquities of boarding-school life.

QUALIFICATIONS

Precious little. 7 O-levels. I should have been made to do much more, but education in the late 1950s did not reckon on women having careers, let alone becoming MPs.

CHILDREN

Alastair aged 20, Camilla aged 17 and Fergus aged 11. I chose independent schools for them because they provide a good all-round education with careful attention to the individual's needs and a strong input of Christian teaching.

POINTS TO CONSIDER WHEN CHOOSING A SCHOOL

Academic achievement, staff motivation and involvement, a school which is 'alive' with enthusiasm, and opportunities to develop all facets of a child's character and skills.

MY VIEW OF TODAY'S EDUCATION SYSTEM

State education is very variable but I have two excellent grammar schools in my constituency. State education must raise the standards and expectations of children of all abilities. State schools must also place more emphasis on Christian teaching to provide a sound moral framework and code of behaviour.

GOLD STAR CELEBRITIES

6 OPTING OUT

| **6a** | OPTING OUT | **187** |

OPTING OUT

It was hailed by ministers as the ultimate example of 'parent power'. The government's idea of allowing parents to vote to take their children's state schools out of local council control was one of the most controversial policies when it became law under the landmark 1988 Education Reform Act. Since then, despite heated debates and opt-out battles, the number of grant-maintained schools has grown steadily, though not uniformly, across the country. In some areas the move has seen schools at the centre of impassioned battles between pro- and anti-opt-out campaigners. Allegations of 'dirty tricks' have been rife, and complaints of alleged ballot-rigging have surfaced in some areas. Some parents clearly think the future of their child's school would be best served by cutting ties with the town hall and going it alone. They are convinced that the benefits of grant-maintained status outweigh those of being governed by local councillors of whatever political persuasion.

Other parents prefer safety in numbers and want to stick with what they see as the relative security of the local education authority. However, ministers have already warned that reforms to both the school system and local government mean that some local education authorities will simply not exist in any meaningful form in a few years' time. The government has set itself a target of 1,000 grant-maintained schools by the end of 1993 and 1,500 by April 1994.

SELF-GOVERNING STATE SCHOOLS

A grant-maintained school is a self-governing state school funded by tax-payers. It receives its funding direct from Whitehall instead of the town hall. Governors have overall responsibility and control for all aspects of the school's running, including the budget. This degree of independence means the school does not have to refer back to an LEA to make decisions. But they are state schools, so the education on offer is still free to those who receive it. Though independent within the state sector, they cannot charge fees.

Government reforms mean that schools still under LEA control must be given at least 85% of their budget to spend as they see fit. The remaining 15%, soon to be reduced to 10%, is retained by the council for central administration. A grant-maintained school receives 100% of its budget in the form of a 'maintenance grant' from Whitehall. It also receives grants to ease the transition to grant-maintained status and can qualify for extra cash for building projects or improvements.

HOW DOES A SCHOOL OPT OUT?

Parents are the critical force behind any school's move to become grant-maintained. They must vote in favour of opting out before the school can formally apply to become a self-governing state school. But it is the Secretary of State for Education who has the final say on whether any such application should be approved. The school must hold a ballot of all parents if either the governors pass a resolution, or enough parents petition, for the school to opt out.

Any petition must be signed by parents equal in number to at least 20% of the school's pupil population. So a school of 1,000 pupils would require the signatures of at least 200 parents for an opt-out move to be put to the vote. The petition is then sent to the chairperson or clerk to the governors.

The 1993 Education Act removed the requirement of a second governors' resolution before parents can be balloted. On receipt of a positive petition from the parents, or after a positive resolution by the governing body, the governing body must arrange with the Electoral Reform Society to hold a ballot within a specified time.

Power to the people. Head-teacher Graham Locke and pupils at Audenshaw High School in Greater Manchester celebrate becoming one of the first schools to opt out of council control and receive direct funding, as a grant-maintained school, from Whitehall.

Picture by Jim Hutchinson, courtesy Daily Mail

If the majority of parents vote to back the opt-out move, and more than half the eligible voters take part, the 'Yes' vote is carried. If fewer than half the eligible voters take part, a second ballot must be held within 14 days. The result of the second ballot is final, no matter how many parents vote. If parents vote against the idea, another ballot cannot normally be held for 12 months.

In the case of a 'Yes' vote, the governors must publish and submit proposals to the Secretary of State for Education within six months, explaining how a new governing body would run the school under grant-maintained status. The proposed start date must normally be at the start of April, September or January. The Secretary of State must allow two months for objections to be aired before reaching a final decision.

The government stresses that each case is decided on its merits, and that opting out will not be sanctioned simply as a means for a school with a doubtful future to avoid closure.

ORGANISING A PARENTS' PETITION

As already explained, parental petitions must be signed by parents numbering at least 20% of pupils.

PARENTAL PETITION IN FAVOUR OF GRANGE HILL SCHOOL APPLYING FOR GRANT-MAINTAINED STATUS

1 We, the undersigned, in accordance with section 60 of the Education Reform Act 1988, request the governing body of Grange Hill School to hold a ballot of parents on the question of whether grant-maintained status should be sought for the school.

2 We confirm that we are parents of pupils registered at the school.

Name and address of parent   Signature

1...

2...

3...

However, in considering the required numbers it is important to note that when both of a child's parents sign the petition, each signature counts separately. A model parental petition, as set out by the Department for Education is shown on the preceding page.

It is important that wording such as that in the example is at the top of EVERY sheet, to prove that all parents are absolutely clear about what they are agreeing to.

Once the required number of signatures has been reached, plus a few more to be on the safe side, the petition can be handed over to the governors. The governors do not have to meet formally to receive the petition. The clock starts ticking as soon as it is handed over to the governors' chairperson or clerk.

WHO IS ELIGIBLE TO VOTE IN AN OPT-OUT BALLOT?

To be eligible to vote you must be the parent of a registered pupil at the school 14 days after the governors' resolution or the presentation of the parental petition. The parents are entitled to one vote each, regardless of how many children attend the school from a particular family.

KEEPING CONTINUITY

If parents vote 'Yes' in the ballot on opting out, part of the proposal submitted to the Secretary of State will include details of the new governing body that will run the grant-maintained school. The government is keen that there should be as much continuity as possible. So if any existing elected parent or teacher governors are interested in serving on the new grant-maintained governing body, they are permitted to do so, as long as their term of office does not expire before the change-over. If there are more governors willing to carry on than there are places available, some will have to stand down. If the appointments cannot be agreed, the matter must be decided by drawing lots. If fewer elected governors than needed are willing to serve on the new governing body, elections must be held to make up the required numbers.

New legislation in 1993 reduces the minimum size of a grant-maintained governing body from 15 to 11, comprising:

- three parents

- one teacher governor

- the head-teacher

- six 'first' or 'foundation' governors.

'First governors' are chosen by other governors as representatives of the local community ready to show a long-term commitment to a non-denominational school. 'Foundation governors' serve the same function but represent a religious or charitable foundation in a voluntary or Church school.

TAKING THE ROUGH WITH THE SMOOTH

Although many schools opt out with very little controversy, not all change-overs go smoothly. In some cases, where parents have voted to opt out against the wishes of the governing body, many of whom have been appointed by the LEA from which the school is parting company, there

Dirty tricks claim in opt-out battle

have been conflicts. Attempts by the prospective or 'shadow' governors to prepare for the change-over have been hampered by the 'old guard' or by the LEA itself.

The 1992 White Paper noted: 'On occasion, prospective governing bodies have met with undesirable obstruction which has severely hampered their legitimate work.' New legislation in the 1993 Education Act requires prospective grant-maintained governors to be given 'an unequivocal right of access to the school at reasonable times'.

SPONSOR GOVERNORS

The new act also allows for 'sponsor' governors from business and industry to be appointed in grant-maintained and voluntary-aided schools. Ministers believe that partnerships between schools and sponsors can play a large part in helping schools to specialise.

POWER TO ACT

The new 1993 legislation gives the Secretary of State powers to remove 'first' governors in grant-maintained schools where the governing body is failing the school. This follows events at controversial Stratford School in East London, at which a clique of governors were accused of acting beyond their powers.

> ❛ Various obstacles have been erected to discourage balloting for grant-maintained status. When ballots have been held, parents have been denied a balanced presentation of the arguments. In some cases the tactics have been intimidatory. ❜

Education Secretary John Patten in his 1992 White Paper 'Choice and Diversity'

INTO THE WAR ZONE

Be warned. Getting involved in an opt-out battle can be a nightmare. In some areas the policy has become highly politicised. The teaching unions are split on the issue. The head-teachers' and moderate classroom teachers' unions take the pragmatic view that many of their members now work in grant-maintained schools, so to castigate them would be counter-productive. Other unions, like the National Union of Teachers and the National Association of Schoolmasters/Union of Women Teachers, are openly hostile and have produced special guides aimed at scuppering any opt-out initiatives. Tempers and emotions can run high, whichever side you may support.

The 1993 Education Act aimed to create a 'level playing field' between parents and the local council. The Act limits the amount of cash LEAs can spend on any information campaign. It also allows a school's governing body to spend an equivalent sum, out of the public purse, on putting its case. Both sums will be roughly equivalent to the cost of producing and distributing one leaflet to parents.

'Choice and Diversity', the White Paper setting out the proposals, noted: 'In a small number of cases, schools have faced great hostility from local education authorities who have used their considerably greater resources to try to undermine governing bodies' attempts to inform parents properly about the grant-maintained option. The government intends to restore the balance.' It added 'This will allow informed debate on the educational issues involved and give the opportunity to all parents to reach a considered view about whether grant-maintained status is right for their child's school.'

GETTING HELP

The Grant Maintained Schools' Foundation and the Grant Maintained Schools' Centre give parents and governors detailed advice on how to opt out, and highlight the pitfalls they may encounter along the way. They can also arrange visits from head-teachers and governors who have been through the process.

SUPPORTERS SAY OPTING OUT:

- frees schools from town-hall bureaucracy

- gives schools greater freedom to make decisions and to spend their budgets as they see fit

- allows schools to develop their own character and ethos

- puts money where it matters – back into the classroom

- enables schools to 'shop around' for the best and most cost-effective educational goods and services.

CRITICS OF THE SELF-GOVERNING SCHOOL POLICY SAY:

- opting out is divisive and sets school against school

- the opt-out ballots set parent against parent

- the government is using cash 'bribes' to persuade schools to go it alone

- the policy is a 'back-door' attempt to reintroduce selection

- self-governing schools are cast adrift from the 'safety net' of LEAs.

The lobby group Local Schools' Information, funded by LEAs, provides information that is generally useful to those parents and governors who wish to resist any attempt to opt out.

OPTING OUT IN 'CLUSTERS'

Small primary schools can opt out in 'clusters' under new provisions in the 1993 Education Act. If successful, they will have a single governing body controlling the budget, staffing and overall running of the group of schools. Each school will continue to have its own admissions arrangements. Budgets will be divided up largely according to pupil numbers. The policy is aimed mainly, though not exclusively, at rural schools.

Each school must ballot its parents separately on the issue of grant-maintained status. Any small primary can seek 'cluster' grant-maintained status as long as it bands together with at least one other primary, which can be from a neighbouring LEA area.

THE 1993 EDUCATION ACT:

- requires governors of all schools run by LEAs to decide annually whether or not to press for grant-maintained status, and to explain their decision to parents.

- simplifies the opting-out process by removing the need for a second governors' meeting.

- limits the amount LEAs can spend on their own campaigns. School governing bodies will receive an equivalent amount from the public purse.

- allows special schools to opt out.

- requires failing council-run schools rescued by 'hit squads' to become grant-maintained.

- allows local groups to set up their own grant-maintained schools.

- gives the Education Secretary new powers to remove governors who are failing their schools.

There is no limit to the size of a cluster, although the Education Secretary would expect proposals to make 'geographical sense'. Cluster ballots must be triggered by a governors' resolution. The ballot paper will specify schools proposing to take part in the cluster. Where the parents from all schools in a proposed cluster vote 'Yes' to opting out, the schools put forward their proposals, to the Secretary of State, for approval. If some, but not all, of the schools vote to opt out, those which voted 'Yes' will still be able to put forward their proposals, but are not obliged to do so.

Once the decision has been made, the cluster schools form a single joint governing body. Parents from all the schools involved form a single electoral college to elect five parent governors. Two teacher governors are elected in a similar way by the staff. Heads elect their own head-teacher governor from among their peers each year.

> ❝ The growth of grant-maintained schools will lead to a greater number of state schools becoming stronger, more independent, more like prep schools. ❞
>
> *Roger Trafford, Headmaster of the Dragon School, Oxford*

CLUSTER 'ASSOCIATE MEMBERS'

Church schools, voluntary-aided schools and special agreement schools can become full members of a cluster. Because this involves losing autonomy, they will be allowed, as a right, some representation in the form of a 'foundation' governor on the new cluster governing body. This is to help protect the unique character that Church and other voluntary schools were established to provide. Foundation members have the right of veto over any changes to the religious character of their school.

Church and voluntary schools can also opt for a looser form of co-operation as 'associate members' of a cluster, retaining more of their autonomy and special character. They keep their governing bodies, but take part in many joint arrangements with the 'cluster' governing body. Associate member schools are not required to ballot parents.

ONE OUT, ALL OUT

A secondary school and its main feeder primary schools may seek some form of association in order to opt out together. Ministers say there are great benefits to be had from such links, including more effective curriculum management, use of resources and staff development.

❝ Will grant-maintained schools pose a threat to independent schools? I hope so.**❞**

Sir Robert Balchin, Chairman of the Grant Maintained Schools' Foundation

Grant Maintained Schools' Foundation and the Grant Maintained Schools' Centre
36 Great Smith Street
London SW1P 3BU

Tel: 071-233 4666
Fax: 071-233 2795

For information critical of opting out:

Local Schools' Information
11–13 Charterhouse Buildings
Goswell Road
London EC1M 7AN

Tel: 071-490 4942
Fax: 071-250 1075

Electoral Reform Society
Ballot Services Department
6 Chancel Street
Blackfriars
London SE1 0UU

Tel: 071-928 9407

★ NICK OWEN ★

OCCUPATION

Breakfast TV presenter

SCHOOLS

Kingsland Grange (7–13), Shrewsbury School (13–18), both independent

SCHOOL REPORT

'Nicholas is enthusiastic but extremely messy.' Art report at age 3 while at Egerton School, Berkhamsted, Hertfordshire. It was prophetic. I have always been hopeless at anything practical.

TEACHER WHO MADE A BIG IMPRESSION

Les Rogerson, who taught me in the 1950s. He was football daft (Manchester City fan) and he made me realise that teachers could be human.

MOST IMPORTANT LESSON LEARNED AT SCHOOL

To speak up for yourself and take the positive line. In other words, go for it! I held back too much until I was in my late teens.

SOMETHING I WISH I'D DONE DIFFERENTLY AT SCHOOL

I wish I had realised at an earlier age that I should believe in myself more.

SWOT POINTS

Guitarist in a dreadful group. Played trumpet in school orchestra. Head of house at Shrewsbury, house captain of football.

Nick Owen and Michelle Pratt, 'Child of Courage', 1992
Picture by Steve Poole, courtesy Daily Mail

EMBARRASSING AND PAINFUL MOMENT

Being stung on the willy by a wasp when I was 12

QUALIFICATIONS

8 O-levels, 3 A-levels and a BA (Hons) degree in Classics from Leeds University

CHILDREN

Independent schools for Andy aged 13, Tim aged 12, Chris 6 and Jenny 4

★ ANGHARAD REES ★

OCCUPATION
Actress

SCHOOLS
Rhiwbina Infant School,
Cardiff and
Commonweal Lodge,
Woodcote, Surrey

SCHOOL REPORT
'Angharad spends too
much time daydreaming'.
It was true.

**TEACHER WHO
MADE A BIG
IMPRESSION**
Miss Clarke for English
and Miss Diana Budd
for drama who saw something in me that no
other teacher had seen – a small talent that
could be nurtured. They were both
excellent and inspiring teachers.

**MOST IMPORTANT LESSON LEARNED
AT SCHOOL**
The kindness of my own parents.

**SOMETHING I WISH I'D DONE
DIFFERENTLY AT SCHOOL**
As I was dyslexic, I would have liked to
have waved a magic wand to achieve all the
things I so dearly wanted. I was ambitious to
do well without the capability.

**BEST MOMENT AT SCHOOL AND
'SWOT POINT'**
Winning the drama cup.

**WORST MOMENTS
AT SCHOOL**
When the headmistress
held up my teeth brace
in assembly and said
'This was found in the
orchard. To whom does
it belong?' I nearly died
having to collect it from
her in front of the
whole school.

**EMBARRASSING
MOMENT**
My boyfriend's letters
being intercepted by the
headmistress.

QUALIFICATIONS
8 O-levels and a scholarship to drama school.
Certificate for Cours de Civilisation Française
(Sorbonne). Similar thing from Madrid from
Madrid University. Teaching diploma in
English and drama.

CHILDREN
Linford, 18, Rhys, 16, educated at
independent school

**MY VIEW OF TODAY'S EDUCATION
SYSTEM**
On the whole I have been very satisfied with
my children's education. The head-teachers
are so important in creating the style for the
school. Unfortunately, all schools are able to
absorb and give protection to teachers who
should not be allowed near children!

★ GOLD STAR CELEBRITIES ★

Picture by
Graham Trott,
courtesy Daily Mail

7 GOING PRIVATE

PAYING YOUR WAY

Good independent schools can offer excellent facilities, smaller classes, a high-quality education, and a strong ethos. Independent senior schools do, however, vary enormously and you must really do your homework well before you make your choice. It is important to remember that independent schools are not all academic 'hothouses'. You do not necessarily have to be brilliant to get in. David Jewel, Master of Haileybury, points out that his school is not selective, and is therefore more 'comprehensive' than most. Some schools even make a selling point of the remedial help they offer.

As in the state sector, the key is to find a school that will best exploit your child's natural aptitudes and abilities, while at the same time ensuring he or she leaves as a rounded individual. The school should suit your child's temperament, as well as his or her talents. One advantage of going private is that you may be less constrained by bureaucracy or catchment areas, and can spread your search further afield, particularly if you consider boarding. But good schools are still likely to be oversubscribed and the entrance exams for highly selective schools can be very tough.

The section on prep schools sets out one way of easing the transition. Many parents send their children to state primary schools until they are either 8 or 11, and then switch them to a prep school to prepare for the Common Entrance exam, which is the passport into the best schools.

A wide variety of guide books give a flavour of what is on offer, but there is no substitute for visiting the school. The number of single-sex schools is shrinking as many traditionally boys' schools turn coeducational, either in the sixth form or throughout the school. You also need to bear in mind how long you are willing, or need, to spend apart from your children. The three possibilities are day schooling, full boarding or weekly boarding. Weekly boarders return home at weekends.

SEE ALSO:
Prep Schools

> **❝My time at Haileybury helped me to cope better with my conditions and to avoid confrontation with the guards.❞**
>
> *Lebanon hostage John McCarthy speaking to sixth-formers at his old school*

FAMOUS NAMES

Eton and Harrow are probably the two names that trip most readily off the tongues of even those people unacquainted with the public school system. Yet they are very different from each other. The traditions, atmosphere and ethos of the schools vary enormously. Academically, Eton is highly selective; Harrow is less so.

PACKING A PARACHUTE

It is no secret among the heads of fee-paying schools that they are looking over their shoulders at the competition from the growing grant-maintained sector. However, if parents fail to get their child into a good state school, they are often prepared to spend hard cash to secure a place at an independent school.

THE BENEFITS OF INDEPENDENCE

• Smaller classes

• More choice of school, particularly if boarding

• The chance to 'escape' from state schools that fail to meet your expectations

• The chance to 'open doors' for your child

THE DRAWBACKS OF INDEPENDENCE

• The cost

• The possible narrowness of the social mix

Independent schools are not compelled to follow the National Curriculum or to take part in national tests at 7, 11 and 14. Depending on your view, this could be either a drawback or a benefit.

GETTING IN – HOW THE COMMON ENTRANCE EXAM WORKS

The Common Entrance exam is used to determine entry to many independent senior schools. It is taken by prep school pupils before they transfer. Girls normally take the exam at 11+ and boys at age 13+ (although it is sometimes taken at age 12). Papers are set by examiners appointed by the Common Entrance Board, but the answers are marked by the senior school for which the pupil is entered. The senior school sets the minimum standard it requires. A school that selects only the most academically able may demand an average pass mark of 65%. A less selective school may set 45% as its requirement.

Candidates are normally entered only when:

- they have already been offered a place subject to passing the exam

- they have to take the exam as a preliminary to a scholarship paper

- they are entered for a 'trial run' where the prep school marks the papers.

Pupils usually sit the exam in their own junior or prep school. The 13+ exam is usually taken in about early June, for entry in September. However, it is possible to sit the exam during other terms. The 11+ and 12+ exams are usually taken in the spring term, but can also be taken in the autumn.

The Common Entrance exam comprises papers in:

English	French
Geography	History
Latin	Scripture
Science	Mathematics

There is an optional paper in Greek.

The Examination Officer Common Entrance

Jordan House
Christchurch Road
New Milton
Hampshire
BH25 6QJ

Tel: 0425 621111
Fax: 0425 620044

GIRLS' PUBLIC DAY SCHOOL TRUST (GPDST)

The 26 schools in the Girls' Public Day School Trust offer a high-quality independent education for 18,000 girls at reasonable cost. Schools range in size from 500 to just over 1,000 pupils. The Trust was set up in 1872 and pioneered education for girls. Tuition fees for schools in the London area are about £1,500 per term, with fees outside London at around £1,300.

Fees are paid to the Trust's head office which deals centrally with most of the administration, allowing schools to keep fees relatively low.

Girls' Public Day School Trust

26 Queen Anne's Gate
London SW1H 9AN

Tel: 071-222 9595
Fax: 071-222 8771

WHO SPEAKS FOR INDEPENDENT SENIOR SCHOOLS?

Mostly they speak for themselves, but many also belong to one or more of the umbrella bodies below.

Independent Schools Information Service (ISIS)
Speaks on behalf of the major associations of independent schools.

201

FACT FILE

There are about 2,500 independent schools in the UK and Eire, educating about 600,000 pupils. This compares with 31,000 state schools educating 8 million pupils.

Although only 7.4% of children go to independent schools, the results they achieve are out of all proportion to their small number.

- Some 75% of children in independent schools leave with five or more GCSEs. In state schools the figure is 24%.

- The number of children leaving independent schools with one or more A-levels is 65%. In state schools the figure is 14%.

Headmasters' Conference (HMC)
Represents more than 230 boys' and coeducational senior schools, including Eton, Harrow, Winchester and Westminster.

Girls' School Association (GSA)
Represents more than 240 girls' senior schools including Roedean, Cheltenham Ladies' College, St Mary's, Wantage and St Paul's Girls'.

Independent Schools Association Incorporated
Has more than 300 member heads from schools catering for all ages.

Society of Headmasters and Headmistresses of Independent Schools
Has 69 members, mostly with a long boarding tradition.

Independent Schools Yearbook, A&C Black
It is the official reference book of the major independent school associations, and gives details of all their members.

FIRST-TIME BUYERS

Some 40% of parents who send their children to independent schools are in fact 'first-time buyers'. That means a significant part of the sector's income derives from people who themselves have no direct experience of independent schooling. These customers have become increasingly important to independent schools in recent years. Many parents, however, still feel intimidated by the concept of independent schooling. You should not. Remember, schools need your cash to survive. And behind all the imposing buildings, the sometimes bizarre uniforms and quaint customs, most of the heads and teachers are genuinely interested in helping your child fulfil his or her potential.

THE PRICE OF INDEPENDENCE

Does it cost an arm and a leg to send your child to an independent school? The answer is 'yes' unless you are rich, have secured a generous government-funded assisted place, or been awarded a school bursary. The chances are that great sacrifices will be called for if you choose to go independent.

Shocking as it may seem, financial experts have estimated that the cost of putting your child through independent school from the age of 8 to 18 as a boarder could be as much as £200,000. Financial planners Towry Law, which carried out a survey of fees, said that they rose four-fold between 1979 and 1992. The company's divisional director Mr Charles Levett-Scrivener said: 'Ten years ago it would have cost you in the region of £4,000 a year to educate your child at public school. Today that sum can be nearer £12,000 a year.' His report adds that the figures do not necessarily take account of extras such as music, school trips and sports fixtures. Obviously fees for day pupils would be less than those quoted.

- Fees rose by 12.6% in 1990–91, by 12% the following year, and by 8.3% in 1992–93.

- Almost a quarter of pupils receive assistance with fees, either from

PAYING YOUR WAY

school scholarships and bursaries, or from government funds.

The soaring cost of fees, often ahead of the rate of inflation, means that the investment is equivalent to buying a luxury yacht, a rural manor house or a chateau in France. The fact that so many parents are prepared to make the sacrifice dispels only part of the myth that says that a good education comes far behind a house and a car in the priorities of most British parents, particularly English ones, since most of these parents already own a house and a car by the time they spend their money on their children's education.

WHY SO EXPENSIVE?

The answer, say the independent schools, lies mainly in the cost of teacher salaries. The annual census prepared by the Independent Schools Information Service notes: 'Teaching and non-teaching staff salaries are the largest item in any school budget. They account for up to 80% of a day school's costs and up to 60% in a boarding school. A spate of big increases for teachers in the state sector has washed over into the private sector.' ISIS director David Woodhead said: 'Parents usually cite small class sizes as one of the main reasons for choosing independent schools. But small classes mean more teachers. So this, coupled with rising staff salaries and continued investment in buildings, meant fees had to go up.'

WHAT PARENTS SPEND ON FEES

- The parents of a boy born on 1 December 1987, who begins preparatory school in September 1995 and continues his education at a public school, will face fees of £153,373, if boarding throughout.

- For a girl the boarding fees will be £151,308.

- The figure will be roughly halved for day-school pupils.

- In 1970, parents putting their child through a public boarding school faced average termly fees of £225. They rose to £1,200 in 1980, £3,132 in 1990 and £3,665 in 1992.

The Towry Law report says the three 'golden rules' to solve the fees dilemma are:

- Plan as early as possible – and put down an initial lump sum.

- Avoid or reduce payment of tax on the investments whenever possible.

- Use capital, particularly from grandparents wherever possible, to avoid paying more inheritance and income tax than necessary.

GETTING ADVICE

ISIS holds a list of independent financial advisers, insurance firms and accountants who specialise in school-fee planning, and which conform to certain basic standards of good practice and efficiency.

PACKAGE DEALS

Financial planners will usually put together a package consisting of tax-efficient savings accounts, life insurance policies and personal equity plans. Parents pay into them each month and build up a fund gradually over the years. Obviously, the earlier you start your fund, the better. The policies and plans will then mature and pay out at regular intervals to cover the fees each year.

2001: A SCHOOL FEES ODYSSEY

Let us take the fictitious case of John and Jane Barrett. Their joint income is £30,000 a year. They have a son, Dominic, aged five in 1993. They want him to go to an independent school when he is 13, in the year 2001. An expensive day school or a medium-priced boarding school would cost, at current prices, about £2,500 per term, or £7,500 a year. BDO Binder Hamlyn, chartered accountants, worked out a fee-plan using 50% Personal Equity Plans and 50% endowment insurance policies. The calculations assume a 10% annual rise in fees. The plan would mean an outlay by the Barretts of almost £62,700, but would fund fees to the value of £108,000. To cover that sum, Mr and Mrs Barrett would have to pay £515 a month for eight years. But beware, because obviously markets and interest rates change. Couples with two or more children would have to stagger their policies.

TAKING OUT A SECOND MORTGAGE

This seems an obvious solution to high fees, but Peter Lewiston, school fees plan expert at BDO Binder Hamlyn, warns: 'This is an expensive method of financing. Since the interest is not tax-deductable, it is not tax-efficient. It may, however, be the only way to provide for your child's education.'

Independent Schools Information Service
56 Buckingham Gate
London SW1E 6AG

Tel: 071-630 8793

PREP SCHOOLS

WHAT IS A PREP SCHOOL?

Preparatory or 'prep' schools are the fee-paying primary and middle schools of the independent sector. There is a wide range, from the ultra-traditional to the relaxed. They cater mainly for pupils aged 6 to 11 or 13, though some schools also have 'pre-prep' nursery wings attached, which take pupils from the age of three or four.

Prep schools prepare their pupils for the Common Entrance exam, which is the passport into independent senior schools such as Eton, Harrow, Winchester and Westminster. But good prep schools should do much more than that. They should give pupils a rounded education suited to their individual needs, and instil sound moral and social values.

In the past many prep schools were run for profit by the proprietor, who might also have been the head-teacher. Nowadays most are funded by charitable foundations. The image of prep schools as old-fashioned crumbling piles run by tyrannical masters or little more than finishing schools for genteel dimwits still persists, but is wide of the mark in most cases. Today's typical prep is a mixed day school. Some preps now specialise in helping children with particular learning or behavioural problems and the majority have smartened up their act to fit in with life in Britain as it approaches the 21st century.

Unlike state schools, prep schools do not have to follow the National Curriculum, but many have tailored their lessons to cover some aspects of it, incorporating many of its targets. Most prep school heads, however, believe that the National Curriculum is simply the basic entitlement that pupils should expect. Prep schools, they argue, offer much more. Pupils may, for instance, learn French from an early age, or tackle Latin, which many fear is being squeezed out of the state school timetable. Up to the age of nine, children are usually taught by class teachers. Beyond that, many prep schools have introduced secondary-trained specialists to take classes in specific subjects.

WHAT DO PREP SCHOOLS OFFER?

What can you get at a fee-paying prep school that you couldn't get at your local state primary for free? It's the £5,000-a-year question, because that, or more, is what you could be

SEE ALSO:
Paying Your
Way

paying for the privilege of going private. Robin Peverett, for 20 years the Head of Dulwich College Prep in Cranbrook, Kent, and now the Director of Education for the Incorporated Association of Preparatory Schools, said: 'It is up to the schools to prove to parents that they are worth that sort of money.'

A PREP SCHOOL SHOULD PROVIDE:

- good teaching

- classes of 15–22 pupils

- excellent facilities

- an all-round education

- academic opportunities

- preparation for the Common Entrance exam

- a passport to a good public school

- attention to pupils' special academic or behavioural needs.

Prep school heads are pretty realistic about what motivates parents to use the private system, and their consciences are not troubled by charges of 'élitism' or 'competition' that might worry some state school heads. If they weren't realists they'd soon go out of business.

GET ON THE FAST TRACK

If you have set your heart on getting your child into a particular public school, your choice of prep school could be crucial. Links between the preps and the senior schools operate on a number of levels. Some leading public schools, like Haileybury in Hertfordshire and King's Rochester in Kent, have their own prep or junior and, in some cases, even pre-prep schools. Transfer to the senior school would not be automatic, but would depend in part on performance in the Common Entrance exam; though your child would have a head start on the field.

Other prep schools have links with particular public schools that are informal but no less strong. The fashionable Dragon School in Oxford, for instance, sends about 10% of its boys off to Eton each year. Roger Trafford has taken over the helm at the Dragon after a decade as headmaster of Clifton College Preparatory School in Bristol. 'A good prep school tends to feed good senior schools,' he said. There are two main reasons for this. Firstly, the pupils are prepared academically for the challenge of getting through the Common Entrance exam at a level sufficient to gain entry to the senior school of their choice.

'We want them to play rugger at Oxbridge!'
Courtesy Mahood of the Daily Mail

Secondly, the prep school is likely to have established close formal or informal links with the public schools it feeds. By joining a good prep school you are therefore patching into a ready-made network.

Some prep schools are resisting the temptation to put all their eggs in one basket, as they might have done a generation ago. By developing strong links with a number of senior schools, they can point pupils towards those that will best suit their academic ability, aptitude and character.

GETTING TO KNOW YOU

As with many things in life, it is not always what you know, but who you know. Knowing the right people to talk to can be vital, says the Dragon's Mr Trafford. 'It is useful if you know a housemaster or a director of admissions. Personal contact makes a lot of difference. If they know a face and can put a name to it, it can help a lot.' However, you should be extremely tactful and resist overdoing the sales pitch. Pestering housemasters about your wonderful darling child or, even worse, intimating that you will 'make it worth their while' to see your child accepted, will get you nowhere.

WHEN TO APPLY?

Start your research as early as possible. Pupils are normally taken on from the age of six. Those preps that feed highly academic public schools are themselves highly selective. Competition for places is intense and the schools close their lists very early. A good start is the annual *Independent Schools Yearbook*, the official reference book of the main independent school associations. See which schools are in your area and contact a few of the head-teachers to arrange visits.

The biggest prep school body is the Incorporated Association of Preparatory Schools (IAPS), representing more than 500 urban and rural institutions. It is a good source of information.

John Morris
General Secretary
IAPS
11 Waterloo Place
Leamington Spa
Warwickshire
CV32 5LA

Tel: 0926 887833
Fax: 0926 888014

STATE SCHOOL TRANSFERS

If your child doesn't start at a prep school at age six, don't fret that you have left it too late. Many children attend state primary schools until they are 9, 10 or 11, and then transfer across. Some prep schools

find they have to set up an extra class to cope with the demand. Another reason for the boom in transfers at 11, apart from this being a natural break in the state system, is that pupils then become eligible for government-funded assisted places.

CHOOSING YOUR PREP SCHOOL

Above all, it is important to check whether a prep school belongs to one of the official independent school organisations. Though not a guarantee of satisfaction, it does give you an element of security. Member schools in England and Wales are subject to inspection overseen by the Independent Schools Joint Council. Inspections are usually carried out by a former government inspector using the same criteria as those used by the Department for Education. All boarding schools must be inspected by social services and conform to certain standards as part of the 1989 Children Act.

> **❝If a pupil is not particularly academic, the prep school must help that child find talents early enough to let them flower. ❞**
>
> *Roger Trafford, Head of the Dragon School, Oxford*

SEE ALSO: Assisted Places Secondary Schools (Choosing a Secondary School)

WHO'S FEEDING WHOM:
SOME WELL-CONNECTED PREP SCHOOLS

Caldicott School, Farnham Royal, Buckinghamshire

90 day boys, 160 boarders

Tuition fees £1,825, boarding fees £2,490 (per term)

Emphasis on the creative activities makes it a favourite with the arty, theatrical 'gin and Jaguar set', as one head put it. The school sends many pupils on to Radley. Boys also leave for Eton, Harrow, Rugby and Wellington College.

Dragon School, Oxford

340 day boys, 240 boarders

Day fees £1,635, boarding fees £2,595 (per term)

Fashionable school with a liberal regime. Many children of Oxford dons. Many parents were themselves pupils. The school prepares pupils for all major public schools, with about 10% going on to Eton.

Holmewood House, Tunbridge Wells, Kent

460 girls and boys

Day fees £1,300, boarding fees £2,744 (per term)

Feeds The King's School, Canterbury.

Ludgrove, Wixenford, Wokingham, Berkshire

187 boys

Fees £2,525 (per term)

Small and select, Ludgrove's pupils have included Prince William and Prince Harry. Set in 130 acres of its own grounds, it prepares boys for a variety of top public schools.

Packwood Haugh, Shropshire

86 girls, 190 boys, mainly boarding

Day fees £1,675, £2,160 boarding fees (per year)

Feeds Shrewsbury and Malvern College, Moreton Hall for girls and is well represented at Eton, Harrow and Wycombe Abbey.

St Paul's Preparatory School (Colet Court), London

370 day boys, 30 boarders

Tuition fees £5,730, boarding fees £3,270 (per year)

Known almost universally as Colet Court, this exclusive and highly academic prep school prepares boys on a fast-track for St Paul's School.

Sunningdale School, Berkshire	*The Pilgrims' School,* Winchester, Hampshire
120 boarders	75 day boys, 90 boarders
Fees £1,950 no extras (per term)	Day fees £4,800, £6,555 boarding fees (per term)
Exclusive school that has prepared many boys, including Prince Michael of Kent for Eton, also Harrow, Stowe and Radley.	Very close links with Winchester College, the headmaster of which is on the governing body.

CHECKLIST FOR PREP SCHOOLS

- Is it affiliated to one of the official independent school associations, such as IAPS?

- Are there 'hidden extras' in the fees?

- Do you like the head-teacher?

- Would you feel happy leaving your child with this man/woman?

- Would you feel happy leaving your child, if boarding, with the housemaster/mistress and matron?

- Does the school combine a good academic record with plenty of breadth?

- Is the school clean, tidy and well cared for?

- How good are the facilities?

- How full is the school? Is there a waiting list?

- Is there lots of building work, expansion, investment?

- Are there lots of sporting, artistic and cultural activities going on after lessons?

- What size are the classes?

- How is discipline?

- Do you like the school ethos?

We have ways of making you learn German

'Guten Morgen', chorus the four year-olds at King's School, Rochester in Kent. The 240 pupils in the pre-prep and prep school receive at least half an hour's tuition in German every day. Practice continues in the lunch-breaks and on the sports field. Headmaster Dr Ian Walker said, 'British school-children stand little chance of competing on equal terms with their peers in the Common Market unless they begin to learn at least one foreign language from the age of five.'

CHOIR SCHOOLS

Though obviously an option only for vocally talented children, choir schools do ease the financial burden of many parents, as 90% of choristers receive some help with their fees through bursaries and scholarships. This assistance ranges from 10% to the full cost of fees.

The vast majority of choir schools are independent preparatory schools. They are attached to cathedrals, college chapels and parish churches throughout the British Isles. The 39 members of the Choir Schools' Association educate more than 14,000 pupils, of whom some 830 are choristers who sing regularly at church services.

Once the domain of male pupils, these schools may now be able to offer your daughter a place: two thirds of choir schools are now mixed.

While girls may be seen in the classroom, it is rare for them to be heard in the cathedral as choristers. There is broad agreement in the choir world that boys' and girls' voices should not be mixed in the same choir. Only St Mary's Music School in Edinburgh has dared to break that taboo, back in 1972. When Salisbury Cathedral formed its first all-girl choir, a special appeal, with opera star Dame Kiri Te Kanawa as its president, was launched to set up a foundation to fund scholarships.

Choir schools usually hold informal voice trials to screen young singers who might feel intimidated by the more formal choir setting. The number of pupils put forward for voice trials has been on the decline, so parents whose children can sing should take full advantage of this gap in the market. Schools also ensure that singing is not at the expense of academic work.

More than two thirds of choristers leaving choir schools at age 13 win music scholarships to independent secondary schools. On average, they go on to achieve 8 GCSEs and 2.5 A-levels. Nearly 8 out of 10 then go on to degree courses in higher education.

The Secretary
The Choir Schools' Association
c/o Richard Moore
Cathedral Choir School, Ripon
Whitcliffe Lane
Ripon
North Yorkshire
HG4 2L

Tel: 0765 602134

Salisbury Cathedral Girl Chorister's Fund
Salisbury Cathedral School
The Close
Salisbury
Wiltshire SP1 2EQ

Tel: 0722 322652
Fax: 0722 323569

Choir Schools Today (the annual journal of the Choir Schools' Association) gives full details of bursaries and scholarships, as well as news. Available from:

Choir Schools' Association
Windrush
Church Road
Market Weston
Diss
Norfolk
IP22 2NX

A list of member schools is available free of charge.

The day of the Dolphin

At the Dolphin School at Hurst, near Reading in Berkshire, pupils wear smart but casual clothes, rather than a uniform, and the girls play rugby, though not in mixed matches. Petty or unnecessary rules are out, and religious education is taught as part of the history and English syllabus. But behind the apparently liberal regime is a stiff academic spine.

Picture by Jonathan Hindmarsh, courtesy I.N.S. and Daily Mail

Graduate specialists teach pupils from the age of six. By the age of seven pupils are expected to have a reading age of at least ten. By the time they leave at 13, many of the 250 pupils are scholarship material for major public schools.

Head-teacher Dr Nancy Follett, a 50 year-old silver-haired Californian with a penchant for fast cars and a passion for rugby, draws on the best British traditions to meet today's demands.

INDEPENDENT
BOARDING

High fees, changing life styles and fashions, as well as parents' own bad memories of boarding school life, have all contributed to the decline of boarding.

FACT FILE

- More than 1,000 schools in Great Britain offer boarding facilities.

- Boarding numbers have been declining for a decade.

- In 1993 boarding schools reported a 6% drop in numbers – 6.7% for boys, 5.4% for girls.

- In 1991–92 full boarding dropped 4.7% among boys and 2.8% among girls.

Prep schools have borne the brunt of the decline. By 1992, the number of pupils in IAPS member schools had risen from 69,000 to 117,000 over 50 years. But the percentage of boarders had dropped in the same period from 50% to just 15%. There are 320 schools that take boarders, and 193 schools that take only day pupils. Mr Trafford, Chairman of the IAPS, in 1992 expected these numbers to reverse in five years or less.

Boarding schools today bear little resemblance to those of the past. John Haden, Vice Chairman of the Boarding Schools Association said, 'Impersonal dormitories have largely been replaced by bedsits or shared rooms by two or three pupils. Rooms are crammed with posters, plants and cuddly toys. Uniform sheets and counterpanes have given way to brightly coloured duvets.'

Of some of the more sinister practices, he stresses 'Beatings, fagging and bullying are things of the past.'

> **❝It is now less fashionable to send children to boarding school. It is nothing to do with the facts. Our schools are immeasurably warmer and comfortable, more caring and happier places.❞**
>
> *Roger Trafford, Head of the Dragon School, Oxford, formerly of Clifton College Preparatory*

THE BENEFITS OF BOARDING

- Parents who move house a number of times can take advantage of the continuity offered by a boarding school.

- Children live and mix together in a strong community.

- Boarding encourages independence and self-reliance.

- Boarding puts children in contact with educators and a supportive staff out of school hours – beneficial to children with special needs.

- Boarding gives children more time to take part in a wide range of extra-curricular activities.

SEE ALSO:
Secondary
Schools
(State Boarding
Schools)

Most pupils live within two hours of home, and their parents are welcome at the schools. 'The old and sometimes harmful gulf between school and home has all but vanished,' he says. Pupils may be either weekly boarders or full boarders. Weekly boarders return home at weekends.

BULLYING, ABUSE AND OTHER WORRIES

A report published by the government and the child protection charity Childline in 1992 showed a continuing need for vigilance in boarding schools.

The charity set up an experimental telephone helpline in boarding schools. It received 10,000 calls in a six-month period, of which just over 1,000 resulted in some form of counselling. Bullying and sexual abuse were the two most frequent problems pupils phoned about.

THE TOP TEN WORRIES BY PERCENTAGE OF CALLERS ON THE BOARDING SCHOOL LINE

Bullying	20%
Sexual abuse	15%
Friendship	9%
Physical abuse	5.5%
Parents	5.5%
Staff	5%
Homesickness or isolation	4.7%
Concern about a friend	4.5%
Sexuality	3.7%
Sexual harassment	3.5%

The happy face of modern boarding schools!

Picture courtesy Millfield School

Following the report, the Boarding Schools Association has asked its 400 members to ensure that:

- the Childline number (0800 1111) is displayed near pay-phones in boarding houses where privacy can be assured.

- schools have arrangements for independent and confidential counselling.

- staff do not put themselves into compromising positions.

- supervision arrangements protect, in particular, more vulnerable children.

- children are reassured that the school takes all reports of bullying and abuse seriously.

- a school culture is established in which bullying is seen as unacceptable to all.

Secretary Frank Bickerstaff
Boarding Schools Association
Westmorland
43 Raglan Road
Reigate
Surrey
RH2 0DU

Tel: 0737 226450
Fax: 0737 226775

THE 1989 CHILDREN ACT SAYS THAT BOARDING SCHOOLS MUST :

- check on suitability of staff before appointing them.

- be aware that pupils may suffer physical, sexual or emotional abuse or bullying.

- have a clearly laid down and recognised procedure for dealing with such allegations.

- nominate a senior member of staff to deal with child protection and welfare issues.

- have an effective and confidential system for hearing children's concerns.

- ensure that all pupils know who they can contact at the school if they feel distressed.

- ensure that pupils also have access to an independent outside 'listener' such as a chaplain, school nurse or doctor.

- ensure that pupils can contact parents, relatives and friends in privacy by telephone without having to seek permission (eg via a suitably located pay-phone).

ASSISTED PLACES

Parents who would like to send their children to independent schools but can't afford the fees should look closely at the Assisted Places Scheme. It was set up in 1981 to give bright children from low income families the opportunity to study at a fee-paying secondary school. Thousands of families, whether hit by unemployment, bereavement, divorce, or are simply suffering from lack of cash, have taken advantage of the scheme in recent years.

At any one time, approximately 30,000 pupils aged 11 to 18 benefit from a private education through the Assisted Places Scheme. At present some 300 independant schools participate in the programme. Each year a fresh 5,700 pupils from England and Wales will begin to have all or part of their tuition fees paid as part of the scheme, which is means-tested according to a sliding scale of parental income. Your own sons or daughters might therefore be eligible to receive free, or at a greatly reduced cost, an education that would normally cost up to £10,000 a year. Scales setting out levels of parental contribution are revised by the government each spring, in line with inflation.

THE SCHEME

A Tory government introduced the plan to replace the old 'direct grant' system which, from 1926 to its abolition by Labour in 1976, had provided a ladder of opportunity to thousands of pupils. These include Labour luminaries like Denis Healey, Gerald Kaufman and Jack Straw, as independent schools take great delight in pointing out. Opinions are divided sharply on the merits and morality of the Assisted Places Scheme. The Conservative party and the public schools claim it gives intelligent children from working-class or disadvantaged backgrounds an opportunity which would otherwise be denied them on financial grounds. They say it also creates a better social mix and helps to dispel the idea that independent schools are the preserve of the rich.

Critics, including the Labour party, which wants assisted places scrapped, say that the £70 million cash subsidies would be better spent on existing state schools. The schools retort that they are actually saving tax-payers' money by educating 30,000 pupils who would otherwise have to be found places in state

FACT FILE

In February 1992, a MORI poll commissioned by the Independent Schools Information Service looked into the backgrounds of pupils taking part in the Assisted Places Scheme. The survey of 3,500 assisted place holders in England, Wales and Scotland showed that:

- more than a third (38%) were from working-class homes.

- nearly two thirds (64%) came from families earning less than the national average wage (£15,000 a year).

- nearly one third (32%) received full assistance with fees.

- 1 pupil in 10 was from an ethnic minority family, the majority of these being Asian.

schools. Some local councils opposed in principle to private education have refused to publicise the Assisted Places Scheme to parents in their own areas, so many parents may not have heard about it.

WHO IS ELIGIBLE?

The Assisted Places Scheme is open to all children, whether they attend a local state-funded school, an independent school or an overseas school run by the Armed Services. However, 60% of all assisted-place pupils must have entered direct from a state-run or Services school. To qualify, a child must be 'ordinarily resident' in the United Kingdom, Channel Islands or Isle of Man for two years before the start of the calendar year in which the award takes effect. Parents applying for places in September 1995 therefore needed to be resident

from 1 January 1993. British parents who work abroad on contract may still qualify as 'ordinarily resident'. There are special rules for the children of workers from the UK and other EC countries moving within the Community, and for refugees.

AGE LIMITS

Entry age to a school is normally 11 or 13, but varies from school to school. The advantage of applying at 11 is that pupils who have been at state primary schools can move at a time when there is a natural break. They will then receive two years' education at a preparatory school, which could make the transfer to a senior independent school less traumatic. Some schools also offer places for pupils going straight into the sixth form, having taken their GCSE exams elsewhere.

MOVING HOUSE?

A pupil who already has an assisted place, but whose family then moves to a different area, can be admitted to an assisted place at another school. Pupils must, however, be the same age as children in the school who entered on assisted places in the normal way.

TESTING TIMES: THE SELECTION OF PUPILS

You should get in touch with the school of your choice at the start of the autumn BEFORE you want your child to enter the school. Entry requirements do vary from school to school and also according to the age of admission. As the vast majority of the 300 participating schools have been chosen because of their academic record, pupils will usually have to sit a qualifying written test. This usually takes place in the January or February preceding entry. Under the rules governing the scheme, a school 'shall not select a child for an assisted place unless it is satisfied that he is capable of benefiting from the education provided at the school'. If your child passes the test and is judged likely to benefit from the sort of education and ethos offered by the school, he or she will be offered a place, subject to the financial elements being satisfactory.

WHAT ABOUT BOARDING?

The scheme offers help only with day or tuition fees, not with the cost of boarding. However, an assisted place may be offered to pupils whose boarding fees are being met in full, or part, from other sources. Some schools are also able to help with boarding fees, although this is discretionary and you must check details with individual schools. You might also try your LEA, but don't hold your breath.

HOW MUCH WILL IT COST ME?

As already mentioned, the amount you pay towards fees depends largely on how much you earn as a family, how many children or dependents you have, and how many of your children take part in the Assisted Places Scheme. First you must work out your family's 'relevant income', and then check that against the contribution tables produced by the government each spring. Schools participating in the scheme have scales of contributions and can calculate how much you will have to pay.

Relevant income is worked out by taking the total income (before tax) from all sources of both parents. This includes any unearned income, such as share dividends, of your dependent children. From this total, you then deduct a special allowance for each dependent child (other than the assisted place holder) and each of your dependent relatives. The final total is your 'relevant income'.

For the year 1993–94 each allowance was £1,125.

Relevant income does NOT include income from:

- child benefit

- mobility allowance

- some other social security benefits

- scholarships or student awards.

WHEN IS RELEVANT INCOME ASSESSED?

Relevant income is usually assessed for the tax year BEFORE the school year in question. So for the school year 1993–94 it was based on income in the tax year 1992–93. Parents must produce evidence such as a Form P60 or a schedule D or E tax assessment.

Special rules apply if you are:

- divorced or separated

- receive certain disability benefits

- receive income from a business with a special accounting year.

WHAT IF I'M DIVORCED OR SEPARATED?

If you are divorced or separated, the parental contribution will be based on the relevant income of the parent who has custody of the child, plus the income of his or her spouse if the parent has remarried.

WHEN DO I PAY?

Parents will usually be asked to pay their share of fees in three equal instalments, one at the start of each term. The amount of assistance is reviewed each year, so once your child has been awarded an assisted place, you will be asked, at the beginning of each new school year, to make a fresh declaration of your income for the previous tax year.

WHAT IF MY INCOME CHANGES?

In cases of sudden hardship the basis on which your share of the fees is calculated can be revised; it can be calculated on current income, instead of the income from the previous year. If your income rises so much that your child is clearly no longer eligible for assistance, there is no need to send in a return. However, this does not stop you claiming in subsequent years if your circumstances change.

YOUR CONTRIBUTION TO FEES IN SCHOOL YEAR 1993–94

RELEVANT INCOME 1992–93 tax year (after allowances for dependents)	One assisted place holder	For each of TWO assisted place holders
9,226	15	9
10,000	87	66
11,000	219	162
12,000	369	276
13,000	564	423
14,000	774	579
15,000	993	744
17,000	1,473	1,104
19,000	2,049	1,536
21,000	2,709	2,031
23,000	3,369	2,526
25,000	4,029	3,021

Parents with a relevant income of less than £9,226 pay nothing towards the fees.
Source: Department for Education

WHAT ABOUT OTHER EXPENSES ON TOP OF FEES?

Children whose parents are receiving income support are also eligible for free school meals and in addition grants may be available for school uniform. In 1992–93 allowances for uniforms were between £38 and £155, if the relevant income was not more than £10,126. Pupils who live more than three miles from school can also get means-tested assistance with the cost of public transport.

WHAT IF MY CHILD IS NOT ACCEPTED?

Demand varies tremendously from school to school. If you fail to win an assisted place at the school of your choice, ask if the school would consider funding your child through one of its own scholarships or bursaries. The school might also run its own financial help scheme. If you decide this is the school for you, whatever the sacrifice, ask whether there is an ordinary fee-paying vacancy. You should also seek advice about a fees

The proof of the pudding

Pupils who have benefited from assisted places:

- Martin Stoddart, 19, St Ambrose College, Altrincham, Cheshire. Brought up on Manchester's Wythenshawe estate, Martin had to endure constant attacks on his home by vandals. With the help of his mother, a single parent and part-time childminder, Martin eventually found stability with an assisted place at St Ambrose where he achieved four A-levels, two at grade A. He has now started a degree in biology at Aberystwyth University.

- Nadeem Akhtar Afzal, 18, Queen Elizabeth Grammar School, Blackburn. Son of a former subsistence farmer from Pakistan, he had all of his £3,336 a year fees paid. He joined the school's sixth form after being educated at a state comprehensive.

plan, which helps spread the financial burden. Almost 20% of assisted places are not taken up. This is partly because the places are tied to individual schools, and are not transferable. So although all the places at your first choice school may be taken, there will be places going spare at other schools. It pays to find out about them.

For general guidance:

Independent Schools Information Service
56 Buckingham Gate
London SW1E 6AG

Tel: 071-630 8793/4

❝The Assisted Places Scheme is in the ladder tradition. It is about opportunity, access to a variety of schools according to parental preference. It is about maximising individual talent and minimising individual disadvantage. That is why we must fight to preserve it.❞

Averil Burgess, South Hampstead High School

How to Get into Eton

Eton College is probably the best-known school in the world and has a reputation for being the most élite, although Henry VI originally intended it to educate 70 boys, known as the King's Scholars. Founded in 1440 as 'The King's College of Our Lady of Eton Beside Windsor', the school has already lived up to its motto of 'Floreat Etona' or 'Long Live Eton'.

Set up for the worship of God and the training of young men in the service of Church and State, its other mission in life has been stated famously as 'to educate the whole man'. To cast an eye down a list of today's 1,270 pupils would probably provide a sneak preview at many of tomorrow's national and world leaders. The number of British prime ministers (19), pillars of the Establishment, politicians of left and right, finance and business chiefs, foreign heads of state, indeed leaders in every walk of life, is unmatched by any other school. Eton has also been a rich source of literary figures, with George Orwell, Aldous Huxley, Gray, Shelley and Henry Fielding all having studied there. It has also had its fair share of villains.

To walk through Eton's cloistered corridors and quad is to stroll through history. Yet while its customs, quaintly archaic coded language and school uniform of black tails and wing collars may hark back to another age, the boys are learning skills for the 21st century. Lessons ranging from technology and computing to business Japanese will ensure that Old Etonians continue to dominate public life.

So, with such a distinguished pedigree to live up to, what chance have you got of getting your son into Eton? Competition for places is, to say the least, intense. Pupils must show the potential to excel either academically or in other fields, and must be judged likely to benefit from the school's style of teaching. The workload can be tough, though the school resists accusations of being an academic hothouse.

However, the significance of family background is not entirely a thing of the past. The sons of Old Etonians will be at an advantage, if only because their parents are familiar with the entry procedure. Inside knowledge of the public school system will also help. As my Old Etonian insider said, 'Even if entry is purely on merit, you will still find that the people who go there will be the people who went to the best prep schools'.

225

> ❛Proponents of the old boy network begin to sound like classic conspiracy theorists; relying as they do on the basic principle that if you are an Etonian you are more likely to give another Etonian a job. Such theorists do not know their Etonians, who must be numbered among the most ruthless and unsentimental products of English society.❜

Godfrey Smith in The English Companion, *Pavilion Books*

It is as well to be aware right from the start that fees are £12,000 a year. All boys are boarders and range from 13 to 18 years of age. Parents should start their quest by writing for a copy of the school prospectus. This sets out the history of the school and details of the entry procedures. Parents who have seen the glossy prospectuses and brochures from other schools might be surprised at the modest presentation of Eton's simple 12-page, closely typed, unillustrated and massively understated effort. But then, Eton doesn't really need to advertise.

Eton boys

Picture by
Philip Ide,
courtesy Daily Mail

ETON SCHOLARS

Broadly speaking, there are two categories of student at Eton:

KING'S SCHOLARS

Known as 'Collegers', they are the scholarship boys, and form the élite academic backbone of the school. There are usually 70 and each has his own room in what was the original college building.

OPPIDANS

Some 1,200 students called Oppidans are housed in 24 boarding houses. The term 'Oppidan' is derived from the Latin for town. It marks the fact that local gentry and aristocrats later sent their own boys to be educated at Eton, alongside the original 70 King's Scholars, but instead of living in college, they lodged in town.

SOME NOTABLE MODERN-DAY OLD ETONIANS

Bamber Gascoigne, broadcaster and author
Brian Johnston, cricket commentator
Ludovic Kennedy, broadcaster and author
Lord Oaksey, racing commentator

Jeremy Brett, actor
Christopher Cazenove, actor
Daniel Massey, actor

Tam Dalyell, Labour MP
Mark Fisher, Labour MP
Lord Grimond, former Liberal leader
Lord Hailsham, former Lord Chancellor
Rt Hon Douglas Hurd, Foreign Secretary
Lord Thorneycroft, former Chairman of the Conservative Party
Jeremy Thorpe, former Liberal leader
Rt Hon William Waldegrave, Conservative Cabinet Minister

Sir James Goldsmith, international tycoon
Sir Simon Hornby, Chairman of W H Smith
John Menzies, Chairman of John Menzies

Sir Ranulph Fiennes, explorer
Humphrey Lyttelton, jazz musician
Jonathan Porritt, environmentalist
Earl of Snowdon, photographer

HOW TO BECOME A KING'S SCHOLAR

About 14 scholarships are awarded each year to those who pass the Scholarship Examination, which is held at Eton in May. Each scholarship lasts five years. Candidates must be over 12 and under 14 on 1 September of the year in which they sit the examination. Parents must contact the college Registrar with details of their son's entry at least three weeks before he sits the exam. There are no other preliminary registration formalities.

The Scholarship Exam consists of papers in English, French, Latin, Greek, History and geography, Mathematics and Science.

General Paper I (questions requiring thought rather than knowledge)

General Paper II (literature, the arts, moral and religious issues)

The school stresses that candidates do not have to take all the papers, so, for example, not having studied Latin or Greek should not deter applicants. Moreover, they did say that '[in] most papers there is a wide range of questions, so that any clever boy has ample opportunity to prove his worth'. Past exam papers costing about £2 per set can be bought from the Registrar, who can also give information about King's Scholarships. King's Scholars have at least half their fees paid, depending on their financial circumstances.

For further information:

The Headmaster's Secretary
Eton College
Windsor
Berkshire
SL4 6DW

❛ The Battle of Waterloo was won on the playing fields of Eton. ❜

Attributed to the Duke of Wellington

HOW TO BECOME AN OPPIDAN

Parents wanting to get their son into Eton as an Oppidan must register him with the school between birth and age ten and a half. The Eton List Secretary holds the appropriate form. Once a boy is registered on the Eton List, his parents may apply for entry to one of the school's 24 boarding houses, either when he is four years old, or when he has passed the Guaranteed Place Test at the age of 11. Most parents wait until their son has secured a place before deciding on a particular house. Many old Etonians choose a housemaster with whom they already have some acquaintance. Although the school insists there is no advantage to be gained by having your son's name on a particular housemaster's list, it would do you no harm, while visiting the school, to make the acquaintance of one or more housemasters and diplomatically seek to be entered on one of their lists.

WHAT HAPPENS NEXT?

When they are about 11 years-old, all boys registered on the Eton List are invited to the school for an interview and an aptitude test called the Guaranteed Place Test. Successful candidates will be offered guaranteed places, conditional on them passing the Common Entrance exam.

MUSIC SCHOLARSHIPS

If your son is musically gifted, you might consider putting him forward for a Music Scholarship or Exhibition. They are open to all boys. There are eight Music Scholarships available at Eton. Four are worth half the school fees, and the rest are worth one sixth. But any scholarship can be boosted by a bursary up to full value of the fees in cases of need. Six Music Exhibitions are also available. They do not contribute towards the cost of fees, but entitle the holders, like the musical scholars, to free instrumental tuition.

The Music Scholarship Examination is held at Eton in February and entries are accepted by the Registrar up to 15 days before the examination.

STATE SCHOOL SCHOLARSHIPS

Pupils attending state schools have other chances of getting into Eton, over and above the conventional entry system.

1 JUNIOR SCHOLARSHIPS

Pupils attending state primary schools can apply for one of up to four Junior Scholarships that are awarded annually. The exam, held at Eton each February, consists of an intelligence test and papers in English and mathematics. To sit the test, pupils must be over 10 and under 11 on 1 September of the year of the exam. Entries are accepted by the Registrar up to three weeks before the exam. Copies of past papers are NOT available.

Successful candidates spend two or three years at a selected preparatory school as either day boys or boarders. They will sit the King's Scholarship Examination at Eton and, depending on their performance, will join the school either as King's Scholars or Oppidans. Each Junior Scholarship covers the whole or part of the fees at both the prep school and at Eton, depending on parental means.

2 SIXTH-FORM SCHOLARSHIPS

State school pupils have the opportunity to join the Eton sixth form. Up to four scholarships are awarded each year, after tests and interviews that take place in February and March. To qualify, candidates must be under 17 on 1 September in the year of the test. Entries are accepted by the Headmaster's Secretary until the first week of December. Scholarships last for two years, during which time the holders will study three subjects to A-level.

OTHER SCHOLARSHIPS AND BURSARIES

A number of other options are available for boys who might not be able to go to, or remain at, Eton without financial help. They include the Camrose Bursaries, which are open to all, and the War Memorial Bursaries, which are open only to the sons or grandsons of Old Etonians.

LEARNING THE ETONIAN LINGO

Eton has a language all its own. Here is a key to some of the most common expressions:

'absence' – roll-call or register

'beaks' – masters

'burry' – desk in student's room

'colleger' – one of the 70 King's Scholars, the school's academic élite

'colours test' – initiation of new pupils who must learn house and team colours by rote

'debates' – lower-sixth prefects who help their house captain maintain order

'divisions' or 'divs' – forms or classes

'dry-bobs' – cricketers

'halves' – terms

'library' – upper-sixth prefects who lead by example

'messing' – having tea

'mobbing' – teasing someone or fooling around

'PB' or private business – informal tutorials with a tutor of your choice

'pop' – the school's 21-strong, self-electing élite sixth-form club, known officially as the Eton Society

'reading schools' – free periods

'schools' – lessons

'sock' – to treat someone, as in 'sock me a pint'

'specialists' – sixth-formers

'spongebags' – the checked trousers that members of 'pop' are allowed to wear along with brightly coloured individually styled waistcoats

'tap' – the school's specially licensed pub, which sells beer and cider to pupils aged 16 and over. The limit is two pints per pupil per day.

'trials' – internal exams

'tugs' – scholars

'wet-bobs' – rowers

OLD SCHOOL TIES

There was a time when going to the 'right' school would guarantee you a place as a member of the ruling class and a pillar of the Establishment. But do the 'old school tie' and the 'old boys' network' it operates within still have influence in today's so-called classless Britain? The answer is 'yes', but less than they used to.

A glance through *Who's Who,* the bible of the Establishment, shows how little times have changed. Of the 29,000 entries in the 1993 edition, Eton educated 1,245 while Harrow had 253. Thirty years ago, when *Who's Who* had just 24,600 entries, Eton had a slightly larger share with 1,398 old boys listed. So did Harrow with 367. So, the two schools still account for 1 in 20 names in the book of Britain's main movers and shakers.

However, the Independent Schools Information Service describes the idea of independent schools having an 'old boys' network' providing a passport to privilege and power as 'a myth'. Spokesman David Woodhead said: 'This may well have been true in the past. Times, however, have changed. Entry to the professions is increasingly dependent on graduate qualifications. Those from

independent schools have to compete on merit for jobs in today's competitive labour market.' He added 'As for passing on privilege from one generation to the next, the fact is that at least 40% of the children in the independent sector come from families where the parents themselves did not attend public schools.'

Whether in business, finance, law, politics or the public services, the right school tie may no longer guarantee you a place at the top, but it can give you a valuable head start, for example by encouraging a prospective employer to come down in your favour when you've reached the short list.

Tim Devlin, a former *Times* education correspondent and co-author of the book *Old School Ties,* contacted more than 3,000 of Britain's most famous and influential names for his research. About 1,800 of those cited had attended independent fee-paying schools, while some 1,300 had been to state schools. But while those who had a state education had been educated at more than 1,000 schools, the former fee-paying pupils had been concentrated in just 369 schools.

SCHOOLS 'BY ROYAL APPOINTMENT'

Where 16 Royals were educated

THE QUEEN	Private tutors	PETER PHILLIPS	Blue Boys Preparatory School, Minchinhampton Port Regis Prep School, Dorset Gordonstoun
DUKE OF EDINBURGH	Cheam School, Berkshire Gordonstoun		
PRINCE CHARLES	Hill House, Knightsbridge Cheam School, Berkshire Gordonstoun	ZARA PHILLIPS	Blue Boys Preparatory School, Minchinhampton Beaudesert Park Prep School, Minchinhampton Port Regis Preparatory School, Dorset
PRINCESS DIANA	Riddlesworth Hall, Norfolk West Heath School, Sevenoaks		
PRINCE WILLIAM	Wetherby School, London Ludgrove School, Wokingham, Berkshire	PRINCE ANDREW	Heatherdown School, Ascot, Berkshire Gordonstoun
PRINCE HARRY	Wetherby School, London Ludgrove School, Wokingham, Berkshire	DUCHESS OF YORK	Hurst Lodge School, Sunningdale
PRINCESS ROYAL	Benenden, Kent	PRINCESS BEATRICE	Upton House School, Windsor

PRINCESS EUGENIE	Winkfield Montessori School, Windsor		Ashdown House Preparatory School, Sussex
PRINCE EDWARD	Gibb's Preparatory School, Minchinhampton Heatherdown School, Ascot, Berkshire Gordonstoun		Millbrook Preparatory School, Berkshire Bedales School, Hampshire
VISCOUNT LINLEY	Gibb's Preparatory School, Minchinhampton	LADY SARAH ARMSTRONG-JONES	Francis Holland School, London Bedales School, Hampshire

Among the independent schools in the survey, Eton easily predominated, with its old boys meriting 180 entries in the list of top names. Next came Tim's old school Winchester, with 52 mentions, followed by Westminster with 39 and Rugby with 38. Tim said: 'If we had carried out our survey 50 years ago, we would have listed hardly anyone from a state school. Slowly and steadily throughout the century, the independent schools are becoming less dominant in turning out the most famous or powerful people in the country.' But, he concedes, 'there are still pockets of old school tie resistance in the officer class of the Army, the civil service and the City'.

The Princess of Wales takes Prince William and Prince Harry to pre-prep Wetherby School in London's Notting Hill

Picture by Steve Douglass, courtesy Daily Mail

Politics has opened up and there are now many state-school-educated MPs on both sides of the House. 'You have to go back six prime ministers to find one who attended public school,' Tim says. John Major, Margaret Thatcher, James Callaghan, Edward Heath and Harold Wilson all attended state schools. Old Etonian Sir Alec Douglas-Home, later Lord Home, was the last fee-payer to reside at Number 10. 'Even Conservative Cabinets are not dominated by ex-public school boys the way they used to be,' he says.

One reason for the loosening of the old school tie could be that many more young people from state schools now go on to university or college, where they mix with students from the private sector. Barriers are broken down and friendships established.

❛I was subjected to pressures I didn't understand and my parents weren't there to talk to. I suffered at boarding school and it would be hypocritical of me to send my children through the same system.❜

The Duke of Westminster in March 1992, on why his son and heir would not follow in his footsteps to Harrow

★ PAUL ROSS ★

OCCUPATION
TV presenter 'The Big Breakfast'

SCHOOLS
Davies Lane Junior School, Norlington Junior High (comprehensive), Leyton Senior High (comprehensive), Leytonstone, East London

SCHOOL REPORT
'A disruptive influence who thinks his dubious charm will compensate for his lack of effort.' Charming!

TEACHER WHO MADE A BIG IMPRESSION
Form teacher Mrs Brewster at Davies Lane, who made me realise I was bright, showed me I had a lot to learn, and cared enough to push me.

MOST IMPORTANT LESSON LEARNED AT SCHOOL
Bright is good, funny is better.

SOMETHING I WISH I'D DONE DIFFERENTLY AT SCHOOL
Forced myself to attend maths classes

BEST MOMENTS AT SCHOOL
English lessons

WORST MOMENTS AT SCHOOL
Maths and physics lessons

SWOT POINTS
Deputy head boy at junior school

EMBARRASSING MOMENT
I was to sport what Ray Charles was to needlework.

QUALIFICATIONS
7 O-levels and 3 A-levels. BA (Hons) in English

CHILDREN
James John aged 12, Dorothea aged 2, Violet aged 1

POINTS TO CONSIDER WHEN CHOOSING A SCHOOL
I want them all to attend state schools because fee-paying schools are socially divisive and expensive. The most important factor is the quality of teaching. The rest is spinach.

MY VIEW OF TODAY'S EDUCATION SYSTEM
Under-resourced, it is kept going by the dedication of the teachers (and parents).

★ GOLD STAR CELEBRITIES ★

Picture by Steve Douglass, courtesy Daily Mail

8 EXTRA-SPECIAL CHILDREN

GIFTED CHILDREN

Your child may be very bright. But is he or she gifted? Or even a genius? Psychologist Dr Joan Freeman, who has made a 20-year study charting the progress through life of more than 200 gifted individuals, has some important tips for parents who think their children are extra special. The whole area of giftedness is fraught with difficulties because experts have differing ideas about what it is. One measure of ability is the Intelligence Quotient or IQ test, but it is not the only standard. Dr Freeman says that, statistically, half of children should be above average ability, the top 15–20% might be considered very bright, about 10% might be considered gifted in one or more areas, and just 2% could be classed as all-round gifted.

THE INTELLIGENCE PYRAMID

A
genius

All-round gifted
2%

Gifted in one or more areas
10%

Bright ——————15–20%

Above average ———— 50%

Geniuses are much rarer. More than just gifted, they can, if their potential is realised, push back the frontiers of knowledge to change our perception and understanding of the world, whether in science like Einstein and Newton, in music like Mozart and Beethoven, or in art like Picasso. Your child may be gifted in one or a number of areas, but, either way, unless this talent is tapped, it will go to waste. Gifted children need the opportunity to express their talents and develop them. All children are born with potential, and it is your job as a parent to ensure that as much as possible of your child's is realised.

IQ TESTS

IQ stands for Intelligence Quotient. There is great controversy about the use of IQ tests and what they really tell you about a child's abilities. In fact, they have been condemned in some quarters for a long time. Critics have argued that they are easier for people familiar with the culture in which the tests were developed. Hence they may discriminate against those from other cultures and classes. In spite of this, they are still in use.

IQ is calculated by assessing a child's mental age from the score he or she achieves in a test administered by educational psychologists. This is divided by the child's chronological age, then multiplied by 100 to round it off

$$\frac{\text{Mental age}}{\text{Chronological age}} \times 100 = IQ$$

Children of average intelligence usually score around 100 and are therefore said to have an 'IQ' of 100. Some 60% of children have an IQ of between 90 and 110. About 10% of children have an IQ score of 120 or more, which suggests that they are very bright. Gifted children will have an IQ of between 135 and 170, depending on the type of test being taken. Membership of the high IQ club, Mensa, requires an IQ of at least 140.

TELL-TALE SIGNS OF A GIFTED CHILD

'Parents are usually the first to spot the fact that their child is brighter than normal,' says mother-of-four Dr Freeman. 'I have great faith in parents' judgements.' She says gifted children show clear signs of being distinctly ahead of their age groups, even as babies and toddlers.

Dr Freeman says the fact that a child can crawl around or walk earlier than normal means the child can experience more and therefore learns more. There is no evidence that gifted children are more susceptible to emotional problems. In most ways gifted children are just like other boys and girls. 'They wake up in the morning, play football, go to school, go to bed,' she says.

Adam Dent

A t the age of 12, Adam Dent won a place at Oxford University after first being taught by his parents and then, effectively, teaching himself. Adam, from Buckinghamshire, passed the entrance exam to read chemistry at St Hugh's College after having already secured four grade A GCSEs at age 11. He is set to join in 1994 after spending a year mugging up his maths and physics. He was taken out of state school at the age of eight, along with his brother and sister, because his parents were dissatisfied with the education they were receiving. His mother Jessie and father Steve found that their son was leaping ahead of the work they set him, and teaching himself from commercially produced GCSE science books.

GIFTED CHILDREN

BRIGHT OR GIFTED TODDLERS OFTEN:

- learn to sit up, crawl, walk, speak and pass other developmental 'milestones' earlier than is usual

- talk a lot

- appear to have an unusually mature grasp of language and argument

- demonstrate lively and enquiring minds

- have an outstanding memory

- have an ability to concentrate on one thing for long periods

- learn to read earlier than normal.

It is a myth that gifted children:

- inevitably get bored

- sleep less than other children

- are smaller than other children

- are less emotionally stable than other children.

INTO THE 'HOTHOUSE'?

There is a world of difference between exposing children to a myriad of stimulating experiences, which Dr Freeman sees as positive, and the idea, imported from the USA, of 'hothousing' children by cramming them with facts and figures for almost every waking hour. 'Those children who have been "hothoused" don't usually end up very well balanced. There is no doubt that children who are hothoused can retain tremendous amounts of information and knowledge. But psychologically it is not very healthy. It depends what you want out of life.'

'DO IT YOURSELF'

If you think your child is extremely gifted, there is much you can do yourself. Parental involvement is probably the most important influence. Take your son or daughter to the library, visit parks, galleries and museums, go on walks into the countryside, read books together and

239

explore the world of knowledge. This is not to say that parents aren't enjoying these activities with their children of all levels of ability. The National Association for Gifted Children also runs 'enrichment' classes to stimulate bright young minds.

SHOULD WE TELL THE TEACHER?

If you suspect your child is very bright but is not being pushed at school, you should indeed tell the teacher. Many parents worry about being branded

Lucinda Cash-Gibson

By the age of three, Lucinda Cash-Gibson had learned to play the violin and piano. By four she had become the youngest member of Mensa with an IQ of 161. Life hit a sour note, however, when she started at her local primary school in Camden, North London. Her mother, Coral, did not believe Lucinda, known as Lulu, was being properly stretched. 'She was not being stimulated. She became distraught, frustrated and bored. She started blacking in pictures. It was a cry for help. At school the teachers said Lulu could not fill in the missing numbers from one to ten. Yet at home, with me, she was doing fractions and multiplication tables.' Mrs Cash-Gibson has fought lengthy legal battles in an attempt to have her daughter's giftedness recognised as a special need under the 1981 Education Act, which caters mainly for pupils with learning difficulties. She said 'I'm doing this for Lulu. But there are thousands of other children who could benefit. Being gifted can be just as much of a disability as being a slow learner.'

Gifted Lucinda Cash-Gibson

Picture by Jenny Goodhall, courtesy Daily Mail

Ganesh Sittampalam

At the age of eight, maths genius Ganesh was celebrating a grade A GCSE. He progressed to a top A-level and crowned his achievements in 1992, at the tender age of 13, by collecting a first class degree from Surrey University. Like a typical schoolboy, Ganesh reads the *Beano* and plays all the latest computer games. Though he has continued with his maths one day a week at the university, he spends the rest of his time in normal lessons with his classmates at King's College, Wimbledon. 'People seem to think that I must love school, but I just think it's OK, like the other kids,' he said. 'Besides, I'm not ahead of them, or different, in anything except maths.' The youngest graduate in modern times lives with his parents, both of whom are keen mathematicians, in Surbiton, Surrey.

Maths genius Ganesh Sittampalam

Picture by Mark Richards, courtesy Daily Mail

'pushy'. But you owe it to your children to ensure that they are getting the level of education necessary to stretch them. Most parents know their own children better than a teacher, and may pick up on things which are missed in the classroom.

SEE ALSO:
Home Alone
Dyslexia

HONESTY WITH MODESTY

'Be honest, but be modest,' says Dr Freeman. Teachers can become very defensive if they feel their profession-alism is being challenged or that they have missed something they should have recognised. So use some tact and diplomacy. Tell the teacher what you have observed. It may be that your child is reading voraciously, or working out all the angles and measurements for your family's latest DIY project. Mention it and ask how this undoubted talent might be enhanced in lessons. Most teachers and schools will be happy that you are taking the interest and keen to do the best for your child.

Not all teachers or LEAs are so understanding, however. Some councils simply refuse to accept that pupils can be 'gifted', equating the term with élitism. The stock response in these cases is: 'All our schools cater for the individual needs of all our pupils.' Some parents have fought lengthy battles in a bid, usually without success, to have their child's high intelligence recognised. If you feel that you are banging your head against a brick wall in this way, call for help. The National Association for Gifted Children has special expertise in counselling. The Schools Psychology Service, which you can contact through your LEA, can also test your child and provide potentially useful evidence to support your case.

Bright as a Button (Optima) and *Gifted Children Growing Up* (Cassell), both by Dr Joan Freeman

National Association for Gifted Children
Park Campus
Boughton Green Road
Northampton NN2 7AL
Tel: 0604 792300

The Schools Psychology Service
Check with your LEA for details of educational psychologists.

Ruth Lawrence

One of the country's most famous child prodigies, Ruth Lawrence arrived at St Hugh's, Oxford, aged 12, to read maths. Her father's intensive one-to-one teaching methods meant that they shared rooms, meals, tutorials and even a bicycle. After graduating, she went on to study at Warwick University.

CHILDREN WITH SPECIAL NEEDS

Parents of children with disabilities or learning difficulties have had a raw deal for many years. The main complaint from parents has been that their children have not been offered schooling appropriate to their needs. Many LEAs have ignored their pleas. Part of the problem has been that the all-embracing term 'special needs' covers so many diverse conditions – from Down's syndrome to dyslexia, and from physical disabilities to slow learning, emotional and behavioural problems. It is estimated that 1 in 5 pupils has some form of learning difficulty; 1 in 50 has such severe learning difficulties that special measures are needed. Your child has a right to an education that meets his or her needs, regardless of any disability or learning difficulty. This includes being provided with the opportunity to follow all the subjects of the National Curriculum to the best of your child's ability.

The government has made clear that pupils with special educational needs should be educated in mainstream schools wherever possible. This principle was established in the 1981 Education Act. Now new legislation in the 1993 Education Act should strengthen parental rights. Ministers announced there would be a new code of conduct governing the service children with special needs and their parents can expect. From autumn 1994 schools must have a written policy on special needs provision that all parents can inspect. Parents of all children with special needs will be able to state a preference for the school at which they want their child taught. There is no guarantee that their wish will be granted by the LEA, but parents can appeal if they are dissatisfied with either the school they are offered or the amount of extra help provided. In the past, frustrated parents who wanted to contest a LEA's decision had to take their case to an appeal panel set up by that very authority, but now a fully independent tribunal will hear such complaints.

If you believe your child needs extra help, there are a number of levels on which it can be given. It may simply involve a period of additional tuition at school. For more serious problems, you, the school or the

PUPILS WITH SPECIAL NEEDS HAVE DIFFICULTIES IN SIX MAIN CATEGORIES:

- physical

- mental

- sight, hearing or speech

- emotional or behavioural

- specifically related to mathematical or language work (such as dyslexia)

- general difficulties covering some or all aspects of school work.

The Department for Education estimates that:

- about 20% of all pupils have some form of special need at some time

- about 2% have been 'statemented'. 1.5% are in special schools and 0.5% in mainstream schools.

LEA may decide that a formal assessment by experts, including educational psychologists, may be the best option. In the event of the most severe difficulties, affecting 2% of all pupils, children are given a 'statement' setting out exactly what additional help the child must by law receive. Such pupils are often referred to as having been 'statemented'. Here are the main steps you may have to follow to get the best deal for your child.

ASK FOR ADVICE

Special educational needs is an area dogged by pitfalls. You will encounter professionals and bureaucrats, not all of whom will be on your side. Mistakes made by you in the early stages of

any process may rebound on you later, and spoil your chances of getting a fair settlement. I would therefore advise any parent embarking on a special needs case to seek independent assistance. Your LEA will have a list of local voluntary groups with expertise in this field. It is also worth contacting the Advisory Centre for Education, an independent educational charity that has a long track record of dispensing valuable free advice to parents (address and telephone number at the end of 8b).

GET HELP AT SCHOOL

If you think your child may need extra help at school, the first step is to talk to the class teacher or head-teacher about your worries. Schools should be prepared to accommodate any child who has learning difficulties. This may take the form of assistance from an extra teacher or helper in the classroom, a period of intensive tuition, a specially designed learning programme, or visits to a specialist centre or special school. Many primary schools have a teacher with particular responsibility for special educational needs, or share one with other schools. Secondary schools may have a special needs unit. For the majority of pupils with special needs, such help within the school may be enough, but for the minority with more severe learning difficulties more formal steps may need to be taken.

SEEKING AN ASSESSMENT

If you fear your child is falling badly behind his or her classmates, you have a legal right to ask your LEA to arrange a full assessment of his or her special educational needs. This request must be met, unless the local authority can show that it is unreasonable. Your child's head-teacher can also request the assessment.

If the LEA wants to assess your child, it must give you prior notice and provide the name of a council official who can give more information. The council must then give you at least 29 days in which to agree to the child undergoing an assessment and to give your own views about his or her needs. If the LEA decides to go ahead with an assessment, it must inform you of that decision and gather information about your child's special needs.

This includes:

- your observations

- educational advice from your child's school

- advice from the local health authority

- advice from an educational psychologist.

It must use the evidence to decide whether your child's needs are such that they require a 'statement of special educational needs'. If the LEA rejects an assessment request by you, or your child's school, you can appeal (see following page).

Attached to the statement must be copies of the professional advice sought during the assessment. You will be sent a draft statement and given 15 days to comment on it before a final version is issued. Once this comes into force, the local authority has a legal duty to provide your child's school with any extra resources required.

WHAT IS A 'STATEMENT OF SPECIAL EDUCATIONAL NEEDS'?

It is a document drawn up by the LEA, setting out what extra or special teaching your child requires. This usually follows evidence from educational psychologists or other experts. Once a child receives a 'statement', the LEA has a legal obligation to comply with it, providing whatever additional help is set down. Each statement is set out in five parts:

Part 1 names your child, and you, the parents.

Part 2 sets out your child's special educational needs.

Part 3 specifies in detail the special provisions your LEA considers will meet those needs.

Part 4 describes the type of school deemed appropriate for your child. The statement will normally name a particular institution, which may be a special school.

Part 5 gives details of non-educational assistance needed by your child, such as home – school transport or physiotherapy. The LEA must arrange for this to be provided.

SPECIAL EDUCATIONAL NEEDS TRIBUNALS

If you are unhappy with the statement your child receives, or you wish to appeal for one of the reasons below, you may take your case to a tribunal.

- Parents have a right to appeal against an authority's refusal to assess their child under section 9(1) of the 1981 Education Act.

- Parents have a right to appeal against an authority's refusal to reassess a child who already has a statement under section 9(2).

- Parents can appeal against an authority that decides to cease maintaining a statement.

- Parents can appeal against the LEA's choice of school.

In all appeal cases, parents have to set out clearly:

- the grounds on which they oppose the LEA's decision.

- what they believe should be done instead for the child.

- why they believe this should be done.

NEW SPECIAL NEEDS PROVISIONS IN THE 1993 EDUCATION ACT SAY THAT:

- pupils with special educational needs should be educated in mainstream schools to the maximum extent possible.

- parents whose children have 'statements' will be given a right to express a preference about which named school their children should attend.

- all schools must publish their stated policy on special needs.

- all 'statements' should normally be prepared within six months, after which time parents can complain directly to the Education Secretary.

- a new independent special education needs tribunal will hear appeals from parents dissatisfied with the result of their bid for a statement.

THE VERDICT

The tribunal works as an independent, informed adjudicator. It has powers to establish the facts in the case and to uphold, dismiss or amend the statement as it sees fit. The tribunal must give reasons for its decision. Its judgement is binding on all parties. If you are still unhappy with the progress of your case,. further appeals against the tribunal's decision are possible, but only on points of law to the High Court.

Where the Local Education Authority is alleged to have failed to arrange the special educational needs provision specified in a statement, complaints will be heard by the Secretary of State for Education. The Minister can then take action if satisfied that the authority was acting unreasonably.

Advisory Centre for Education (ACE)
Unit 1B
Aberdeen Studios
22–24 Highbury Grove
London N5 2EA

Advice line: 071-354 8321

ACE also publishes detailed guidance on special educational needs.

Special Needs Division
Department for Education
Sanctuary Buildings
Great Smith Street
Westminster
London SW1P 3BT

National Association for Special
Educational Needs (NASEN)
York House
Exhall Grange
Wheelwright Lane
Coventry CV7 9HP
Tel. and Fax: 0203 362414

UNDER THE 1981 EDUCATION ACT:

- a child has a 'learning difficulty' when he or she has a significantly greater difficulty learning than most other children in the same age group, or a disability that prevents the child from using the facilities provided in schools.

- a child has 'special educational needs' if he or she has a learning difficulty which calls for special educational provision.

- special educational provision for children under the age of two means any educational provision. For those aged two and over it means anything provided in addition to, or otherwise different from, what is normally provided in state schools.

- a child is NOT considered to have a learning difficulty solely because the language in which he or she is taught at school is different from that used at home.

SEE ALSO:
Dyslexia

★ ANTHEA TURNER ★

OCCUPATION
Broadcaster, 'Blue Peter' presenter

SCHOOL
St Dominic's Grammar School for Girls
(direct grant)

SCHOOL REPORT
'Anthea has excellent social skills.' This was
actually meant to be an insult.

**TEACHER WHO MADE A BIG
IMPRESSION**
My maths teacher was so frightening, she
put me off the subject until I left school and
put £ signs in front of numbers.

**MOST IMPORTANT LESSON LEARNED
AT SCHOOL**
To be a contributor to society

**SOMETHING I WISH I HAD DONE
DIFFERENTLY AT SCHOOL**
I should have concentrated more.

BEST MOMENTS AT SCHOOL
Winning the drama prize and arranging the
best sixth-form dance ever.

WORST MOMENT AT SCHOOL
Every maths lesson

SWOT POINTS
Prefect

EMBARRASSING MOMENT
Went up in the loft with some pals to see
what was up there and got stuck

QUALIFICATIONS
7 O-levels and 2 A-levels

**POINTS TO CONSIDER WHEN
CHOOSING A SCHOOL**
• A school offering a sound educational base.
• A school strong on arts subjects.
• Happy pupils

GOLD STAR CELEBRITIES

Picture by
Michael Floyd,
courtesy Daily Mail

9 GETTING INVOLVED AS A PARENT

PTA AND CLASSROOM HELPER

ACTIVE PARENTS

Many parents do want to play an active part in the life of their child's school, but are not sure how to go about it. There are a number of ways of getting involved, and most schools will welcome your support and interest with open arms. The options are many and varied, from helping out in class to fund-raising, or simply showing a keen interest in your own child's education and development.

Many schools, particularly primaries, welcome classroom volunteers. These parents may listen to children read, prepare the classroom for art lessons and photocopy lesson materials. They are providing a valuable extra pair of hands and often find the experience extremely rewarding.

For more formal involvement, you may consider joining a parent/ teacher association or becoming a school governor. The main point to remember is that you are not expected to be an expert. What is much more important is your help, enthusiasm and common sense.

PARENT/ TEACHER ASSOCIATIONS

Most schools have some form of home−school link. The most common is a parent/teacher association or PTA, though it may not go by that name at your particular school. Other names include Friends of [the school] or simply Home−School Association.

The National Confederation of Parent Teacher Associations represents more than 10,500 such groups, which between them include more than 8 million parents and teachers. Most do extraordinarily good, and sometimes unsung, work.

The big fear most parents have about PTAs, however, is that they will be taken over by a small clique of domineering old wind-bags and prod-noses who will bore the pants off the rest of the mums and dads. In the worst-run associations this undoubtedly happens. The second worry is that the professionals will take over and intimidate the very people they are supposed to be serving, or hijack meetings to set

251

SEE ALSO:
Partnership?

their own agendas. This 'teacher knows best' attitude sends any right-thinking parents running for the hills.

But Margaret Morrissey of the National Confederation of Parent Teacher Associations says the vast majority of PTAs work hard to encourage even the most reluctant parents to play an active part in the life of their child's school. She believes they help foster good relations between staff and parents and organise social events, which often involve children. 'Only on very few occasions do we receive complaints or concerns that parents feel for different reasons excluded from the PTA.'

She urges worried parents to have an informal chat with the head-teacher or the PTA teacher liaison member in advance of any meetings. That way they can deal with their worries, and perhaps meet some of the other parents beforehand.

'We also recommend that PTAs make sure that new members are befriended and not left out. This so easily happens when everyone else knows one another. But it is this lack of thought that makes new parents feel the PTA are a clique.'

Many PTAs in fact tend not to push new members too hard, for fear of frightening them off. But this can be mistakenly interpreted as disinterest.

Mrs Morrissey also stresses that parents who do not wish to become involved in PTAs should not feel guilty. 'The important thing is that parents get involved where they feel most comfortable.'

Partnerships benefit both the school and parents, she says. 'Parents can become part of the partnership of educating their children and know how to support at home the work done in school.'

Fund-raising, while often a valuable part of school life, is not the most important. No association should exist solely for this purpose, says Mrs Morrissey. And fund-raising, when it does happen, should be done with a sense of fun.

For more information contact:

The National Confederation of Parent Teacher Associations (NCPTA)
2 Ebbfleet Industrial Estate
Stonebridge Road
Gravesend
Kent
DA11 9DZ

Tel: 0474 560618
Fax: 0474 564418

Field of dreams

Parents at rural Criftins Church of England Primary School know the value of banding together. They raised £8,000 to turn a farmer's field into a long-desired sports ground for the school's 60 pupils in the sleepy hamlet of Dudlestone Heath in Shropshire. Their efforts even won praise from the Duke of Edinburgh, President of the National Playing Fields Association.

Mrs Angela Spicer, Secretary to the Criftins School Field Trust, said the villagers pledged to buy the one-acre field next to their school when it came up for auction. Then they set about transforming it into an arena for sports, in time for the school's 60th anniversary. It was to cap the celebrations for the school, whose scout hut was used as a chapel by General de Gaulle during his evacuation to the village during the Second World War.

Villagers and local businesses were asked to sponsor parts of the pitch, while sponsored tree plantings and fun runs were held. The local Women's Institute, church and amateur dramatic society all played a part in raising cash.

Broadcaster and writer Gyles Brandreth, Chairman of the National Playing Fields Association and now MP for Chester, opened it in September 1991.

Mrs Spicer said 'We keep reading about the decline of school sport and we feel that in one small primary school something has been done to reverse that.'

The Duke of Edinburgh wrote 'This is a tremendous achievement and everybody involved deserves congratulations. I am sure the field will be appreciated by many generations of pupils at Criftins School.'

Gyles Brandreth and children

Picture courtesy News Team International and Daily Mail

253

BECOMING A GOVERNOR OR LAY INSPECTOR

SCHOOLS NEED GOVERNORS

The power of school governors has increased dramatically in recent years. They are responsible for running organisations that may employ 100 or more people, serve up to 1,000 'customers' a day and have a budget of anywhere between £500,000 and £3 million a year. They also hire and fire staff.

You should be aware of the power and responsibility you would be taking on were you to become a school governor. But you should not let it put you off. The vast majority of school governors are people like you. Each brings with him or her a variety of skills, common sense, energy, enthusiasm and willingness to tackle some difficult issues. Ann Holt, a governor at St Saviour's First and Christ Church Middle Schools, both in Ealing, west London, spearheaded the 1992 'Schools Need Governors' campaign. She said the responsibility

should not be taken lightly, but most reasonably educated people can do it.

Governors must be over 18 years-old and usually serve for a term of four years. Schools and ministers have gone to great lengths to dispel the idea that governors are predominantly white, middle-class, professional, busybody men, and to recruit them from a wide variety of backgrounds. Even so, a government survey of 7,000 governors in 1992 showed that 39% of governors were in professional jobs and 20% were managers or administrators. Nearly 6 out of 10 were men and 98% were white.

HOW MANY GOVERNORS?

The number of parent governors in a school is determined by the number of pupils on the school roll. Secondary schools range quite a bit in size. A school with 600 pupils is considered small, 1000 is considered large and the largest has 1700 pupils. Once schools have more than about 800 pupils, it may be difficult for teachers

THE MAIN REASONS FOR GOVERNORS WANTING TO BE IN OFFICE WERE:

- the enjoyment of being involved in the working life of the school

- the ability to contribute skill and experience

- the sense of achievement, satisfaction or fulfilment

- the wish to serve the local community.

to know all the pupils and children may feel anonymous. An average-sized comprehensive will have about 16 governors, of which one can be the head if he or she chooses.

ELECTIONS

Four parent and four teacher governors are elected by their peers once every four years. Along with the local authority-appointed governors, this group can then co-opt the rest of the body, which must be drawn from a cross-section of the community. One governor, whether elected or not, must have a business background.

Parent and teacher governors should normally be elected, unless fewer parents stand for election than there are places. The governing body elects its own chairperson and vice-chairperson. The full board must meet at least three times a year, but five or six times is more usual. Often work is delegated to committees.

Grant-maintained school governors are initially appointed by the school's

governing body, with subsequent governors being elected. In Church schools the co-opted seats are normally set aside for foundation governors. The term 'foundation' marks the fact that these governors are appointed by the religious or charitable foundation that set up the school.

WHAT DO GOVERNORS DO?

Some people suggest that the governors are like a board of directors headed by a chairperson, while the head-teacher is the managing director. In a well-balanced school, the governors and head-teacher work in partnership, with the governors setting the broad overall policy, and the head responsible for the day-to-day running of the school. In an ideal situation, the governors will delegate sufficient power to the head, and trust him or her to exercise it well. The head should, in turn, keep the governors informed of progress. Difficulties or 'power struggles' can develop if the head and governors fall out over the exact division of responsibilities.

SEE ALSO:
How are
Schools Run?
Opting Out

255

TYPES OF GOVERNOR

Each governing body comprises a mixture of elected and appointed governors.

PARENT GOVERNORS

They are elected by parents and must have a child at the school at the time they are elected.

TEACHER GOVERNORS

They work at the school and are elected by their colleagues.

LOCAL EDUCATION AUTHORITY GOVERNORS

They are appointed by the LEA in schools run by the council. They are sometimes members of political parties or people known for their involvement in the community.

CO-OPTED GOVERNORS

They are chosen by the rest of the governing body, either because they come from a specialist group, such as the business community, or because they have a particular skill. Sometimes they are chosen to widen representation on the governing body.

FOUNDATION GOVERNORS

They are appointed by the church or charitable foundation in voluntary or special agreement schools.

FIRST GOVERNORS

This is the name given to the governors who take over the reins of a school that opts out of council control to become grant-maintained.

SPONSOR GOVERNOR

A new category introduced with the 1993 Education Act, these governors are appointed by companies which agree to sponsor a voluntary-aided or grant-maintained school.

HEAD-TEACHERS

They choose whether or not to be governors.

FACT FILE

- There are more than 300,000 school governors in England and Wales.

- Governors are unpaid volunteers.

- The law says governors must be given 'reasonable time off' by their employers to carry out their duties.

- Employers may give their employees PAID time off, but are not compelled to do so.

If you are interested in becoming a governor, the best start is to ask about elections and the co-opting at your own child's school.

BROADLY SPEAKING, GOVERNORS:

- set the aims and policies of the school

- ensure the school follows the National Curriculum and sets statutory tests

- decide how the school's budget will be spent in line with the needs of individual pupils and within the law

- appoint, promote and discipline staff, including the head-teacher

- ensure the school follows the law on religious education and collective worship

- give outside advice and act as a link between the school and the local community

- decide how the school will be used outside school hours.

Governors also hear formal and informal complaints from parents about a wide range of matters, including the curriculum and exclusions.

National Association of Governors and Managers (NAGM)
21 Bennetts Hill
Birmingham B2 5QP

Tel: 021-643 5787

❝ The days when all a governing body did was to meet once a term to hear a report from its head-teacher are over for good. Governing bodies nowadays wield real power. ❞

Education Secretary John Patten launching the 'Schools Need Governors' campaign in April 1992

257

BECOMING A LAY INSPECTOR

The new private teams of inspectors who monitor standards in the nation's schools must, by law, include one lay member. This is to ensure a commonsense view of what goes on in a school, which will be considered alongside the assessments of the professional team members. In the inspection lay inspectors play a full part, offering parents the chance to take an even more active role in the educational process.

Lay inspectors are defined in law as those without personal experience of managing or teaching in any school. They may come from all walks of life. Early indications from the Office for Standards in Education (OFSTED), which oversees the inspection of 6000 schools a year, described the lay inspectors' backgrounds as 'wide and impressive'. They included consultants, nurses, police officers, small business managers, parents at home with children, auditors and engineers. OFSTED noted 'Many have previous involvement with schools as governors'. School governors and voluntary helpers can become lay inspectors, but not in the schools where they are governors. To be a lay inspector, you must be a 'fit and proper person'; in other words, your background will be checked.

SEE ALSO:
An Inspector
Calls
Information

‘OFSTED will be the finger on the pulse of England's schools.’

Dr Stewart Sutherland, Her Majesty's Chief Inspector of Schools

TRAINING

Training for lay inspectors involves a preliminary session of two half-days in schools, followed by a five-day course. This includes coverage of the 'Framework for Inspection' which sets out what must be judged. The training is tailored to this role.

The names of those who satisfactorily complete the training will be held on a list.

Office for Standards in Education (OFSTED)
Elizabeth House
York Road
London SE1 7PH

Tel: 071-925 6800

★ CAROL VORDERMAN ★

OCCUPATION
TV presenter, programmes include 'Countdown'

SCHOOLS
Ysgol Mair RC Primary, Rhyl, North Wales and Blessed Edward Jones RC High (mixed comprehensive), Rhyl, North Wales

SCHOOL REPORT
'Carol has a masterly hold over mathematical computation which should prove profitable later on.' Class report, aged 8.

TEACHER WHO MADE A BIG IMPRESSION
My primary head-teacher Fred Jennett was totally committed to stretching each child to the utmost of his or her talents. Every pupil left with a minimum reading age of 11 – most with a reading age of 14 or above. He often put a child 'up a year' if they were bright enough, and many graduated to the high school at the age of 10. The majority of children were from poor backgrounds, but many have gone on to be successful professionals or business people.

He was also an extremely strict, hilariously funny, well-loved man who forced us all to say a prayer for Manchester United every Friday in the hope that they would win another match. Slightly tough on those who supported Everton, however.

MOST IMPORTANT LESSON LEARNED AT SCHOOL
That different people have different motivations, talents and circumstances

THINGS I WISH I'D DONE DIFFERENTLY AT SCHOOL
Worked harder and taken slightly different subjects at A-level in preparation for university

BEST MOMENT AT SCHOOL
Collecting my A-level results, knowing that I had done enough to get into Cambridge

WORST MOMENT AT SCHOOL
Trekking down to the playing fields, a mile away, for hockey

SWOT POINTS
Distinctly avoided most swot points

EMBARRASSING MOMENT
Caned in primary school for talking and playing slap-hands. Hiding in the toilets at lunchtimes.

QUALIFICATIONS
12 O-levels (9 grade A), 3 A-levels, Special paper maths, degree in engineering from Cambridge

CHILDREN
Katie, aged 1 year. Undecided about state or independent sector. This will depend on local schools.

POINTS TO CONSIDER WHEN CHOOSING A SCHOOL
Academic excellence • Coeducational • Good technical facilities • Plenty of after-school activities • Not too rough

★ GOLD STAR CELEBRITIES ★

Picture by
Mark Richards
courtesy Daily Mail

10 WALES, SCOTLAND, NORTHERN IRELAND

WALES

Apart from the teaching of the Welsh language, the school system in Wales follows broadly the same pattern as that in England. Education in both countries is governed by the same legislation. In Wales, however, schools are the responsibility of the Welsh Office, and not of the Department for Education which oversees only those in England.

Y CWRICWLWM CENEDLAETHOL

Welsh is a compulsory part of the National Curriculum – or 'Y Cwricwlwm Cenedlaethol' – for all school-children in Wales. Its status in individual schools depends upon whether Welsh or English is the main language for teaching pupils.

In schools where all lessons are taken in Welsh – usually in predominantly Welsh-speaking areas – it joins English, maths and science as a core subject. Where English is the main language of instruction, Welsh is treated as a foundation subject and taught in the manner of a second language – even though it is the country's native tongue.

Some schools in Anglicised areas where Welsh had not been studied before were granted extra time to introduce Welsh into the curriculum. Finding sufficient Welsh-speaking teachers has also been a problem. Inspectors noted in spring 1993 that some schools were slipping behind the timetable.

Pupils over the age of 13 are exempted from studying Welsh if they have not already studied it for at least one of the three preceding academic years. This is to take account of pupils moving into Wales who might not have been exposed to the language.

STANDARDS

As in England, government inspectors in Wales in 1993 reported poor standards in between a quarter and a third of lessons they visited, depending on the subject and whether the school was primary or secondary.

> ❝ In the Welsh language the word for school (ysgol) is the same as the word for ladder. There are those who think that the word for school in English is the same as the word for flattening out; iron, perhaps, or steam-roller might be appropriate. ❞
>
> *Averil Burgess, Headmistress, South Hampstead High School*

261

In the core subjects of Welsh, English, mathematics and science, work is satisfactory or better in more than 3 out of 4 lessons. But there are 'weaknesses' in more than 1 in 4 lessons.

Work in the foundation subjects of Welsh as a second language, technology, history and geography 'is rarely consistently good, and is unsatisfactory about 1 class in 3 overall.'

Another inspectors' report looking at underachievement in Welsh secondary schools (*Achievement and Underachievement in Secondary Schools in Wales 1991–92*) said the heart of the problem was that too many 16 year-olds were leaving school with few or no qualifications: 'The period since the mid-70s has seen an unprecedented level of public and political interest in educational standards.' It said the problem was a widespread perception that many pupils were underachieving and that there were too many variations in the nature, quality and effectiveness of educational provision (Published by the Office of Her Majesty's Chief Inspector Wales).

Welsh Office Education Department
Phase 2
Government Buildings
Ty Glas Road
Llanishen
Cardiff CF4 5WE

Tel: 0222 761456

FACT FILE 1991–92

- Nearly 487,000 pupils are taught by almost 27,700 teachers in Wales.
- The average pupil:teacher ratio in Welsh secondary schools was 15:6.
- In Welsh primary schools the ratio was 22:3.
- Welsh was taught to 90% of primary and secondary pupils in 1991–92.
- In Welsh, 85% of seven year-olds reached or surpassed the National Curriculum bench-mark target (level 2). Almost a third achieved level 3.

NEW FROM 1993

- The school reforms in Wales mirror those in England.
- The Curriculum and Assessment Authority for Wales has been set up to oversee lesson content and testing from April 1994.
- It replaces the former Curriculum Council for Wales and takes over some of the functions previously held by its English curriculum advisers.
- The School Funding Council for Wales takes over responsibility for paying cash to grant-maintained schools and shares responsibility for planning with LEAs in areas where opt-out schools become a real force.

SCOTLAND

Legend has it that the education given to pupils in state-funded Scottish schools is superior to that dished out in England. Certainly, Scots with aspirations have traditionally placed great value on the benefits of a good education, particularly in the state sector. But the image of the disciplinarian dominie (teacher) giving a traditional, no-nonsense but rigorous schooling has taken a bit of a knock in recent years as concern over low standards has grown. Some cynical Scots blame the problem on fashionable Sassenach ideas invading from the South.

Scottish education is quite different from that in England and Wales, and it too is going through a period of reform. A report by Professor Howie of St Andrews University in 1992 recommended sweeping changes in the courses and examinations in secondary schools. This reform was designed to 're-establish the Scottish education system as one of the best in the world'.

ORGANISATION

North of the border, state schools funded by tax-payers are known as 'public' schools, just as they are in the United States. The Scottish Office Education Department has a 'national overview' of the system and offers advice to schools and education authorities. Central guidance comes in circulars from the Scottish Education Department, Her Majesty's Inspectors of Schools and the Scottish Consultative Council on the Curriculum (SCCC).

Education in Scotland has until now been the responsibility of nine regional councils and three island councils known as education authorities. Local government reorganisation may change this.

The authorities are responsible for a variety of educational provision, including special needs, sport and Gaelic in Gaelic-speaking areas. School boards are the equivalent of governing bodies in England and Wales. Opting out, though possible in Scottish schools, has not really taken off in the way that it has south of the border.

CURRICULUM

Instead of the National Curriculum , schools in Scotland follow the 5–14 Development Programme, which is optional, not compulsory. This gives Scottish schools much more flexibility about what they teach.

263

THE FIVE AREAS OF THE PRIMARY CURRICULUM:

- languages
- mathematics
- environmental studies
- religious and moral education
- expressive arts.

THE EIGHT AREAS OF THE SECONDARY CURRICULUM:

- language and communication
- mathematical studies and applications
- scientific studies and applications
- social and environmental studies
- technological activities and applications
- creative and aesthetic activities
- physical education
- religious and moral education.

EXAMS

STANDARD GRADE

The main exam taken at age 16 is the Scottish Certificate of Education 'Standard Grade', which is broadly equivalent to the GCSE. It replaced the more traditional O-grade (similar to O-levels) from 1986.

SCOTTISH HIGHERS

The Scottish Higher is normally taken at 17. The Highers are taken one year after Standard Grade and usually cover four or five subjects. The exams differ from English and Welsh A-levels in that they cover more subjects in less depth. Four Highers are regarded as

roughly equivalent to two A-levels.

CERTIFICATE OF SIXTH YEAR STUDIES (CSYS)

Taken by Scottish 18 year-olds a year after Highers.

TESTING

National testing in reading, writing and mathematics was introduced from 1993 and differs markedly from the system in England. Scottish teachers can choose whether or not to test their pupils, drawing on a bank of tests to check their own assessments. Pupils are graded against five levels, from A to E, through primary school to their second year of secondary school.

Scottish Vocational Education Council (SCOTVEC)

New St Andrew's House
St James's Centre
Edinburgh EH1 3TG
Tel: 031-556 8400

The body responsible for work-related qualifications. It is similar to the National Council for Vocational Qualifications in England and Wales.

Scottish Office Education Department

New St Andrew's House
St James's Centre
Edinburgh EH1 3TG
Tel: 031-556 8400

NORTHERN IRELAND

Unlike England and Wales, where the comprehensive revolution took hold, Northern Ireland has retained a selective school system. Pupils who pass the eleven-plus exam go to grammar schools, while the rest go to secondary intermediate schools. Most schools are divided along religious lines, catering either for Protestant or Catholic children, though some pioneering steps at integration have been attempted. Government studies of performance have shown that pupils in Northern Ireland do generally perform better in maths and English than pupils in England and Wales. However, ministers and teachers are concerned that the number of pupils leaving school in Northern Ireland with few or no qualifications is too high.

REFORM

Many of the reforms that have taken place in England and Wales since 1988 have been echoed in Northern Ireland. The Education Reform (Northern Ireland) Order of 1989 heralded the changes.

CURRICULUM

A full-scale review of the primary curriculum in Northern Ireland was announced in June 1993. This was because of fears that the volume and content would become excessive as the full range of subjects came on stream.

The curriculum comprises religious education and six other study areas. These are:

- English
- mathematics
- science and technology
- the environment and society
- creative and expressive studies
- language studies.

Programmes of study for English, maths, science and Irish (in Irish-speaking schools) were introduced in September 1990, followed by history, geography, PE, art and design, music, drama, modern languages, home economics and business studies.

There are also a number of cross-curricular themes to be woven through the main curriculum subjects. These are:

- education for mutual understanding
- cultural heritage
- health education
- information technology
- economic awareness
- careers education.

265

TESTING

Pupils are formally assessed in compulsory subjects at ages 8, 11, 14 and 16. The idea is that the teacher's own assessments should be backed up by externally-set tests sat by all pupils at age 8, 11 and 14, with GCSE exams at 16. However, in 1993 the government announced an extension for the pilot tests so that 'more manageable arrangements' could be developed. This contrasted with the decision to press ahead with the tests on the mainland, which lead to a boycott by teachers.

ORGANISATION

State education is administered centrally by the Department for Education Northern Ireland (DENI), and locally by five education and library boards. These are the equivalent of the English and Welsh education authorities. The boards are wholly responsible for the schools under their management. Reforms mean that schools now have control of most of their budgets. The board of governors decides how to spend the cash.

TYPES OF SCHOOL

The terms 'controlled' and 'maintained' schools are used differently in Northern Ireland.

CONTROLLED SCHOOLS

Provided by an education and library board and managed by a board of governors, these schools are mainly Protestant primary, secondary intermediate, grammar or special schools.

VOLUNTARY MAINTAINED SCHOOLS

Provided by a voluntary school authority and managed by governors, these are mainly Roman Catholic schools.

INTEGRATED SCHOOLS

Protestant and Catholic children can be educated together if their parents vote in a secret ballot for their school to become integrated. Financial assistance will also be given to parents who want to set up their own integrated schools.

INDEPENDENT SCHOOLS

There are very few independent schools in Northern Ireland. They tend to cater for wealthy parents whose children do not get into grammar school.

Department for Education Northern Ireland (DENI)
Rathgael House
Balloo Road
Bangor
County Down
BT19 7PR
Tel: 0247 270077

★ JAMES WHALE ★

OCCUPATION
Broadcaster

SCHOOLS
Ewell C of E Primary and Longmead County Secondary, Epsom, Surrey

SCHOOL REPORT
A Miss Gentry said of me at age 7, 'James has not quite grasped the written word, but he does speak well which, I'm sure, will stand him in good stead for the future.'

TEACHER WHO MADE A BIG IMPRESSION
The only teacher I can remember is Mr Stone and he shouted a lot. Teachers made me realise that just because you have a certain position in life, you don't necessarily deserve respect.

MOST IMPORTANT LESSON LEARNED AT SCHOOL
You can achieve anything you really want. Whatever your so-called betters say, you must use your own judgement.

SOMETHING I WISH I'D DONE DIFFERENTLY AT SCHOOL
Not worried so much

BEST MOMENT AT SCHOOL
Leaving

WORST MOMENTS AT SCHOOL
My first day and failing the eleven-plus

SWOT POINTS
Nothing at school but I was the under-15 Surrey archery champion in 1965.

EMBARRASSING MOMENT
Being sent home for wearing a green shirt with a white collar, which was very fashionable at the time.

QUALIFICATIONS
None listed for school. Diploma at the London School of Broadcasting in 1969, which was a joke anyway. So nothing really. But I have lied about my qualifications to get a job.

POINTS TO CONSIDER WHEN CHOOSING A SCHOOL
I want all schools to be first class so choice is not necessary.

MY VIEW OF TODAY'S EDUCATION SYSTEM
Not much better than when I was at school. Teachers and politicians must stop bickering and start thinking. Good teachers should be given respect and bad teachers must be removed.

★ GOLD STAR CELEBRITIES

11 THE BIG DEBATES

BULLYING

Bullying exists in every walk of life, but most victims encounter it first in school. It is just as rife among girls as it is among boys, but whereas girls tend to use verbal and psychological weapons, boys tend to be more physical, using actual or threatened violence.

It is too often a hidden problem, but it brings heartache to thousands of pupils every year, and has sometimes ended in tragic suicides. Experts on the subject agree that bullying flourishes most easily in schools that refuse to acknowledge that they have a problem. This creates a 'conspiracy of silence' in which children are frightened to raise the matter with teachers, believing that their complaints will not be given the attention they merit. Getting your mates together and 'sorting out' a bully may be extremely effective in some cases, but it does not always work.

Educational psychologist Michele Elliott, director of child protection charity Kidscape, says that a good school will have a whole-school policy on bullying. This will make clear to all pupils and staff that such behaviour will simply not be tolerated, and words will be backed up by action. This includes not allowing bullying anywhere inside or outside the school, breaking up bully gangs, supporting children who are victims and telling parents if their children are bullies or are being bullied. Teachers sensitive to the problem will ensure that the bully and the bullied pupil are not questioned together, but are seen individually.

Kidscape has produced a range of pamphlets and books setting out strategies for pupils, parents and teachers to adopt in the battle against bullies – many of whom have themselves been bullied at either home or school. Some schools have set up 'bully courts' where pupils, under the guidance of teachers, 'try' their classroom persecutors. Reported incidences of bullying halved in 8 out of the 30 schools that took part in a pilot scheme in 1990. Other schools have adopted 'good-behaviour pledges'.

Unless they are stopped at school, many bullies carry their anti-social behaviour on into adult life by bullying at work or in their own homes. Some will drift into criminality or find it difficult to sustain relationships. Often the root problem is low self-esteem and a sense of inadequacy that leads to an attempt to over-compensate. Michele Elliott said, 'Children who are worried about being bullied or who see their friends being bullied have a hard time concentrating on learning. Children who are bullies are seldom our best pupils.'

All schools have a duty to ensure good behaviour among pupils. A range of anti-bullying strategies, developed by the Scottish Council for Research in Education, has already been made available in English and Welsh schools. Ministers have also funded a £175,000 research programme, at Sheffield University, aimed at helping schools beat the bullies.

SIGNS OF POSSIBLE BULLYING

Michele Elliott and Kidscape have drawn up a number of tell-tale signs for spotting bullying in its early stages and practical responses for dealing with the problem.

Your child may be a victim of bullying, if he or she:

- is reluctant to go to school.

- starts doing badly at school.

- returns home regularly with damaged clothes or books.

- becomes withdrawn, distressed or stops eating.

- appears to 'lose' pocket money or dinner money or begins stealing cash (to pay the bully).

- has nightmares or cries at bedtime.

- has unexplained cuts, bruises or scratches.

- refuses to say what is wrong.

- gives improbable answers to your questions.

You can help by:

- being aware of the symptoms.

- asking your child directly if he or she is being bullied.

- taking the problem seriously and discussing it openly with your child.

- talking to the teacher or head-teacher.

- helping your child practise strategies to cope with bullying, such as shouting 'No', walking with confidence and, as a last resort, running away.

- talking to parent governors at the school about beefing up the policy on bullying and bringing the subject out into the open.

- arranging to meet your child, if the bullying is happening on the way to or from school.

- considering whether self-defence lessons would help your child feel more confident.

- making sure your child is not attracting the intolerance of others because of an unpleasant habit such as spitting or nose-picking.

Pupils can help themselves by:

- telling an adult they trust.

- reminding themselves they don't deserve it.

- getting their friends together to confront the bully.

- staying in large groups.

- trying to ignore it and not showing they are upset.

- learning to be more assertive – by practising shouting 'No' in front of a mirror.

- remembering that fighting may make it worse.

- taking self-defence lessons.

TAKING BULLIES IN HAND

Pupils keen to banish bullying from the playground queued up to sign good-behaviour pledges at Westbourne First School in Manningham, Bradford. Staff became aware there was a problem when the subject began to crop up in children's essays and poems. The pledge, drawn up by staff, reads: 'I have signed my name below to say that I will not become involved in gangs or bullying at Westbourne.' Children caught bullying are punished by being made to hold a teacher's hand for a week in the playground. Second-time offenders must hold a teacher's hand out of lesson-time inside school for the same duration.

Kidscape
152 Buckingham Palace Road
London SW1W 9TR

Tel: 071-730 3300
Fax: 071-730 7081

DYSLEXIA

Dr Harry Chasty, Director of the Dyslexia Institute, defines the condition as an organising disability that impairs manual skills, short-term memory and perception. This inhibits an individual's ability to master the three Rs, particularly reading, writing and spelling. The problem occurs regardless of the intelligence of the child or adult. It is interesting to note that 75% of dyslexics are male. Famous dyslexics include actress Susan Hampshire, politician Michael Heseltine, Olympic swimmer Duncan Goodhew and architect Richard Rogers.

Intense debate still surrounds the subject. Some LEAs and educationalists refuse to recognise it as a condition and others remain sceptical. That is why it is sometimes referred to as a 'specific learning difficulty' rather than dyslexia. Some experts believe the disorder may be genetic, as it appears to run in families. Child development and education may also play a part.

Research in the United States suggests that abnormalities in the arrangement of nerve cells, combined with the way the right and left sides of the brain function, conspire to 'short-circuit' the brain and scramble its ability to decode signals. The result is that a child attempting to say or write 'roller-skate' may instead produce 'skate roller'.

SPOTTING DYSLEXIA

The Dyslexia Institute says the following may be early symptoms of dyslexia:

- being bright in some areas but having 'blocks' in others.

- being uncertain which hand to use for eating.

- having difficulty dressing, including putting on clothes in the wrong order or having problems with buttons or laces.

- using spoonerisms such as par cark.

- having difficulty reciting nursery rhymes.

6 Parents will have to struggle for their dyslexic child. But early identification and intervention give the best hope of success. 9

Martin Turner, Principal Psychologist at the Dyslexia Association

FACT FILE

- About 1 person in 25 shows signs of serious dyslexia.

- It is four or five times more common in boys than girls.

- It appears to be hereditary.

If, in addition, your child is slow to crawl, walk or talk, you might be well advised to seek help.

Between the ages of 7 and 11 symptoms include:

- difficulties with reading or spelling.
- putting figures and letters the wrong way round, such as 16 for 61, b for d, or 'was' for 'saw'.
- reading a word correctly and then getting stuck with it later on the page.
- confusing left and right.
- poor concentration for reading and writing.
- being able to answer questions verbally but having difficulty writing them down.
- being unusually clumsy.

From age 11 to adulthood signs can include:

- poor and inaccurate reading.
- poor spelling.
- difficulty taking notes, planning and writing essays or reports.
- confusion with opposites like 'on' and 'off', or 'under' and 'over'.

HOW TO HELP

If in doubt, it is worthwhile seeking professional advice from your school, the LEA, a qualified educational psychologist or a recognised body like the Dyslexia Institute. You can ask to have your child assessed.

Children can be taught strategies to help overcome their 'word-blindness' problems. Experiments with tinted overlays on spectacles have shown some success, for example. You can also help your child by giving him or her confidence and encouraging speech with all activities such as washing and dressing. Developing a beat or rhythm by clapping, tapping or clicking fingers helps link what children do with what they hear, see, say and understand. 'Simon Says' and nursery rhyme games also reinforce the linking of words to actions.

The Dyslexia Institute
113 Gresham Road
Staines
Middlesex
TW18 2AJ

Tel: 0784 463851

British Dyslexia Association
98 London Road
Reading
Berkshire
RG1 5AU

Tel: 0734 668271

SEE ALSO:
Children with
Special Needs

EXCLUSIONS

Pupils have been expelled for bad behaviour as long as there have been schools. Today, however, the jargon used to describe this process is 'exclusion'. Ministers and teachers have expressed alarm at the dramatic rise in the number of pupils being excluded in recent years. This is partly because schools, whose budgets are tied to the number of pupils they attract, are less willing to put up with disruptive children who might interfere with the education of others and drag down the school's reputation. There are conflicting views about whether such a hardline policy is a good or a bad thing. Consider the following imaginary situation:

Bash Street School excludes lots of pupils. Is that a bad sign, because it means the school has lots of unruly pupils? Or is it a good sign, because it means Bash Street is taking a firm line on discipline and will not stand for any

> **❝The reason why we are so oversubscribed and others are not, may be because they do not exclude pupils.❞**
>
> *Roger Perks, Headmaster, Baverstock grant-maintained school, Birmingham*

nonsense? Grange Hill, by contrast, excludes very few pupils. Is that a good sign, because it means there is little trouble? Or is it a bad sign because it means the school is letting disruptive pupils get away with murder?

Only the head-teacher can exclude a pupil, and pupils should be aware of the sort of behaviour likely to lead to exclusion. What is considered and exclusion offence can vary dramatically from school to school, although exclusion should be for only the most serious misdemeanours. Parents can appeal against their child's exclusion if they feel it is unjustified.

THE TWO TYPES OF EXCLUSION

FIXED-TERM EXCLUSION

This can be up to 15 days in any one term to give schools flexibility in dealing with difficult or disruptive pupils. It could be a single five-day exclusion, extended up to 15 days, or a series of short fixed-period exclusions.

PERMANENT EXCLUSION

The pupil is not allowed back to the school at all. Only in the case of permanent exclusion is the pupil struck off the school roll.

'SIN BINS'

Pupils who are excluded may be taught at home, at another school, or in serious cases, at a special 'pupil referral unit' set up by the local council. These units, nicknamed 'sin bins' because they deal with the most disruptive pupils, offer a broad and balanced education, but will not follow the National Curriculum. They will, however, seek to prepare pupils for return to mainstream schools or for entry into the world of work.

Ministers have made it clear that they believe there are too many exclusions, that the sanction should be used only as a last resort and that excluded pupils should be returned to mainstream schools as soon as possible. They are also disturbed that Afro-Caribbean pupils appear to be excluded proportionately four times as often as other children. The government therefore wants schools to develop early intervention strategies to keep pupils in school and to make exclusion procedures clearer to pupils, parents and teachers. It also wants to help schools develop strategies for the early identification of the minority of pupils with emotional and behavioural problems, so that they can be helped before disciplinary measures are necessary.

THE 1993 EDUCATION ACT:

- abolished the category of 'indefinite exclusion' on the grounds that it was too open-ended, leaving pupils and parents hanging on in uncertainty.

- puts a duty upon LEAs to find alternative education for pupils who are excluded.

- allows LEAs to operate 'pupil referral units' to educate excluded children.

- attempts to give schools an incentive to persevere with troublesome children by reducing per capita funding as pupils are permanently excluded.

- sets general time limits on the operation of exclusion procedures.

The new provisions are timetabled to begin from September 1994.

APPEALS

Parents can appeal against a head-teacher's decision. Appeals are normally heard by the governing body or one of its committees. Allegations must be put in writing and there must be a chance to respond to the charges. The appeal panel must listen to both sides of the story, with both parties able to respond to, or contradict, the other side's claims. The head-teacher must leave the appeal hearing after giving evidence and should not be present during the governors' deliberations. If you are still not satisfied, you can seek a judicial review of the decision in the High Court, although this will require professional legal advice, which could be costly.

A recent survey noted that decisions taken to exclude a pupil are rarely overturned on appeal. Of the 6,743 permanent exclusions ordered over two years by head-teachers, only 330 were reversed, 170 by LEAs and 160 by governors. Some 213 parental appeals were lodged, of which only 37 were successful.

Of those pupils permanently excluded:

- 45% were said to be receiving home tuition.

- 30% secured a place in another mainstream school.

- 19% were sent to special units.

- 6% went to a special school or changed special school.

FACT FILE

Research on exclusions carried out for the Education Department over the two years from 1990 to 1992 shows that:

- a total of 6,743 permanent exclusions were reported over the period.

- exclusions in primary schools accounted for 13.5% of the total.

- pupils with statements of special educational needs accounted for 12.5% of the total in year one and 15% in year two.

- many more boys than girls were excluded; the ratio was 4:1 in the first year, rising to 5:1 in the second.

- 15 was the peak age for exclusions for both boys and girls.

- Afro-Caribbean pupils, who make up about 2% of the pupil population, accounted for between 8.1% and 8.5% of the exclusions.

FITNESS

Concern about the performance of the nation's sports stars often turns to worries about the fitness of the nation's children. Although physical education is a compulsory National Curriculum subject, many pupils would rather be excused games. The abandonment of competitive individual sport in some schools in the 1960s and 1970s is often cited as a root cause of Britain's current lack-lustre sporting performance in the world arena.

Middle-class children are the least fit for school sport according to one study of primary school pupils. Despite far greater access to expensive sports facilities than poorer working-class children, they prefer to spend their time playing computer games or watching television. Children from poorer and ethnic areas, who were found to be generally fitter, also find the whole idea of exercise a bore. The result is a new generation of unfit 7–11 year-olds who fail, or come close to failing, standard fitness tests for children. Many pupils are so out of condition that they can't even take part in basic playground games like skipping, running and hop-scotch, the report said.

The two-year study was carried out by education chiefs in Peterborough, Cambridgeshire, who monitored the fitness of children aged between 7 and 11, after concern about reduced levels of exercise over the previous 10 – 15 years. The project received £30,000 funding from the Sports Council, which said it was alarmed by the findings. Children from seven of the city's junior schools were put through a rigorous test involving running, jumping and throwing. Most found it too difficult. Study leader Chris Blackshaw said: 'We need to get back to basics. These children could be our sports stars of tomorrow.' He believes his report may have national implications on how sport is taught in schools up and down the country. 'It will mean redefining the PE curriculum', he said. 'The majority of PE in schools is very limited: apparatus, netball and rounders with no enthusiasm introduced into it.'

Youngsters in Peterborough have been encouraged to take up more novel sports like short tennis and kwik cricket to keep them interested. The study has been so successful that fitness rates in the seven test schools have already been raised and the project will be extended to Peterborough's remaining 50 primary and special schools. 'It takes about a year to get a child who is sub-standard back to proper fitness', said Mr Blackshaw.

HEAD-LICE

LICE TO SEE YOU

Many myths abound about head-lice. But the reality is that no one is immune from the odious little creatures. Even Prince William's exclusive London school was hit by an outbreak of lice. Though the traditional school visit of the 'nit-nurse' has been gradually abandoned in favour of giving parents information, most adults are still prone to panic when the topic of lice rears its ugly head. Yet the school is not the most likely source of the problem. In fact, the incidence of head-lice is biggest at the start of the autumn term. During the long summer holiday children often come into contact with new people and are susceptible to their bugs. Cuddles with adults – including elderly family members – can be responsible. The peak ages for infection are about six and seven.

> 6 When head-lice appear, schools panic and they panic the parents. We are not dealing with epidemics of head-lice, but of head-lice hysteria. 9

Dr John Maunder, Director of Medical Entomology at Cambridge University

Regular checks with a fine comb can help spot the problem. But you have to be extremely thorough and know what you are looking for. And washing and combing will only get rid of the elderly louse. Commercial louse creams will be needed to kill the egg infestation.

Louse expert Dr John Maunder, Director of Medical Entomology at Cambridge University, is fascinated by the insects he has studied for more than 20 years. 'Some people can't stand lice,' he says. 'But after studying them for so long, they start to grow on you.' Yet lice, nits, dickies or whatever you choose to call them, are no joke if you catch them, or live in fear of catching them, he concedes.

20 THINGS YOU NEVER KNEW ABOUT HEAD-LICE BUT WERE ITCHING TO LEARN

1   The average male louse has sex 24 times a night. Female lice outnumber males by 3 to 1 and mate before each egg-laying. As they lay eight eggs a night, each male must perform 24 times. As

Dr Maunder noted, 'You can always tell a male louse by the look on his face'.

2 The biggest lice grow to 3 mm long, the size of a match-head. The six-legged insects can't jump or fly, and have difficulty walking on flat surfaces.

3 The parasites move from one person to another by walking along hairs during head-to-head contact.

4 Most lice are dead within a fortnight, though one 'super-louse' hand-reared in a laboratory lasted 66 days. The female can lay up to 200 eggs in her lifetime.

5 Lice eggs are called 'nits'. A louse is not a nit, even though lice are popularly, but incorrectly, called nits.

6 A louse can change colour once to camouflage itself in hair from blond to black.

7 About 750,000 people a year are infected by lice, half of them adults, estimates Dr Maunder.

8 Despite the stigma attached to catching lice, the insect is actually more attracted to clean, frequently washed hair than to dirt.

9 Grandparents are a more likely source of lice than school chums.

Unlike children, adults are often desensitised to the bites of these blood-sucking insects, and are less likely to itch or scratch. Older people don't notice they are carriers and unwittingly pass on their lice to children who then display symptoms of infection in schools while the source remains hidden.

10 Tracing adult lice carriers is more important than treating individual pupils in schools, and has a bigger impact in stemming infections, says Dr Maunder. The policy has led to a dramatic decrease in lice outbreaks over the last decade.

11 Research by Dr Maunder and his team saves the NHS about £10 million a year by reducing the number of infections, he says.

12 Britain is one of the least lousy countries in the world because of the success in tracing carriers.

13 Blood-sucking lice do not generally carry serious diseases.

14 The louse has worked its way into the English language. While sucking blood from the scalp, lice inject saliva into the bloodstream which, over time, will make the person feel out of sorts or 'lousy'. If this malady affects a pupil's work, he may be described as a 'nitwit'. Anyone who is particularly fussy

may be accused of 'nit-picking'. Over time, thousands of eggs or 'nits' can become glued to hair. Running one's hand through these empty eggshells gives a rough sensation as the fingers get down to the 'nitty-gritty'. Scottish poet Robert Burns immortalised the creature with his *Ode to a Louse*.

15 People with short hair are more likely to catch lice than those with long hair. Scientists have discovered that lice spread during head-to-head contact lasting long enough for the rubbing hairs to warm up. Short hairs warm up faster than long hairs.

16 Lice develop a pressure of 40lbs per square inch – twice that of a car tyre – when injecting anti-blood clotting saliva into their victims.

17 A louse cream is better than a louse shampoo for killing the eggs, says Dr Maunder. The cream, available for a few pounds from chemists, should be left on for at least two hours, but preferably for 12 hours.

18 There are up-market and down-market louse creams. The latter smell more. Some people, however, don't think a cream is working unless it smells. The louse lotion of the aristocracy is Derbac. It is also used for other parasites and is an anagram of 'de-crab'.

19 Tell-tale warning signs of louse infection are dirtier than normal pillows and shirt collars. Louse waste resembles a black and gritty fine powder.

20 After receiving about 10,000 bites, victims set up an allergic reaction to chemicals in the louse's saliva, which includes a local anaesthetic and an anti-blood clotting substance. By the time you start scratching, you will have had head-lice for at least six weeks, and possibly for three months.

RESOURCES

A 15-minute video called 'Let's Lose Lice' has been produced by the Royal Society of Medicine, 1 Wigmore Street, London.

A Bug Busting Pack including advice on how to detect lice is available from Community Hygiene Concern, PO Box 1233, Weymouth, DT3 4YE at £9.95.

The Louse Watch Helpline can be contacted on 081-341 7167.

RE AND COLLECTIVE WORSHIP

Religious education has been compulsory in state schools since 1944, but parents do have the right to withdraw their children from lessons. It is an area that demands great sensitivity from parents and teachers, as each individual's beliefs may differ markedly in what is becoming an increasingly diverse society.

The role of religious education was strengthened substantially in the 1988 Education Reform Act and then tightened up again in the 1993 Education Act. The latter changes followed concern expressed by government ministers, Christian groups and parents about some schools and local councils flouting the law in the way they teach religious education.

The 1988 Education Reform Act says RE lessons must 'reflect the fact that the religious traditions in Great Britain are in the main Christian', whilst taking account of the teachings and practices of the other principal religions represented in this country. Government ministers have made clear that the subject should be seen as an ideal vehicle for teaching pupils certain 'moral absolutes', such as the difference between right and wrong. This has provoked much philosophical, religious and political debate.

RELIGIOUS EDUCATION:

- Schools must provide RE lessons for all pupils aged 4 to 18.

- RE lessons must reflect Britain's mainly Christian culture.

- They must take account of the teachings and practices of the other principal religions represented in Great Britain.

- Parents have the right to withdraw their children from RE lessons.

- RE lessons must not seek to convert pupils to the doctrines of any particular religion or denomination.

Schools under the control of the LEA must follow an agreed syllabus drawn up by a conference of teachers, church leaders, representatives of other faiths and councillors. They are helped by a local Standing Advisory Committee on Religious Education, or SACRE, which is similarly composed. Church schools offer RE as laid down in their own trust deeds, which are usually in accordance with the beliefs of their particular denomination or faith.

'WITH GOD ON OUR SIDE'

The problem was that by 1992 some two thirds of local authorities had still not revised their RE syllabuses to comply with the 1988 legislation. And there was more trouble: Christian campaigners decried some of those that had been revised as being totally inadequate. They pointed to one syllabus that failed to mention either God or Jesus Christ, and accused others of putting the study of witchcraft, occultism and communism on the same level as Christianity.

PRAISE THE LORD... PASS THE AMMUNITION

Behind the controversy lies a polarisation of belief about how religious education should be taught. This has led to vicious verbal battles, with all participants seeking ammunition

'And now for our plan to put Christianity back in the classrooms... let us pray for a miracle!'
Courtesy Mahood of the Daily Mail

with which to attack their opponents. Some academics and church leaders favour a thematic approach in which pupils might compare and contrast what happens in a range of religions by looking at subjects such as prayer, belief systems and festivals. Critics say this approach too often neglects the legal requirement that lessons reflect the mainly Christian nature of British

THE 1993 EDUCATION ACT:

- compels LEAs to speed up the drafting of agreed syllabuses setting out how RE in each area should be taught.

- allows grant-maintained schools to choose a syllabus from any area – not just its own.

society and puts too great an emphasis on non-Christian religions, and even atheism.

It was largely in response to these concerns that the government tightened up the legislation, forcing the 2 out of 3 LEAs that had not already done so to revise their agreed syllabuses. The new legislation also allowed grant-maintained schools, which had opted out of council control, to choose an agreed syllabus from anywhere in the country, rather than being forced to adopt the one developed in its own locality. Go-it-alone schools now have greater freedom to choose a religious education syllabus that fits in with their ethos.

COLLECTIVE WORSHIP

It used to be known as morning assembly. In most schools that is still the traditional and most convenient time for it to take place, but in some schools morning assembly has all but disappeared. The 1988 Education Reform Act requires that daily acts of collective worship in schools must be 'wholly or mainly of a broadly Christian character'. However, schools can apply to have this requirement lifted if they believe it is not suitable because of the religious backgrounds of the pupils. This could, for instance, be the case in an area where the majority of children are Moslems or Hindus. Schools can seek exemption by putting their case to the local Standing Advisory Council on Religious Education (SACRE) to ask for what is technically termed a 'determination'.

GOVERNMENT GUIDELINES

Guidelines issued in 1991 say the content of an agreed syllabus should:

- be based on the traditions, practices and teaching of Christianity and other principal world religions.

- extend into wider areas of morality and the way religious beliefs and practices affect people's lives.

- have regard to the national, as well as the local, population.

Thou shalt not forget the Ten Commandments

S chools are still failing to teach pupils the Lord's Prayer and the Ten Commandments, according to a survey by Christian campaigners. They observed that the Bible is rarely read in class. Even in some Church schools few pupils have studied the Apostle's Creed, and many could not name the parts of the Holy Trinity. Many pupils were unable to name even six of the Ten Commandments and few children had read or studied Psalm 23, the Lord is my Shepherd, or had read the gospels of Matthew, Mark, Luke and John. Most did, however, know that Jesus was born on Christmas Day, was crucified on Good Friday and rose again on Easter Day.

While Christian teaching appears to be on the wane, non-Christian festivals like Diwali are commonly observed, sometimes without the permission of the pupils' parents, according to Lady Olga Maitland, Conservative MP for Sutton and Cheam and Chairwoman of the pressure group 'Christian Call' which carried out the survey in 1993. She said the government must be vigilant against the 'multi-faith mish-mash' which is eroding traditional Christian teachings in schools.

MUSLIM SCHOOLS

All British pupils, regardless of their background, are likely at some point to study Islam as part of their RE lessons. The teachings of the prophet Mohammed can be covered by schools as long as the main thrust of lessons takes account of the fact that Britain's religious traditions are 'mainly Christian'. It is against this background that many British Muslims have been campaigning to have their own state Muslim schools that would teach pupils according to Islamic rather than Christian traditions. They are backed in this quest by many Conservative peers and politicians of the traditional right, who believe that if state funding is available to Church of England, Roman Catholic and Jewish schools, it should also be extended to Muslim schools.

The Muslim campaigners and their Tory allies argue that it is a question of parental choice. By contrast, some critics with more 'liberal' inclinations are against the idea of state-funded Muslim schools on the grounds that they might lead to

SCHOOL VALUES

Government guidelines say: 'Schools should be expected to uphold those values which contain moral absolutes.'

- Pupils must be taught the difference between right and wrong.

- Teachers must act as 'moral agents' in the classroom.

School values should include:

- telling the truth

- keeping promises

- respecting the rights and property of others

- acting considerately towards others

- self-discipline

- helping those less fortunate and weaker than oneself

- taking personal responsibility for one's actions

School values should reject:

- bullying

- cheating

- deceit

- cruelty

- irresponsibility

- dishonesty

greater segregation and add to, rather than ease, racial and religious intolerance. Government ministers insist that each application for state funding by a Muslim school will be considered on its merits. A test case involved the Islamia School in Brent, London, set up by singer Cat Stevens, who converted to Islam and changed his name to Yusuf Islam. In August 1993, the school lost its bid for state funding. There is nothing in law to prevent state funding, provided the schools follow the National Curriculum and conform to certain other standards. Ministers are, however, sensitive to the political ramifications of such a move and to worries about the impact of Islamic fundamentalism.

READING

The ability to read is probably the most important skill your child will acquire. It unlocks the door to so many other skills, and may be the start of a love of books. As a parent you can play a crucial role in helping your child to read and in fostering his or her enjoyment. Studies have shown that children's reading abilities improve dramatically if parents take an active interest at home. 'Strong parental support and involvement is associated with higher reading standards,' government inspectors have reported. The impact can be 'huge', they say.

THE VITAL 15 MINUTES

Many schools now run schemes in which parents are encouraged to take part in 'paired reading'. This means parents spend about 15 minutes a day reading with their children during lesson-time or each evening at home. Parents may be asked to keep a log or diary charting their son's or daughter's progress and noting down words or word patterns with which their children have difficulty. This allows the teacher to concentrate on overcoming these problems in lesson-time. It is in the interest of all schools to get parents on board to help raise standards, because a good early grasp of reading will help children in all other lessons.

A number of pioneering schools have also been holding special lessons for parents who want to improve their own reading skills. The logic is that the parents' improved ability and boosted confidence will rub off onto the children.

Again, research tends to bear this out. Mothers, in particular, play a crucial role in boosting the reading ability of their children, the Adult Literacy and Basic Skills Unit has found. That is why it launched a campaign to help mums who were poor readers, so that they, in turn, could help boost the literacy levels of their children.

Sadly some parents, albeit a minority, have reported getting short shrift from their schools when they have tried to get involved. This has even gone as far as teachers telling parents not to interfere. If you encounter such resistance, try talking through the problem with the teacher concerned. If you are still unhappy, try the head and the governors. The last resort of moving your child to another school may not be an option for some parents.

READING BETWEEN THE LINES

Controversy about how reading is best taught in schools, and whether standards are going up or down, has raged for some time. Government inspectors have reported that the teaching of reading is not up to scratch in 20% of lessons. One of the main battles has been between the supporters of the 'phonics' approach and what is called the 'real books' method.

'PHONICS'

The 'phonics' approach is essentially the traditional, structured method of teaching in which pupils are taught to match letters or groups of letters to sounds, such as 'buh-aah-tuh spells BAT'. Phonics systems usually involve following a specially written and structured reading scheme. A 'blend' can be defined as joining the sounds represented by two or more letters with minimal change, such as 'gr' in grow or 'spl' in splash. Children's TV programmes like 'Sesame Street' draw on this method when they nominate a letter of the alphabet for each show, and then spell out a series of words beginning with it, such as 'G is for green, F is for friend' and so on.

'LOOK AND SAY'

In this method children learn to read by recognising the shape of whole words such as 'boat' or 'train'.

'REAL BOOKS'

Using this approach, teachers do not follow specially written schemes or kits. Instead, pupils choose from a selection of appropriate books and read them either under the guidance of the teacher or on their own.

Pioneered by the Canadian academic Frank Smith, it is called the 'real books' method because it rejects the use of reading programmes that take a more formal step-by-step approach to learning. The books chosen are therefore 'real' story books, and not specifically written to teach reading skills. Supporters of the 'real books' system include primary teacher Glenys Kinnock.

> ❝ The impact of parental support on reading standards was huge. In almost all the schools where the children's progress was good, there were signs that parents took an active interest in helping them to read at home. ❞

Report on reading by Her Majesty's Inspectorate, published March 1992

IN VOGUE

There has recently been a shift back towards the more traditional phonics method by ministers. The government's 1993 draft blueprint on English teaching said that all primary schools should put the emphasis on this approach. Phonics was an 'essential component' of learning to read, said the authors. However, a great many government inspectors' reports have stressed that a mixture of methods is the best way to teach a child to read. Most schools insist, and inspectors back them up, that they do use a mixture. The argument, however, is really about where the balance of the mix is best struck.

READING THE RIOT ACT

The most recent controversy about reading standards began in June 1990 when a group of education psychologists, led by Martin Turner, released hitherto secret figures of reading tests carried out in nine local education authorities. Mr Turner said that the alarming results pointed to the biggest drop in reading standards since the Second World War. Although a House of Commons Education Select Committee rejected his conclusions, the government was not convinced. Ministers ordered their inspectors and exam advisers to

> ❝ Watching television leads in the long run to a reduction in reading comprehension. This also applies in reverse. Children whose reading skills are mediocre gradually watch more television. ❞

Child and Media Study Group, University of Leiden, The Netherlands

investigate. The inspectors' report concluded that the teaching of reading was poor in 1 out of 5 primary school classes, a situation that Kenneth Clarke, then Education Secretary, described as 'deplorable'; it meant 700,000 pupils were not being properly taught how to read.

In a letter to head-teachers, Eric Bolton, then Senior Chief Inspector, said: 'While a very small proportion of pupils fail to read at all, some 25% or so are not as fluent, nor as accurate readers, as they should and need to be at age 11.' A report by the National Foundation for Educational Research (NFER) added that where a decline in standards could be detected, it was concentrated among the children of lowest ability. Subsequent research by the NFER did, however, provide evidence of a more widespread decline in reading standards between 1987 and 1991.

WHAT CAN MAKE A DIFFERENCE AT HOME?

A report by the government's Assessment of Performance Unit (APU) in 1991 showed some of the home factors that affected reading standards among children.

- The more books a pupil owns, the higher his or her performance in reading and writing is likely to be in primary and secondary school.

- Pupils who spend less than two hours a week reading for pleasure perform less well at reading and writing.

> **6** The misconception is that teachers who do not use reading schemes have no cogent approach to their task. But those of us who do not use reading schemes do use properly conceived and applied reading systems. ... It saddens teachers like me that there are so many dogmatists, literacy Luddite, who are not prepared even to consider important international developments of recent years. **9**

Primary teacher Glenys Kinnock, writing in defence of 'real books' for The Guardian *in March 1991*

- Children who borrow books from a library more than once a month get higher reading scores than those who claim not to use a library at all.

- Primary school pupils aged 5 to 11 who watch more than six hours of TV a day score significantly lower in reading tests than pupils who watch between two and five hours per day.

TEACHING YOUR CHILD TO READ

- Set aside 15 minutes of every day to read with your child.

- Make the experience enjoyable and try not to turn it into a test.

- Ask questions about the book such as: 'Why do you think she did that? What do you think will happen next? Shall we see?'

- Take turns reading to each other.

- Read your child stories at bedtime.

- Surround your child with as many stimulating books as possible to encourage an appreciation for them.

- Join a library and visit it regularly with your child.

- Teach your child to recite the alphabet.

- Buy a simple dictionary and encourage your child to use it.

COULD DO BETTER

In the 20% of primary school classes where the teaching of reading for 700,000 pupils was judged poor, government inspectors identified the main problems as:

- inadequate classroom planning that 'looked good on paper'.

- 'haphazard', infrequent and ineffective teaching of reading skills.

- poorly organised and managed work leading to chronic time-wasting.

- 'lacklustre' presentation and use of resources that failed to fire pupils' imaginations.

- poor assessment of pupils' strengths and weaknesses.

Inspectors noted a 'stark contrast' between the quality of the best and the worst classes of similar-aged pupils in broadly similar schools.

SEE ALSO:
National
Curriculum
Testing
Dyslexia

- Take an interest in your child's reading at school.

- Ask your child's teacher for advice on how to help and for details of home–school reading schemes.

- Contact the school if you are unhappy with your child's progress.

For details of the phonics approach:

Reading Reform Foundation
Mona McNee
UK Chapter Secretary
2 The Crescent
Toftwood
East Dereham
Norfolk
NR19 1NR

Tel: 0362 695109

❝ The 5% of teachers who described their approach as 'real books' gave too little attention to the systematic teaching of skills for tackling print. Many simply assumed that the children's repeated experiences of hearing stories and sharing books would enable them to gain independence and discern essential patterns in the print with minimal help from the teacher. ❞

Report of Her Majesty's Inspectorate into the teaching and learning of reading in primary schools, published in January 1991

SEX EDUCATION

FACTS OF LIFE MADE EXPLICIT IN SCHOOLS

Sex education is now a timetabled subject that must be taught in schools. The change, brought about by the 1993 Education Act, is a substantial shift. Previously, sex education was a bit of a hotch–potch subject, with bits of it being covered in science lessons, and the rest left to the school governors to decide exactly what, if anything, should be taught. The new legislation gives sex education, as a subject, roughly the same status as religious education. However, the legislation does give parents the right to withdraw their children from sex education lessons.

What to tell your children, and when, can be a nightmare for any parent balancing up educational, moral and health factors, not to mention the potential for embarrassment. Many parents simply avoid the decision and wait until they are asked. Polarised arguments rage between those parents and campaigners who say sex education in school promotes promiscuity and immorality, and those who say it is a sensible and potentially life-saving way to educate children about the

facts of life and healthy living. That is why Health Minister Tom Sackville provoked a storm when he suggested in 1993 that pupils should be given free condoms at school to cut down teenage pregnancies.

'If the Government issued 1,000 free condoms to this school today, how many fewer free school meals would they have to provide in five years' time?'
Courtesy Mahood of the Daily Mail

291

Before the changes, the government issued guidelines, the main points of which are likely to survive. They said that sex education in schools must emphasise morality and family values, while tackling controversial subjects like AIDS, contraception and abortion. They also stressed that anything appearing to advocate homosexual behaviour or to present it as 'the norm' was to remain outlawed in the nation's classrooms.

The circular to all schools emphasised the need for sex education to be seen within a 'clear moral framework' and emphasised the key role parents have to play in teaching their children the facts of life. Pupils should be taught to consider the importance of 'self-restraint, dignity and respect', for themselves and others. Pupils must also learn to recognise 'the physical, emotional and moral risks of casual and promiscuous sexual behaviour' and be taught that both sexes should behave responsibly in sexual matters. 'Pupils should be helped to appreciate the benefits of stable married and family life and the responsibilities of parenthood', said the guidelines.

New from 1993:

- Sex education is a separate subject under the National Curriculum.

- HIV, AIDS and other sexually transmitted diseases become part of sex education lessons. Previously they were part of science lessons.

FACT FILE

- More than 8,500 girls under the age of 16 become pregnant each year; equivalent to two at every secondary school.

- 69 out of every 1,000 girls aged 15 to 19 become pregnant. That is six times the rate in The Netherlands.

- Section 28 of the Local Government Act prohibits local authorities from promoting homosexuality or from promoting in state schools the 'teaching of the acceptability of homosexuality as a pretended family relationship'.

- Sexual intercourse with a girl under 16, homosexual acts between males if one or more parties is below 21, and indecent acts against children are against the law.

- All schools must provide sex education.

- Parents have a right to withdraw their children from sex education lessons.

- Science lessons will continue to cover reproduction.

SEX AND THE CHURCH

Sex education should be taught to all pupils in school before they learn about it behind the bike sheds or from television. Guidelines issued by the Church of England's National Society, which promotes religious education, admit that sex education is 'a delicate subject' but stresses that it is better for children to learn about it in school, rather than from less reputable sources.

‘We are clear that all sex education should take place within a framework which encourages pupils to consider the moral dimension of their actions. It should recognise the value of family life and understand the importance of loving relationships and mutual respect. ’

Education Secretary John Patten, launching sex education guidelines in 1993

'If they're not going to allow condoms in school, my dad says at least they should provide a creche.'
Courtesy Mac of the Daily Mail

293

> Parents are the key figures in helping their children to cope with the physical and emotional aspects of growing up, and in preparing them for the challenges and responsibilities which sexual maturity brings. The teaching offered by schools should be complementary and supportive to the role of parents.

Education Secretary John Patten in the government's 1993 sex education guidelines

'Learning about sex is an inescapable element of school and home life. Pupils talk with each other about it at play, as well as in the school classroom. Many children are likely to be aware of the presence of overt sexual issues through television, videos and newspapers. Left unchecked, this can lead to growth in the minds of even quite young children of misunderstanding, distorted information and irrational fear.'

The report goes on to add: 'The fact is we all fall short of the perfection enshrined in the gospel.'

Alan Brown, Director of the Church of England National Society's Religious Education Centre and RE Schools Officer of the General Synod's Board of Education, conceded: 'Homosexuality is a difficult area, but there is a difference between answering children's questions honestly and organising lessons specifically about homosexuality.'

Family Planning Association
27–35 Mortimer Street
London W1N 7RJ

Tel: 071-636 7866

or

Family Planning Association (Wales)
4 Museum Place
Cardiff CF1 3BG

Tel: 0222 342766

The Family Planning Association has a number of booklets in its *Growing Up* series, covering the whole range of questions children ask about sex.

> There is a condom culture in the classroom. Most of the booklets and videos have no religious or moral basis at all. They are simply about kids having sex and using condoms. Homosexuality is put on a par with heterosexuality. Look what happens. There are more abortions, illegitimate pregnancies and family breakdowns. We have had 30 years to learn the lessons.

Valerie Riches, Director of the Family Education Trust

TRENDY VERSUS TRADITIONAL

TRENDY TEACHING.
DOES IT EXIST?

The great education debate is sometimes presented as a polarised battle with the 'trendies' on the left, and the 'traditionalists' on the right. The terms 'trendy' and 'traditional' have therefore become a convenient shorthand to describe different approaches to teaching. Critics, particularly teachers, dismiss such descriptions as horrendously simplistic. They undoubtedly are, but there is a useful grain of truth in them.

'Traditional' usually means pupils sitting at rows of desks facing the blackboard at the front of the room and being taught as a whole class. The traditional teacher employs formal methods, which tend to mean drilling children with facts and making them learn by rote. The individual needs of each child are not taken into account; all are treated en masse. Those who are average fare best. Those who cannot work at the pace of the group suffer. Bright children are held back.

'Trendy' usually refers to the child-centred approaches introduced during the 1960s and '70s, in which the balance shifted towards letting the child follow its own instincts and learn by discovery. Pupils are arranged in groups around tables and follow individual projects under the teacher's guidance. Creativity is valued above rote-learning. In some classrooms the blackboard has been

❝ Much of the government's disregard for the views of heads, deputies and teachers stems from a pathological belief that the teaching profession is riddled with left-wing loonies who are sworn enemies of the government's reforms, belonging to professional associations dedicated to the undermining and destruction of government policies. ❞

David Hart, General Secretary of the National Association of Head Teachers (annual conference, May 1993)

295

abolished altogether as the teacher may rarely 'teach from the front'. A fatal flaw in the 'trendy' approach was that while many of these 'progressive' methods might have worked well in theory, the practice was difficult. There were too many pupils in classes, the rooms were the wrong shape to be easily divided into work areas, uncarpeted floors made the sound of pupils moving about and dragging chairs a deafening noise. The organisational problems were compounded by some teachers' lack of expertise in managing children who were now working at their own pace, being encouraged to talk in lessons and move about. With hindsight, the scope for chaos is apparent.

Education experts maintain that a mixture of methods is central to successful teaching, but it is the balance of the mix that makes the difference. The government's own advisers have now acknowledged this and are advising that a greater proportion of class time be spent in using more traditional methods.

Schools are asked to examine how much time is spent teaching pupils as a whole class, for example. One of the most compelling arguments used by experts to support this return to 'traditional' methods is one of efficiency. If a teacher is concentrating on one pupil or one small group at a time, how can he or she be paying sufficient attention to the others in the class?

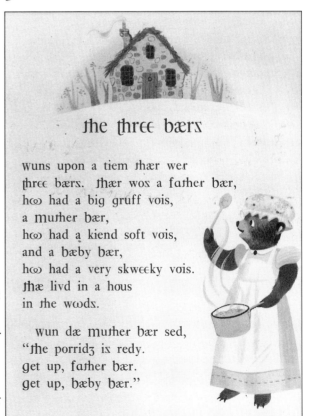

the three bærʒ

wuns upon a tiem thær wer
three bærʒ. thær woʒ a father bær,
hꝏ had a big gruff vois,
a muther bær,
hꝏ had a kiend soft vois,
and a bæby bær,
hꝏ had a very skweeky vois.
thæ livd in a hous
in the wꝏdʒ.

  wun dæ muther bær sed,
"the porridʒ iʒ redy.
get up, father bær.
get up, bæby bær."

The Three Bears
© Initial Teaching Publishing Co Ltd 1964

Fairy tale or horror story?

I have no truck with those who try to pretend that 'trendy' methods do not exist. I experienced them myself at primary school in the early 1960s. My parents had me reading in a rudimentary fashion before I started in the infants. But then I had to unlearn it as part of an ill-fated experiment called the 'Initial Teaching Alphabet' or ITA. Though the bizarre squiggles seemed more like notes in shorthand, they were part of a phonetic alphabet through which the word 'once' became 'wuns', 'lived' became 'livd' and 'was' became 'woz'.

The memories came flooding back when retired teacher, Mrs Gina Habgood from Stratford-upon-Avon, sent me a copy of the book I'd studied years before, which included the tale of Goldilocks and the Three Bears. It had been the latest fad from the education experts who had chosen her Bolton school, like mine, as a test-bed for their experiment. But Mrs Habgood had resisted. She said, 'It was like trying to learn Chinese. I told the powers that be that I would resign immediately if I was ordered to use the children as guinea pigs. I said "If you think I'm going to have a big block of children passing through my hands who have spelling and reading difficulties because of these crackpot ideas, I'm leaving." They told me it was a great honour for the school to be chosen. I said it was an honour spelled M-U-G.'

My spelling is not a disaster, but it could be better. We did switch to more conventional reading lessons later. I wonder how my classmates fared?

TRUANCY

Truancy goes by many names, but whether you call it 'playing hooky', 'skipping lessons' or 'bunking off', it can be a real headache for parents and teachers. Truancy simply means unauthorised absence from school and, if it is left unchecked, can lead to pupils missing vital lessons and parents facing legal action. Survey findings vary as to the exact extent of truancy, but ministers accept that the figure is too high, that truancy is a serious barrier to raising standards and that it appears to increase the chances of children becoming involved in crime.

A survey, commissioned by the government and conducted by academics at the University of North London in 1993, showed that more than a third of pupils admitted having played truant, with 1 in 5 admitting having done so at least once a month. Some 8.2% played truant at least once a week with a hard core of 1.5% saying they did it every day.

Truancy is not always a clear-cut affair of children simply failing to turn up; some pupils arrive for registration and then disappear for all, or part of, the rest of the day.

Reasons given by truants vary from boredom to unhappiness with teachers, but may include the fear of being bullied. Often parents are the last to know about their children playing truant. Truancy does rise dramatically as pupils get closer to the end of compulsory schooling at age 16. This is particularly a problem with teenagers who see no point in continuing to attend school.

PARENTAL RESPONSIBILITIES

Parents have a legal duty to ensure that their children are educated either at school or otherwise, which can include at home. Parents of persistent truants could find the LEA slapping an educational supervision order on them. This requires the parent to work in partnership with an educational welfare officer (EWO) to solve the problem. The supervising officer can make specific demands about how the child's behaviour must change. If parents refuse to co-operate or decide to turn a blind eye to their child's truancy, they can face hefty fines in the courts.

In 1993 ministers released millions of pounds to help schools develop new methods to deal with the problem. In July 1993 four parents in the London Borough of Tower Hamlets received fines of up to £700 each after failing to ensure that their children attended school. The borough's education chairman, councillor Stewart Rayment, said: 'We are not in the business of persecuting people, but at the end of the day the local education authority will not shrink from its responsibility in ensuring that children get their chance in the education system.'

HI-TECH SOLUTIONS TO OLD PROBLEMS

One of the most popular methods for combating truancy has been electronic registers. These come in a variety of forms. In some schools, pupils are issued with special cards that have a magnetic strip on the

> ❝Ask any police officer or probation worker, and he or she will tell you that the slide of a boy into criminality often has a depressingly familiar pattern. It starts with hanging around street corners, drifting into shoplifting and stealing bicycles, progresses to petty burglary, perhaps becoming involved with drugs, and then moves on to stealing cars or criminal damage. Before long, the journey from street corner to prison cell is complete. The boy is a habitual criminal, and a significant part of his life may then be spent behind bars. This cycle of criminality is too often triggered by being truant from school. ❞

Education Secretary John Patten in his 1992 White Paper 'Choice and Diversity'

From 1993:

- Schools have their truancy rates published in performance 'league tables' and in their prospectuses.

- LEAs can direct any state school to take a child who would otherwise be without a place. Such action is subject to consultation with the governing body, which can appeal to the Secretary of State.

back, rather like a credit card. When they arrive at school in the morning, they run their card through a special terminal outisde the classroom door.

The beauty of such a system is that pupils have to clock in before every lesson. A computer logs the time, so can also tell whether pupils are late. Some schools and LEAs also mount truant patrols to check for children who are on the streets when they should be sitting at their desks.

In 1993 the fast-food giant Burger King opened a special academy in conjunction with the charity Schools in Cities and London's Tower Hamlets. It caters for persistent teenage truants who cannot fit into life in mainstream schools. It provides intensive tuition and concentrates on basic skills, and also insists on a firm set of rules to which the teenagers must sign up.

> 'Children playing truant are not necessarily going to become criminals, but they are exposed to juvenile crime and many are sucked into it. Unless there is change, the present worsening position is going to lead to a massive explosion in juvenile crime. We fear that juvenile crime – shoplifting, drugs, car thefts, vandalism – could double in five years.'

John Findlay, National and Local Government Officers' Association spokesman for social workers in education

UNIFORM

School uniforms are part of the fabric of many schools, particularly secondaries. Opinions do vary, however, about their desirability. There is no direct link between the standards of dress and the standards of academic achievement, but many head-teachers do believe that smartly turned out pupils – whether in uniform or not – do reflect high standards elsewhere.

The origin of the uniform was in the charity schools for the poor. An element of this philosophy persists in the argument that uniforms mean rich and poor learn together without looking different from one another in terms of sartorial elegance. The reality, however, is more subtle, with the 'rich kids' often sporting clothes that are specially cut from the best quality cloth.

Schools do vary enormously in the dress codes they set and the rigour with which they are enforced. Many rows centre on the wearing or abandonment of ties and the length of skirts. Uniforms can vary from brightly striped blazers or quaintly archaic wing collars and tail-coats to the more relaxed and often specially designed American-style high school bomber jackets.

Those who support the idea of a dress code argue that it helps stamp the school's identity on the public consciousness and sends out a message to pupils about the standards of discipline and achievement expected. Many parents also breathe a sigh of relief because a uniform reduces demands from fashion-conscious children for the latest item of extremely expensive 'in' clothing or footwear.

Decisions about uniform rest with the head-teacher and governors. Schools must tell parents in their prospectuses the details of any dress code and also – though few ever comply with this requirement – the cost. Parents on low incomes or receiving benefits may be entitled to financial help and should ask their LEA for details.

❛ The children were not asked specifically whether they wanted a uniform or not, but they were involved in choosing the colour. The effect was magical. All sorts of people contacted us to say how the children's behaviour had improved. ❜

Stanley Goodchild, a former head of Garth Hill Comprehensive in Bracknell

---